FOUNDATION

CW00569545

NORTHWICK PUBLISHERS

14, BEVERE CLOSE, WORCESTER, WR3 7QH, ENGLAND

Telephone Number: 0905-56876/56529

FOUNDATION SERIES

Other books in the series:

FINANCIAL ACCOUNTING
AUTHOR W. HARRISON, F.C.I.B., Cert.Ed.

LAW
AUTHOR P. GERRARD B.Sc., Ph.D., A.C.I.B.

ECONOMICS
AUTHOR R. G. WINFIELD B.Sc.(Econ) Hons., F.C.I.B.

FOUNDATION SERIES

COST ACCOUNTING

SECOND EDITION

G. J. WILKINSON-RIDDLE B.A., F.C.A.

Head of Department of Accounting and Finance
Leicester Business School
Leicester Polytechnic

NORTHWICK PUBLISHERS

NORTHWICK PUBLISHERS

© G. J. WILKINSON-RIDDLE 1983, 1989

ISBN 0 907135 63 3

Printed in England by Clays Ltd, St Ives plc

First Impression 1983
Second Edition 1989
Reprinted 1990

PREFACE

For too many years my students, and many of my businessmen and women friends, have bemoaned the fact that "beginners" cost accounting books were impossible for a complete novice to understand, <u>unaided.</u>

My aim in writing Cost Accounting has been to rectify this appalling situation. This book is intended to make clear the basics of the subject in a way that absolute beginners will understand, and to show clearly the application of cost accounting to real business decisions. Each topic has many simple worked examples which are followed up by gradually more complicated ones.

While the individual reader can choose at which point to cease developing his or her technical ability – every student using this book should be clear in principle about: (A) How each particular technique introduced works, (B) What it is for, (C) The types of businesses which will use it, and (D) Any practical problems to be expected in using it. Finally all the necessary technical jargon accountants use is explained in ordinary language.

Students taking exams will find "self-assessment" questions at the end of each chapter and an appendix of fully worked answers at the end of the book. These are in gradually ascending order of difficulty, and anyone who can do all of them should have an excellent grounding for G.C.E. "A" level, BTEC National and Higher, Bankers, Professional Foundation and First Year Degree Courses.

Businessmen and women will find the book a clear guide to understanding the costing techniques their accountants use.

For the many small businessmen, who do not have the benefit of in-house accountants, it may suggest techniques that they could usefully implement themselves.

To my professional colleagues, who may find some of my explanations insufficiently "pure", I can only emphasise that this book is for beginners. I have not forgotten what it felt like to be one. There are many excellent texts for the student to progress towards – this one is to ensure the first step on the ladder is not too high from the ground.

Summer 1989   G.J.W.R.

CONTENTS

CHAPTER 1

WHAT IS COST ACCOUNTING AND WHAT IS COST?

CHAPTER OBJECTIVES

Having studied this chapter you should be able to:

* EXPLAIN THE MEANING AND PURPOSE OF COST ACCOUNTING

* UNDERSTAND HOW COST ACCOUNTING ARISES OUT OF THE NEED TO MAKE BUSINESS DECISIONS

* UNDERSTAND THE TWO DISTINCT MEANINGS OF "HOW MUCH DOES IT COST TO MAKE?"

WHAT IS COST ACCOUNTING?

People running businesses, any business, need to know all sorts of information before they can make business decisions. For instance:

"Can we reduce the selling price?"
"Shall we advertise the product on TV?"
"Shall we employ more people?"
"Shall we make a new product?"
"Shall we offer a new service?"
"How can we keep our costs down?"

are all questions which business managers will need to answer. Whether the business is large or small, in manufacturing (e.g. making washing machines) or service industry (e.g. shops) the questions apply. Even in government and semi-government agencies most of the questions apply.

So think of the information you might need before reducing the selling price of (say) the bicycles your business manufactures. A few of the things you would need to know are: present price, present costs, probable future costs, the probable future number to be sold if the price is reduced, the probable future number to be sold if the price is *not* reduced, and if there is factory capacity to make extra bikes. Quite enough to start with and by no means a complete list!

Having assembled all the information you would be in a position to decide. Some of the information would be in money terms – expected costs and sales income (revenues) – and some of it relating to other considerations: for example, marketing, personnel, and raw material supply. This illustration gives us the clue to what cost accounting is: Cost accounting information is *any* information in money terms which is used by managers to help them make decisions about the products and services the business supplies. It is important to be clear that the cost accounting information used in decision-making is not the *only* consideration. In our bicycle example the costs and revenues predicted as a result of reducing the price are obviously important. However, so is the non-cost accounting information: the marketing and raw material supply aspects, for example. It would be no use planning to make and sell more bikes if it were not possible to buy enough steel and tyres to make the extra ones!

So the term "cost accounting" (sometimes also called "management accounting" or "costing") has come to mean a collection of techniques which are commonly used in business to provide information in money terms to help managers make business decisions.

I say "commonly used in business" because there is no law or statute *making* a business use any of the cost accounting techniques. By contrast with Financial Accounts – which all limited companies are required by law to produce – what cost accounting information a business produces is entirely a matter of choice. It could produce none; in which case the people running it would not be able to make their decisions very confidently. Equally, it could develop special types of information of its own that no-one else uses and are not mentioned in this book. In as far as that information was in money terms and helped the managers make decisions about the products and services the business supplies, it would still be cost accounting.

WHAT ARE THE COMMONLY USED TECHNIQUES?

Each cost accounting technique exists because a specific type of question needs answering. The most commonly asked one (at the heart of all decisions managers make about the products their businesses sell) is "How much does it cost to make?" (Note: the term "product" is used generally from now on to include services as well. So "How much does it cost to make?" also includes "How much does the service cost to provide?" Illustrations will be taken from both manufacturing and service industries throughout the book).

PRODUCT COSTING techniques answer this basic "How much does it cost to make?" question.

The next type of question involves planning the future, for example "What do we want to sell/make/buy/start/pay, next year?" "What will this product cost to make next year?" And clearly this leads to *comparing* that planned future with what actually occurs as time goes by: "How did our plans turn out in reality?"

BUDGETING techniques help managers record their future plans in money terms, and help them compare what actually happened with what they planned would happen.

Note although there are particular budgeting techniques, product costing techniques can also be used to help BUDGETS be compiled. In this case the question becomes "What *will* this proposed product cost to make?" and a product costing technique is used not to find out what something has cost, but to help plan (i.e. budget) what something *should* cost.

The third type of question involves evaluating possible future plans and evaluating the way a particular product has performed in the past. "Is it worth making this product?" "Are the risks of this plan too great in comparison with the possible rewards?" "Are we using the business's resources well in continuing to advertise this product?" are all questions which managers need to ask about their future plans and existing products.

APPRAISAL techniques help managers answer this important type of question.

Note: although there are particular appraisal techniques, you will also find that some product costing and budgeting techniques are also used to appraise the performance of existing products and to decide which plan to put into action in the future.

The techniques will be introduced under the broad headings of PRODUCT COSTING, BUDGETING, and APPRAISAL because they grow out of the need to answer the sort of questions mentioned above. However they can often help to answer the other questions as well. For example once you have mastered how to measure the cost of making one extra item in reality; you can use the same method to predict (i.e. plan, i.e. budget) the cost of making one more in the future. These techniques reflect the activity of managers: they plan, (budget) measure the results of their plans (record actual product costs) and evaluate how well or otherwise the plan is turning out in reality. So cost accounting techniques help managers make well informed business decisions.

Diagrammatically the cost accounting techniques dealt with in this book are shown in Fig. 1.

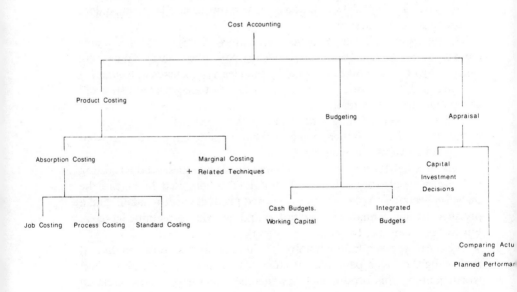

Fig. 1.

The sequence in which the chapters deal with these items is important and I very strongly recommend you work through the chapters in order. For instance if you are to grasp standard costing in Chapter 8 you must have understood all the preceding ones first.

WHAT IS COST?

For a moment, consider PRODUCT COSTING. Most beginners are only familiar with the question "What does it cost?" in a retail sense (i.e. how much money does it cost to buy in a shop). In this retail sense there is no doubt about the question's meaning. The answer may vary only as far as one shop sells at a slightly higher or lower price than another. But the basic *meaning* of the question is clear: "*How much money* do I have to give to the salesman to purchase the shoes/pay for the haircut/buy the jeans?"

And for the individual considering whether or not to buy something, the saving of money by NOT buying is equally clear. If the shoes cost £12, you will save £12 by not spending the money. So for an individual buying something in a shop the questions "What does it cost?" and "what will I save if I don't have it?" are clearly linked.

What this part of the chapter will explain is that for a business providing a service, or making a product, the question "What does it cost to make?" has TWO clear and separate meanings. Furthermore the savings made by NOT making the product are related to ONLY ONE of the two meanings of "What does it cost?"

The two distinct meanings in cost accounting of "What does it cost" depend upon the *use which is going to be made of the answer.*

Take as an example a family of four living in a nice three bedroomed semi-detached house: what does it cost them to live in the house each year?

	£
Mortgage or Rent Payments	1,800
Food	2,080
Gas and Electricity	280
Rates	340
Clothes	400
Train and bus fares	100
TOTAL YEAR'S EXPENSES	£5,000

Fig. 2.

Now there are four people living in the house, so what is the yearly cost per person?

Yearly Cost per person = £5,000 ÷ 4 people = £1,250 per person.

The question "How much does it cost per person to live in the house?" is answered by taking *all of the costs* and dividing them up among all of the people. Using cost-accounting jargon, all the costs are ABSORBED by all the people living there. This illustrates the *first meaning* of "What does it cost?" in cost accounting, when dealing with PRODUCT COST-

ING. An ABSORPTION COST is one which includes all of the costs incurred in making a product and spreads them evenly or fairly over each item produced.

Now for the second meaning. Imagine that the Mother and Father were lucky enough to have another baby, so now there were 5 people living in the house. Assuming that they had all their baby clothes left over from the first two children and that the new child didn't eat too much in the first year, what would the cost of the *extra* child be? Originally we decided the cost per person (in sense one) was £1,250 each. Would the new child cost its Mother and Father an extra £1,250? *No* definitely not. With the extra child (say it ate £60 of food in the first year), the total family expenses would be:

	ORIGINAL FOUR PEOPLE	EXTRA SPENT ON NEW BABY	NEW TOTAL
	£	£	£
Mortgage	1,800	–	1,800
Food	2,080	60	2,140
Gas and Electricity	280	–	280
Rates	340	–	340
Clothes	400	–	400
Train and Bus Fares	100	–	100
	£5,000	£60	£5,060

Fig. 3.

So the SECOND MEANING of "What does it cost?" becomes clear: When "what does it cost?" really means "*what is the extra cost* involved in having the extra child?" the answer is only £60, which of course is a very different answer from the FIRST MEANING.

The jargon used in cost accounting for the *extra cost* of making one more item of the product (e.g. one more bicycle) is the MARGINAL COST.

In our example if asked, "What does it cost for one member of the family to live in the house per year?", you need to know the *use* that will be made of the answer. If someone wants to know the cost per person in full, (perhaps to compare it with the cost last year) assuming the present expenses and number of family members, the answer would be £1,250. But if someone wants to see if he could afford to have another member in his family, £60 would be the correct answer. So under some circumstances the right answer to "What does it cost?" is the ABSORPTION COST, and under others it is the MARGINAL COST.

USING THE ABSORPTION AND MARGINAL COSTS

In business it is important to know what to use these two types of cost for. The absorption cost is mainly used to set a normal selling price for the normal output (i.e. normal number of items made) of a product; because obviously the sales revenue must be higher than *all* of the costs incurred if a profit is to be made. For example, imagine the £5,000 per year is the cost of running a small workshop – including wages, rent, heat, light, materials and everything. Let's say a year's normal output is 500 dresses. The Costs break down as follows (identical to the family's costs in Fig. 2 but with different headings):

	£
Workshop Rent and Wages	1,800
Materials for the Dresses	2,080
Gas and Electricity	280
Rates	340
Sewing Machine Hire	400
Tissue Paper	100
	£5,000

Fig. 4.

We want to make a profit, so the selling price must be higher than the cost. In this instance the sales revenue for the year must be more than £5,000 if we are to make a profit. So the ABSORPTION COST per dress (i.e. the cost which "includes all of the costs incurred in making the product") must be used to base our selling price on: for example:

Total Year's Costs: £5,000
Number of Dresses Made = 500
ABSORPTION COST per dress = £5,000 ÷ 500 = £10 per dress

So if we sold the dresses for £12 each (i.e. a 20% mark up on cost) our profit would be:

	£
Revenue £12 × 500 =	6,000
Less costs	5,000
PROFIT	£1,000

So the ABSORPTION COST is used to set the selling price for the normal output of items produced. In which case what should the marginal cost (i.e. the cost of an extra one) be used for?

Consider the costs listed in Fig. 4. If an *extra* dress were made in the year, which of them is likely to increase? Unless the staff are paid per dress, the only cost that will go up is the materials for the dresses. No more rent, rates, heating, machine hire costs will have to be paid just because an extra dress is made. The extra cost of one more dress will be just the extra material used. What then is the material cost per dress?

Price of Materials for 500 Dresses = £2,080

Therefore, cost per dress for materials = 2,080 ÷ 500 = £4·16p

So the MARGINAL COST of one dress = £4·16; that is the extra cost of making one more dress would be £4·16p. If we put a 20% mark up on the marginal cost and used it as a selling price for the whole batch, we would clearly make a huge loss: £4·99 is £4·16 + 20% so:

Revenue 500 × £4·99 =	£2,495
less Expenses for the	
year	5,000
LOSS	(£2,505)

The MARGINAL COST per dress would be no good for setting a selling price for the *whole batch* of 500 dresses.

What the marginal cost would be useful for is (for example) deciding if it might be worth while *giving* a dress to a shop as a window display item – to help as an advertisement for the other dresses which are for sale. Because if an extra dress were made for this purpose the *extra one would not cost £10* (which is the full absorption cost) it would only cost an extra £4·16. So as the price of the advertisement is quite low – it might be worth doing. There are many other uses of marginal costs, which are dealt with in Chapters 5 and 6. At this stage the important point is that you are clear about what a marginal cost is.

Back at the start of this section I wrote that while there were two meanings of "Cost" in PRODUCT COSTING – namely the "full ABSORPTION COST" meaning and the "extra-cost-of-one-more, MARGINAL COST" meaning – only one of these meanings was related to the savings made if an item of product is *not* made.

Think of our dress example. If instead of making 500 dresses we make only 499 of them, what will we save? The answer is only £4·16. Look at the list of costs in Fig. 4: if one less dress is made, the only expense which will be lower as a result is the materials. Instead of spending £4·16 × 500 = £2,080 we will spend £4·16 × 499 = £2,075·84 i.e. £4·16 less! The marginal cost is therefore also the amount which *will be saved if one less item is made.*

TO SUMMARISE THIS SECTION OF THE CHAPTER

For businesses trying to determine what it costs them to produce an item there are two possible answers to the question "What does it cost?" (A) One which takes into account *all* the costs spread evenly or fairly over *all* the items produced (i.e. over all the "output"). This so called ABSORP-TION COST must be the main guide to setting normal selling prices for normal output.

(B) One which takes into account only the *extra cost* of producing *one more item* – called the MARGINAL COST. This is used when the *point* of asking the question "what does it cost?" is to find out the effect on expenses of making more, or making fewer items.

As the book progresses this important distinction between the two meanings of "what does it cost" will be developed further, and *you will learn that there are many other uses of marginal and absorption costs.* Make sure you are clear so far about this "What is cost" section. If you are not, don't go on until you are really sure of it. If you have grasped it you are well on your way to grasping the heart of Cost Accounting.

SELF-ASSESSMENT QUESTIONS

Make the most of this first set of questions – there are only a few this time!

1. Why does cost accounting exist?
2. The need to answer what sort of question has led to the development of
   (A) Product Costing techniques?
   (B) Budgeting techniques?
   (C) Appraisal techniques?
* 3. A dry cleaning business spent the following amounts on expenses in one year: Wages £15,000, Rent £5,000, Machinery yearly cost £3,000, Electricity and Gas £4,000, Rates £2,000, Cleaning Fluid £7,000. The business cleaned 18,000 pieces of clothing in the year.
   (A) What is the absorption cost per article cleaned?
   (B) If half of the electricity and gas bill expense (i.e. £2,000) and all of the cleaning fluid expense (i.e. £7,000) are the only costs incurred in direct proportion to the number of items cleaned, what is the cost of cleaning one more item (i.e. what is the marginal cost of cleaning an item)?
4. (A) Using the original data in Q.3 and your answer to Q.3(B), what would the total expenses have been if the dry cleaning business had cleaned 20,000 items instead of 18,000?
   (B) Using your answer in (4A) what would the new absorption cost be per item if 20,000 items were cleaned?

NOTE Fully worked answers to all the numerical questions in this book that have an asterisk (*) by them are in the answers appendix at the back of the book.

CHAPTER 2

LEARNING SOME ESSENTIAL COST ACCOUNTING LANGUAGE

CHAPTER OBJECTIVES

Having studied this chapter you should be able to:

* CLASSIFY BUSINESS EXPENSES IN TERMS OF THE BASIC COST-ACCOUNTING TABLE OF COSTS

* DEMONSTRATE THE IMPORTANCE OF THE PRODUCT-BY-PRODUCT APPROACH IN COST ACCOUNTING

* DEFINE THE MEANING OF "OVERHEADS"

SPECIAL COST ACCOUNTING LANGUAGE

Every subject tends to develop its own special language (jargon) and cost accounting is no different. Many of you will be familiar with the typical financial accounting classification of expenses used in the profit and loss account. This financial accounting classification is usually based on what the money was spent on. For example you would expect to see as expenses, in a profit and loss account, headings such as wages, insurance, telephone and postage, stationery, purchases of goods for sale, electricity and gas, motor expenses, rent and rates and machine depreciation.

By contrast a *cost accounting* classification *of the same expenses* would be different. The point of the cost accounting classification being to show not quite so much what the money was spent on; but more *in which area of the business the money was spent.* For instance instead of showing what the total rent and rates paid were (as you would in the profit and loss expense classification) the cost accounting classification would re-distribute the rates expenses, and all the other expenses, in order to show what was spent on operating the factory, what the sales department cost to operate, and so on. Each department's share of the rent and rates expenses, and the other expenses, would be included in that department's total operating costs, in the cost accounting classification.

Below in Fig. 5 is the most commonly used basic classification of costs for cost-accounting purposes;

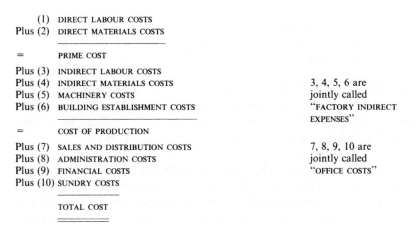

(1)	DIRECT LABOUR COSTS	
Plus (2)	DIRECT MATERIALS COSTS	
=	PRIME COST	
Plus (3)	INDIRECT LABOUR COSTS	
Plus (4)	INDIRECT MATERIALS COSTS	3, 4, 5, 6 are
Plus (5)	MACHINERY COSTS	jointly called
Plus (6)	BUILDING ESTABLISHMENT COSTS	"FACTORY INDIRECT EXPENSES"
=	COST OF PRODUCTION	
Plus (7)	SALES AND DISTRIBUTION COSTS	7, 8, 9, 10 are
Plus (8)	ADMINISTRATION COSTS	jointly called
Plus (9)	FINANCIAL COSTS	"OFFICE COSTS"
Plus (10)	SUNDRY COSTS	
	TOTAL COST	

Fig. 5.

And, of course, Sales income (REVENUE) less TOTAL COST must equal profit.

Some of these new terms need explanation, so starting from the top of the table:

(1) DIRECT LABOUR COSTS: This is defined as the wages paid to the people actually engaged in making the product or providing the service. So in a car factory the men actually welding together the car would be direct labour – while the wages of the foreman supervising their work, or the quality controller checking it, would not be direct labour as these people would not be actually making the product.

(2) DIRECT MATERIAL COSTS: This is defined as the cost of buying in the materials from which the finished product is made. The steel and glass and paint used to make a car are direct materials – the lubricant used to grease the machinery in the factory would not be direct material as it is not part of the finished product.

(3) INDIRECT LABOUR COSTS: This is defined as the wages paid to all the other people in the factory who are not direct labour: e.g. Foremen, quality controllers, factory manager, storemen, cleaners.

(4) INDIRECT MATERIALS COSTS: These are the costs of buying all the other materials used in the factory other than Direct Materials, e.g. cleaning materials, cotton rags, lubricants for the machines.

(5) MACHINERY COSTS: Often this will be just the depreciation charge on the machines used in the factory, but it may include costs of hiring and repairing machines as well. It covers all the costs of using the machines in the factory.

(6) BUILDING ESTABLISHMENT COSTS: Under this heading is included all the expenses of providing the structure of the factory and the services within it. The rent, rates, telephone, heating, electricity, insurances of the building and similar expenses will be included here.

(7) SALES AND DISTRIBUTION COSTS: This includes all the costs of selling the product and of delivering it. The wages of the salesmen, their car expenses, the cost of their cars, the wages of the deliverymen and the cost of their trucks are all included here, together with the rent and rates and telephone costs of the sales and distribution offices.

(8) ADMINISTRATION COSTS: This would include the wages of the Managers, Directors, Accountants, Production Controllers, and similar

people, and all the costs of their offices' rent, rates and telephone. The cost of their cars if they were provided by the business would be included too.

(9) FINANCIAL COSTS: Often businesses borrow money, and have to pay substantial sums to raise it. So this heading would include the interest paid on money borrowed and any expenses incurred in raising the main sum: for example the cost of commission to the people who may have arranged the loan for the business.

(10) SUNDRY COSTS: In any business there are odd expenses which don't seem to fit in – or may need to have special attention drawn to them, and this is included for that reason.

Note the two sub-totals included in the classification (see Fig. 5) that is: PRIME COST (*direct materials* + *direct labour*) and COST OF PRO-DUCTION (*prime cost* + *factory indirect expenses*) are there for a purpose. *Prime Cost* is the absolute minimum possible cost anything could be made for, that is the wages of the makers and the cost of the materials. More importantly the *COST of PRODUCTION* sub-total shows the amount it is costing to run the factory *as a unit separate from the office.* Quite often firms calculate a *factory absorption cost per unit* (Cost of Production ÷ Number of items produced) to ensure the factory is making goods at the correct factory cost. Of course the *full* absorption cost per unit would be Total Cost divided by the number of items produced.

In order that the relationship between the Profit and Loss Account Expense Classification and the Cost accounting classification is clear, and so that you understand each is merely a different way of showing the *same* expenditure. Fig. 6 below shows a typical profit and loss account re-analysed into the cost accounting classification; look at it now.

This is just an example of course; the actual way (for instance) that rent and rates expenses are allocated between factory, sales offices and administration would depend on the floor area of the departments concerned. As long as you are clear that the intention of the cost accounting classification is to find out the costs incurred in particular areas (sometimes called "cost centres") of the business; and that *all* costs incurred in that area are included, then you have grasped the point at issue.

Finally I hope you recall from Chapter 1 that all cost-accounting activity is a voluntary activity on the part of any business. Equally this basic cost classification is only a starting point for learning about the subject. Many businesses will use a different classification which suits their purposes better, and if a particular type of cost were of crucial importance it might be singled out specially. For example electricity costs in aluminium manu-

P L EXPENSE CLASSIFICATION

5000 Wages	500 Insurance	7000 Purchases	3000 Motor Expenses	1500 Telephone & Postage	300 Stationery	2200 Rent & Rates	700 Electricity & Gas	3200 Machinery Depreciation	23400 Total	COST ACCOUNTING CLASSIFICATION	
3000										(1) Direct Labour	3000
		5000								(2) Direct Materials	5000
										= Prime Cost	8000
800										(3) Indirect Labour	800
		1600								(4) Indirect Materials	1600
								2300		(5) Machinery Costs	2300
	200			400	50	1800	500			(6) Building Establishment	2950
										= Cost of Production	15650
700	250	200	2600	600	200	100	50	700		(7) Sales & Distribution	5400
500	50	200	400	500	50	300	150	200		(8) Administration	2350
										(9) Financial	–
										(10) Sundry	–
										= Total Cost	23400

Fig. 6.

facture are enormously high – running to hundreds of pounds per ton of aluminium produced. In this case the electricity cost might well be singled out in the cost classification that this business used.

THE PRODUCT-BY-PRODUCT APPROACH

Another important aspect of cost accounting has been implied in the book so far, but not spelt out. Cost accounting information is generally information about A PARTICULAR PRODUCT. The decisions that cost accounting information helps managers make are decisions *about particular products*. Financial accounts (again by contrast) seek to give information about the business as a whole. The product by product approach of cost accounting is crucial to its usefulness for managers. Figure 6 is an example of the re-classification of a profit and loss account into the basic cost classification. It would only be left like that if the business made one product. If two or more products were made and sold, a separate cost classification for each product would be necessary, so managers could see how each separate product was performing. For example, imagine our Fig. 6 business which had costs totalling £23,400, had revenues of £27,000. The Profit made by the *entire* business would obviously be:

	£
Revenue	27,000
less Total Costs	23,400
PROFIT	£ 3,600

If the business made and sold two products (say bicycles and prams) then the basic cost classification hasn't really told us all that much more than the profit and loss account. It has told us *some* more of course (e.g. what the factory cost to run, how much the sales and distribution costs are, and so forth) but nothing about the performance of the *individual* products sold.

However if we split the cost classification and the revenues between the two products (bicycles and prams), much more information might emerge. For instance:

	TOTAL	BICYCLES	PRAMS
	£	£	£
REVENUES (A)	27,000	14,000	13,000
COSTS			
Direct labour	3,000	2,000	1,000
Direct materials	5,000	3,500	1,500
PRIME COST	8,000	5,500	2,500
Indirect labour	800	500	300
Indirect materials	1,600	1,000	600
Machinery costs	2,300	1,700	600
Building and establishment	2,950	2,000	950
COST OF PRODUCTION	15,650	10,700	4,950
Sales and distribution	5,400	3,000	2,400
Administration	2,350	1,250	1,100
Financial	–	–	–
Sundry	–	–	–
TOTAL COST (B)	£23,400	£14,950	£8,450
PROFIT A—B	£3,600	£(950)	£4,550

Fig. 7.

Now there is a proper *product by product* cost classification there is the chance of some really useful information emerging. In our example the most obvious thing is that prams are very profitable and bicycles are not; but there are other useful things as well. Direct material and direct labour costs for the bicycles are much higher than for the prams, perhaps this might lead the managers to investigate this aspect. As a result they might be able to reduce the costs of the bikes, for example by buying the raw materials more carefully, eliminating wastage and reducing idle labour time.

OVERHEADS

This is the last piece of special cost accounting language you need to learn before starting the product costing work in the next chapter. There is no official definition of overheads and in ordinary life people use the term to mean a variety of things.

For our cost accounting purposes "overheads" mean *all costs except direct labour and direct materials.* Using the basic classification of costs this definition is easily illustrated.

(1)   Direct labour
(2)   Direct materials

(3)   Indirect labour
(4)   Indirect materials
(5)   Machinery costs   } FACTORY OVERHEADS
(6)   Building and establishment   } TOTAL OVERHEADS

(7)   Sales and distribution
(8)   Administration
(9)   Financial   } OFFICE OVERHEADS
(10) Sundry

Fig. 8.

Note that Cost of Production (the addition of items 1–6) includes an overhead *and* direct cost mixture. Note also that the terms "Factory Overheads" and "Factory Indirect Expenses" are used to mean the same items. Using our last numerical example in Fig. 7 the total overheads would be:

	£	£
Indirect labour	800	
Indirect Materials	1,600	
Machinery Costs	2,300	
Building and Establishment	2,950	
FACTORY OVERHEADS TOTAL		7,650
Sales and Distribution	5,400	
Administration	2,350	
OFFICE OVERHEADS TOTAL		7,750
TOTAL OVERHEADS		£15,400

Fig. 9.

SELF-ASSESSMENT QUESTIONS

(1) Into which cost-accounting categories would you put the following expenses of a business making tumble driers and electric cookers:
- a: Electric cooker element
- b: Oven doors
- c: Wages of storemen who issue parts to production
- d: Accountant's wages
- e: Works manager's car expenses
- f: Wages of people working assembling the driers
- g: Electric motors used in the driers
- h: Welding machines used to assemble the cookers
- i: Factory telephones
- j: Repairs to the office block
- k: Cars for salesmen
- l: Servicing the salesman's cars
- m: Fuel for the delivery lorries
- n: Foremen's wages
- o: Interest payments on borrowed money
- p: Electricity used in the offices to run the computer used by the accounts and sales departments
- q: Cost of the computer used in the two departments
- r: Oils used in the factory to lubricate the production line
- s: Fork lift truck hire costs
- t: Wages of fork lift truck drivers working in the stores area
- u: Steel used to make the cookers and driers
- v: Cable used to wire-up the cookers
- w: Switches used on the cookers and driers
- x: Wages of the works engineer
- y: Materials used by the works engineer in maintaining the factory machinery
- z: Roof repairs to the factory

* (2) The data below is from the accounts of Uniproduct Ltd who make only one product – namely distress rockets:

	£
: Factory Wages 65% of which are paid to the production-line staff	40,000
: Rent and Rates 74% of which is for the factory area, sales and admin. offices are of equal size	12,000
: Material purchases. 85% are materials for the rockets, 10% are other factory materials and 5% office cleaning materials	75,000

: Machine depreciation, all of which is factory
  machinery   29,000
: Office wages 50% sales, 50% admin.   18,000
: Telephone and Postage 15% factory, 85% Sales   15,000
: Salesmen's car expenses   9,000
: Delivery costs   15,000
: Advertising costs   17,000

(a) What is the prime cost of the distress rockets?
(b) What is the cost of production of the rockets?
(c) What is the total cost of the rockets?
(d) What are the factory overheads?
(e) What are the total overheads?

If 20,000 rockets were made:

(f) What is the absorption cost per rocket?
(g) What is the prime cost of one rocket?
(h) What is the factory overhead cost per rocket?
(i) What is the total overhead cost per rocket?
(j) What is the cost of production of one rocket?

(3) The Electric Business Ltd makes two products, and its profit and loss
account was:

Sales Revenue = £164,000

£

Expenses
	£
Wages	26,000
Purchases	34,000
Rent and Rates	6,800
Power	15,000
Machine Depreciation	30,000
Insurances	8,000
Motor Expenses	14,000
Telephone	9,000
Stationery	6,000
	£148,800

Net Profit   £15,200

The two products are Radios and Tape Decks. There are now two
stages in this question:

STAGE 1

You are required to convert the expenses to the cost classification:
your researches reveal the following facts:
(a) Wages are 60% direct, 10% indirect, 18% Sales and Distribution,
and 12% Administration.

(*b*) Purchases are 70% direct materials, 15% indirect materials, 5% factory building maintenance supplies, and 10% sales office and administrative office items, split evenly between the two.

(*c*) The factory rent is £5,000 and the office's rent £1,800. The sales office is twice the size of the administration office.

(*d*) The machines and factory heating use £9000 of power each year, the remainder of the amount heats the offices (see point (*c*) for relative office sizes).

(*e*) The insurances are £6,000 for the factory, £1,500 for the sales and distribution and £500 for administration.

(*f*) Motor expenses are £6,000 for salesmen's cars, £5,000 for delivery vans and a total of £3,000 for the chief accountant's and Managing Director's cars.

(*g*) 90% of telephone calls are made by the sales force. The Works management and the Accounts department make 5% of the calls each.

(*h*) £4,000 of stationery is used in the accounts dept. computer, £500 is for clock-cards used by the factory workforce; £500 used by the sales office management staff and £1,000 by administrative staff.

(*i*) The machine depreciation is all for machines used in the factory except for £7,000 which is on the computer used by the accounts department.

STAGE 2

The cost classification you have produced in stage 1 is divided between the two products as follows:

	Radios	Tape Decks
	%	%
Direct labour	50	50
Direct materials	40	60
Indirect labour	30	70
Indirect materials	60	40
Machinery costs	45	55
Building establishment	45	55
Sales and distribution	35	65
Administration	42	58

Sales Revenue is split as follows:

Radios	Tape Decks
£97,000	£67,000

9,700 radios were sold and 3,350 tape decks were sold.

    (*a*) What is the total cost of the radios?
    (*b*) What is the total cost of the tape decks?
    (*c*) What is the absorption cost per radio?
    (*d*) What is the absorption cost per tape deck?
    (*e*) What is the profit/loss made on selling the radios?
    (*f*) What is the profit/loss made on selling the tape decks?

(4) (*a*) What are the total overheads incurred by the Electric Business Ltd (using your answer to Question 3)?
    (*b*) What are the factory overheads for making Radios?
    (*c*) What are the factory overheads for making tape decks?
    (*d*) What are the total overheads for making Radios?
    (*e*) What are the total overheads for making tape decks?

(5) Using the data worked out in Question 3:
    (*a*) What is the prime cost of making the radios?
    (*b*) What is the prime cost of making the tape decks?
    (*c*) What is the cost of production of the radios?
    (*d*) What is the cost of production of the tape decks?

CHAPTER 3

THE COMPONENTS OF AN ABSORPTION COST

CHAPTER OBJECTIVES

Having studied this chapter you should be able to:

* DESCRIBE THE COMPONENTS OF THE ABSORPTION COST OF A PRODUCT
* DESCRIBE IN PRINCIPLE HOW TO CALCULATE THE DIRECT LABOUR COSTS OF A PRODUCT
* CALCULATE DIRECT MATERIAL COSTS USING FIFO, LIFO AND AVCO PRICING METHODS
* DESCRIBE THE METHOD BY WHICH OVERHEAD COSTS ARE GIVEN TO INDIVIDUAL PRODUCTS
* CALCULATE OVERHEAD RECOVERY RATES
* EXPLAIN HOW PRODUCT COSTS ARE PARTLY DEPENDENT UPON THE JUDGMENTS MADE WHEN OVERHEAD RECOVERY RATES ARE CALCULATED

THE COMPONENTS OF AN ABSORPTION COST

Having worked through the book so far, you already know in detail what these components are – that is all of the costs which are listed in the basic table of costs in Chapter 2, Fig. 5. However, in order to make the breakdown of the absorption cost of a product more manageable in size, it is usually split into three components:

	Direct labour
	Direct materials
and	Overheads
=	Absorption Cost of a Product

After your work in the last chapter you should realise that "overheads" is a shorthand form of stating the Factory Indirect Expenses and Office costs which are included in the full cost classification.

So from now on for the remainder of the product costing chapters which deal with absorption costs, we shall talk of the absorption cost of an item in terms of *Direct Labour, Direct Materials* and *Overheads.*

This chapter goes on to explain how a business will collect the data about, and then calculate the cost of, each of the three components. The techniques described can be applied to (A) *actual* costs which have been incurred, i.e. actual data is collected *or* (B) *Estimated* costs which it is thought *will* be incurred in the future, i.e. *estimated* data is collected. Remember Chapter 1? The product costing techniques used to answer the "What does it cost to make?" question can also be used as budgeting techniques to answer "What *will* it cost to make?' In many ways the most important question for a business is "What *will* it cost to make?" Because the selling price of the product must be related to the cost – and businesses must have an idea of a product's cost *before* deciding whether to make it.

For instance it would be no good deciding to make jeans, running up 4,000 pairs, and *then* measuring the costs only to find they came out at £55 each pair! Obviously no one would buy them at a price enabling you to make a profit.

So the way the components of an absorption cost are found can apply to *estimated* as well as *actually incurred* costs. In fact businesses usually (A) estimate the costs of a product (budgeting) (B) make the product and (C) measure the actual costs incurred (product costing). The comparisons between (A) and (C) reveal useful information – as we shall see in Chapter 4 and onwards, and of course come under the heading of *appraisal.*

DETERMINING THE DIRECT LABOUR COST OF AN ITEM

The direct labour cost of a pair of jeans means the wages paid to the people who actually cut out and stitched together that garment. The direct labour cost of a motor car means the wages paid to the people who actually built it on the assembly line. The direct labour cost of a field of potatoes is the wages of the farm workers who ploughed, sowed, weeded and lifted the final crop.

What all of these examples have in common is that in principle the direct labour cost is MEASURABLE. You could go and look in the jeans factory and perhaps you might find the following data – albeit with the aid of a stop watch:

(A) Time taken to cut out one pattern from the roll of cloth: 6 minutes
(B) Time taken to stitch together the pattern: 10 minutes
(C) Time taken to add zip, buttons, studs and labels: 4 minutes

Total time taken: 20 minutes

Imagine you now ask what the people who do operations A, B and C are paid per hour, and you get these answers:

(A) £5 per hour
(B) £6 per hour
(C) £6 per hour

You can now do a simple sum to work out the direct labour cost of a pair of jeans:

(A) D.L. COST PER HOUR = £5

Therefore £5 ÷ 60 = Cost of 1 minute

Therefore $\frac{5}{60}$ × 6 minutes = Cost of 6 minutes = D.L. cost of cutting out one pair.

: $\frac{5}{60}$ × 6 = £0.50p, so D.L. cost of cutting = £0·50

(B) D.L. COST PER HOUR = £6

There £6 ÷ 60 = Cost of 1 minute

Therefore $\frac{£6}{60}$ × 10 = Cost of 10 minutes = D.L. cost of stitching 1 pair.

: $\frac{£6}{60}$ × 10 = £1, so D.L. cost of stitching = £1·00

(C) D.L. COST PER HOUR = £6

There fore 6 ÷ 60 = Cost of 1 minute

Therefore $\frac{6}{60}$ × 4 = Cost of 4 minutes = D.L. cost of finishing one pair.

: $\frac{6}{60}$ × 4 = £0·40p, so D.L. cost of finishing = £0.40

$$
\begin{array}{rr}
 & £ \\
\text{Total DIRECT LABOUR COST of 1 pair of Jeans} = & 0\cdot50 \\
+ & 1\cdot00 \\
+ & 0\cdot40 \\
\hline
& £1\cdot90 \\
\end{array}
$$

This simple example illustrates how all direct labour costs are gathered: i.e. the time actually taken to make the product is measured, and the wages cost of that time is calculated, which becomes the direct labour cost of that product. And if the basic data (i.e. the times and wages) were *estimated* you would have the estimated (budgeted) direct labour cost of a pair of jeans.

Obviously in reality there is not someone standing around measuring how long people work on *every* individual car, or *every* individual pair of jeans. In the jean factory they might do as follows when they checked the costs:

1 week's output of jeans = 5,000 pairs
1 week's wages for the production workers = £9,750
Therefore ACTUAL Direct Labour cost per pair =

$$
\frac{9,750}{5,000} = £1\cdot95 \text{ each.}
$$

(Note if our previous calculation of £1·90 had been the PLANNED, i.e. BUDGETED, cost per pair – we would now know that in this particular week the product was costing *more* than we intended).

In a car factory people generally have particular jobs which they always do. For instance they always put on the wheels, or always assemble the engines, or always paint the cars. In this sort of factory people usually "clock on" and "clock off" – which means they have an individual card which is time-stamped when they start and stop work.

At the end of the week the hours they have worked are calculated from the cards. These hours are used to calculate their wages which (pretending in an individual case the person assembles engines) then become part of the Direct Labour cost of the engines; for example:

CLOCK CARD:		Mr M Hunter			
		DATE: WEEK 15			
	MON	TUES	WED	THURS	FRI
Starting time:	8am	8am	8am	8am	7am
Finishing time:	4pm	5pm	5pm	4pm	4pm	TOTAL HOURS
DAILY HOURS	8	9	9	8	9	43

Fig. 10.

The accounts office will pay Mr Hunter for 43 hours' work; at £3 per hour he will earn = 3 × 43 = £129. If Mr Hunter assembles engines (which the accounts office will know) the £129 becomes part of the Direct Labour cost of assembling engines. If there are 25 people who do that work, and between them they earn £3450 that week, then that is the Direct Labour Cost of making engines that week. If 120 were made then:

$$\text{DIRECT LABOUR COST OF EACH ENGINE} = \frac{£3,450}{120}$$

$$= £28{\cdot}75$$

And this type of data could be used as the basis of estimating the *future* direct labour cost of making engines.

Finally if someone does several tasks and spends, for example, two hours assembling engines, two hours putting on wheels, and four hours painting on one day; there has to be a method of dividing up his or her time so that the cost of the wages can be properly allocated. When this happens a TIME SHEET is used which either a foreman or the individuals themselves fill in. All a time sheet does is to analyse the clock hours over the various types of work the person has done that week.

If Mr Hunter had worked in three departments that week, then his time sheet (which would *reconcile* to his clock card, i.e. agree in total with it) might look like Fig. 11 below .

MR HUNTER: TIME SHEET: WEEK 15						
DEPARTMENTS	MON	TUES	WED	THUR	FRI	TOTALS
ENGINES	3	3	3	4	2	15
PAINT	5	4		4	4	17
WHEEL ASSEMBLY		2	6		3	11
TOTALS	8	9	9	8	9	43

Fig. 11.

And the accounts department, using Mr Hunter's hourly rate of £3, would now allocate his wages cost as follows:

```
                                         £
Engine department D.L. 15 × 3 = 45
Paint department    D.L. 17 × 3 = 51
Wheel department   D.L. 11 × 3 = 33
                                       ----
                                       £129
                                       ====
```

And of course the £129 is what he is paid, which agrees with the original wages calculation following Fig. 10.

TO SUMMARISE

Direct labour costs are in principle measurable and can be allocated between products accurately. The methods of doing this are various; but all have in common the fact that some measurement occurs. In principle time spent is measured, quantity produced is measured, wages paid are measured, and then simple calculations done to produce a DIRECT LABOUR COST PER ITEM.

If the data was in fact estimated rather than actual, the same calculations produce the *estimated* direct labour cost per item.

Now work through the questions in section A at the end of this chapter.

DETERMINING THE DIRECT MATERIAL COST OF AN ITEM

In the main direct materials are bought in from outside the firm, which makes determining the direct material cost of an item easy in principle. Really just a matter of finding out what the business paid its supplier for the particular supplies concerned; then measuring how much is used to make the particular product being costed.

If we use the example of the jeans factory; the direct materials (i.e. the materials out of which the product is actually made) are denim cloth, zips, buttons, studs, and cotton sewing thread. If we confine ourselves to the main item for the moment – the denim cloth – here is how the direct material cost would be found:

1. Measure the length used to cut out one pair of jeans. (Say 2 yards were used.)

2. Find out the cost per yard. (Your examination of the suppliers invoice shows the denim material is bought for £1·50 per yard.)

3. Quantity used × price per unit = Direct Material Cost.

Therefore 2 yards × £1·50 per yard = £3 Direct Material cost per pair.

So in principle the way to determine direct material costs is very easy: find out the amount used and find out how much that amount cost to buy. The amount used is found by measuring; the cost to buy the materials is found from the supplier's invoice.

If estimated direct material costs are required the calculations are the same; but the data has to be predicted. For example you find out what the price of denim will be from your supplier, and estimate the amount of denim needed for one pair of jeans (or even make one test pair to be quite sure).

This holds good for our car-factory example too. The paint shop might start the day with 2,000 gallons of paint. At the end of the shift 600 cars have been painted and 200 gallons of paint are left over for the next day, so:

PAINT USED = 2,000 − 200 = 1,800 gallons

Imagine the Price per gallon = £5 (found from supplier's invoice)

Total Direct Materials Cost for Painting 600 Cars = 1,800 gallons × 5 = £9,000

$$\text{Direct Material Cost per car for PAINT} = \frac{£9,000}{600 \text{ cars}} = £15 \text{ per car}$$

In reality firms always hold a stock of direct materials in their stores, and issue those materials to the production line as they are required. This means that the storemen keep STOCK RECORDS which show the movements of each type of material in and out of the stores. The point of stock records is so managers can quickly check how much of a particular type of material is available. It is no good deciding to spray cars green today if there is no green paint available to use. The stock records enable the people in charge of production (the production controllers) to check that everything they need (for the next day or week or month) is ready. They could go and physically count everything each time they wanted to know of course; but that would obviously take far too long.

Stock records usually record (1) the price per unit of the particular material; (2) the quantity of it in stock; (3) the history of inflows from suppliers; and (4) issues to production. A typical stock card (which might be a physical card, or an image on a computer V.D.U.) would look like Fig. 12 below, look at it now.

On the 25 April 1983 the production controllers know, by checking the stock-card kept by the storemen, that there are 5,000 gallons of green paint available. They can then check if this is enough for their future plans. If it isn't, more can be ordered. The supplier code indicates from whom the paint was purchased, of course.

No problems with direct materials you think – well, unfortunately, the fact that (A) firms keep goods in stock and (B) prices for identical goods change means there can be a catch . . .

Take a stock item that never deteriorates – say a wheel nut (i.e. one of

MATERIAL: GREEN PAINT: PRICE £5 PER GALLON					
RECEIVED	DATE	SUPPLIER CODE	ISSUED	DATE	BALANCE
4,000 gallons	1.2.83	42			4,000
			3,000 gallons	1.3.83	1,000
6,000 gallons	3.4.83	42			7,000
			2,000 gallons	25.4.83	5,000

Fig. 12.

the nuts which holds on the wheels of a car to the axle) sprayed with grease so it doesn't rust. Believe me: I've seen such items, in absolutely perfect condition, that were produced 50 years ago.

Say a regular order is placed for 20 boxes of wheel nuts per month – which is about the number used in production. The business has a policy of keeping one months supply in stock, and over the last four months the price per box has risen from £10 to £15.

Figure 13 below shows the pattern of receipts and issues for the four months, and shows that the opening balance was 20 boxes costing £10 each.

Now we come to the point of the catch. Figure 13 shows the *physical* movements of stock, and the closing *physical* balance. It shows the prices that the stock was bought for. However it doesn't show the *value* of the issued quantities, nor the *value* of the balances in stock.

The *reason* these later prices are not yet shown is because we do not yet know *which* nuts were issued and which remained. For example take the first issue of nuts in MARCH: were the 22 boxes used in production bought for £10 per thousand or £12 per thousand?

Now it is not worth putting a label on each nut (it would cost more than the nut itself!) and it is not worth keeping the nuts separate. Storemen always want to keep the same item in the same place so they know where to find them. Even more importantly as the nuts never deteriorate it is not worth *physically* using them in any particular order. It doesn't matter if a nut remains in store for years and years: it will still be a good item.

So we have this problem (A) to determine the direct material prices we need to know the price of the nuts issued each month, while (B) it is not worth bothering to physically separate the nuts so we *can* do (A).

				BOXES OF TYPE 10 WHEEL NUTS				
RECEIPTS			ISSUES			BALANCE		
QUANTITY OF BOXES	DATE	PRICE/ BOX	QUANTITY OF BOXES	DATE	VALUE OF ISSUES	QUANTITY OF BOXES	VALUE £	
		£10				20	200	
20	MARCH	£12				40		
			22	MARCH		18		
20	APRIL	£13				38		
			17	APRIL		21		
20	MAY	£14				41		
			25	MAY		16		
20	JUNE	£15				36		
			20	JUNE		16		

Fig. 13.

SOLUTION For direct material costing purposes in these circumstances, cost accountants PRETEND THE STOCK IS USED IN A PARTICULAR ORDER. There are three pretend-using-sequences to choose from:

1. Pretend the nuts *Bought First* were *Used First*. This is called "FIRST IN FIRST OUT" or "F.I.F.O." stock usage.

Quick FIFO illustration:

Stock = 20 boxes all mixed up together: 10 cost £10 BOUGHT SEPTEMBER
10 cost £12 BOUGHT OCTOBER
———
VALUE OF STOCK £22
═══

If 10 are issued under FIFO system: *Direct material cost of issues = £10*, i.e. the ones bought first we pretend have been issued first.

2. Pretend the nuts *Bought Last* were *Used First*. This is called "LAST IN FIRST OUT" or "L.I.F.O." stock usage.

Quick LIFO illustration:

Stock = 20 boxes all mixed up together: 10 cost £10 BOUGHT SEPTEMBER
10 cost £12 BOUGHT OCTOBER
———
VALUE OF STOCK £22
═══

If 10 are issued under LIFO system: *Direct Material cost of issues* = *£12*, i.e. the ones bought last we pretend have been issued first.

3. Pretend the nuts were used on average from each delivery. This is called "*Average Cost*" or "*AVCO*" stock usage.

Quick AVCO illustration:

Stock = 20 boxes all mixed up together: 10 cost £10 BOUGHT SEPTEMBER
                                        10 cost £12 BOUGHT OCTOBER

                    VALUE OF STOCK 22

If 10 are issued under AVCO system: Average Cost of 10 boxes = $\frac{£22}{2}$ = £11 per thousand: So *Direct material cost of issues* = *£11*, i.e. the ones issued are issued at the average price.

We can now go on to apply these methods to the wheel-nut stock card in Fig. 13 above. However, before we do, a word to balance your understanding of direct material costs. The FIFO, LIFO and AVCO choice is only necessary when the stock concerned is (i) of low value and (ii) does not deteriorate. For high value items, e.g. TV sets, cars, fridges, gold bars, it is well worth the cost and effort of tracing each individual item in stock (by labelling it and recording its serial number in and out of stock). Then you know exactly which item has been issued. Under these circumstances you have recorded the original cost of each separate item; you have identified its movement into and out of stock as an individual item, so you have no problem knowing its direct material cost when used. In short, because each item has been individually identified and its cost recorded, pricing it when issued from stock presents no problem; because the direct material cost of each item is separately identified in the records.

Perishable items *must be physically used in a FIFO manner*, of course. How would you feel if you bought a bottle of milk that had been standing at the back of the dairy for 6 months? Stock valuations of this type of item *must* be done on a FIFO basis – pretence is unnecessary.

Many people find LIFO, FIFO and AVCO calculations complicated and boring. My own view is that this is true, and that exam-setters give them far too much importance. If you find them difficult, don't be put off. In many ways they are the most complicated and least important part of cost accounting. Nevertheless if you have an exam in mind you must master the methods involved.

So FIFO, LIFO and AVCO costing methods apply to low-value non-perishable direct materials only – and as they often appear in exams you need to know how to apply them. But remember because a particular method is chosen (e.g. AVCO) *it does NOT mean the stock is actually used in that way.* Can you imagine the storeman in the car factory carefully picking out certain boxes from each delivery when asked for 17 boxes of nuts to be issued to production?

FIFO, LIFO, AVCO EXAMPLE

The stock card in Fig. 13 is the basic data for the following illustration of how the valuation systems work in a more complex example. Work your way carefully through them, and be sure you understand how the issues have been priced. You may find it helpful to copy out the stock card and fill it in but be sure you do understand the three methods of "pretend issuing".

FIFO STOCK ISSUING VALUES

NARRATIVE	Quantity of Boxes	Price per Box	Value of Boxes	Analysis of Issues & Balances
		£	£	March Issue in FIFO order:
Opening Balance	20	10	200	(i) 20 @ £10 = £200
Add March Receipts	20	12	240	+ (ii) 2 @ £12 = £24
Balance	40	–	440	= 22 £224
less March Issues	22	–	224	End March Balance =
				18 @ £12 = £216
Balance	18		216	
Add April Receipts	20	13	260	
				April Issue in FIFO order:
Balance	38	–	476	(i) 17 @ £12 = £204
				End April Balance:
less April Issues	17	–	204	1 @ £12 = £12
				+ 20 @ £13 = £260
Balance	21		272	21 £272
Add May Receipts	20	14	280	
				May Issue in FIFO order:
Balance	41		552	(i) 1 @ £12 = £12
				+ (ii) 20 @ £13 = £260
less May Issues	25		328	+ (iii) 4 @ £14 = £56
Balance	16		£224	25 £328
				End May Balance:
				16 @ £14 = £224

Fig. 14.

You should now complete the June issues and receipts for yourself. The closing June FIFO stock should be valued at £240.

LIFO APPLICATIONS

In this case the ones bought *most recently* we pretend are used first.

LIFO STOCK ISSUING VALUES

NARRATIVE	Quantity of Boxes	Price per Box	Value of Boxes	Analysis of Issues & Balances
		£	£	March Issue in LIFO order:
Opening Balance	20	10	200	(i) 20 @ £12 = £240
Add March Receipts	20	12	240	+ (ii) 2 @ £10 = £20
Balance	40	–	440	22 £260
less March Issues	22	–	260	End March Balance:
Balance	18		180	18 @ £10 = £180
Add April Receipts	20	13	260	
				April Issue in LIFO order:
Balance	38		440	17 @ £13 = £221
less April Issues	17	–	221	
				End of April Balance:
				18 @ £10 = £180
Balance	21		219	3 @ £13 = £39
Add May Receipts	20	14	280	21 £219
Balance	41		499	May Issue in LIFO Order:
				(i) 20 @ £14 = £280
less May Issues	25		339	+ (ii) 3 @ £13 = £39
				+ (iii) 2 @ £10 = £20
Balance	16	–	160	25 £339
				End May Balance:
				16 @ £10 = £160

Fig. 15.

You should now complete the remaining month for yourself. The closing June LIFO stock value you should have is £160.

SUMMARY SO FAR

Don't lose sight of the fact that we are learning about PRODUCT COSTING, and are at the moment learning how to find out the Direct Material cost of an item. With low value non-perishable items, this will vary slightly depending upon the pretend-issuing-method chosen. For example if we used FIFO the direct material cost of the 25 boxes issued in May would be £328. If we used LIFO the direct material cost would be £339. This may seem odd, but remember the difference between the two is balanced by the different closing stock valuations. In FIFO *and* LIFO we have *spent* the same amount on wheel nuts:

		£	
Amounts spent:	Opening Stock	200	
	March receipt	240	
	April receipt	260	
	May receipt	280	
	Total spent	£980	

		£	
In FIFO our issues have been *priced* at:	March	224	(Fig. 14)
	April	204	,,
	May	328	,,
So Total Direct Materials *used* are valued at:		756	
FIFO STOCK BALANCE VALUE AT END OF MAY:		224	(Fig. 14)
STOCK + USAGE TOTAL		£980	= AMOUNT SPENT

		£	
In LIFO our issues have been *priced* at:	March	260	(Fig. 15)
	April	221	,,
	May	339	,,
So Total Direct Materials *used* are valued at:		820	
LIFO STOCK BALANCE VALUE AT END OF MAY:		160	(Fig. 15)
STOCK + USAGE TOTAL:		£980	= AMOUNT SPENT

I hope it is now clear to you that there are consequences resulting from the decision – that must be made – whether to use a FIFO or LIFO stock-issuing method. In both cases up until May we have issued and used the *same number* of wheel-nuts as direct materials: 22 + 17 + 25 = 64 boxes issued. However in FIFO (up to May) we will charge £756 as their direct material cost and in LIFO £820. This means that any product cost we calculate will be higher if the LIFO system is used; *and therefore any profit shown will be lower.* (Remember Revenue less cost = Profit.) Having dealt with AVCO these points will be discussed further – suffice it now that you clearly realise that *a management decision* (whether to use FIFO or LIFO) *can affect what we show as the cost of a product.* ∽ effects P+L A/C .

AVCO APPLICATIONS

Under this system we pretend that the items are issued proportionately from each batch in the stores. What this means is that an average price is calculated *every time some new stores are delivered.* This price is then used for all issues until a new delivery makes a new average price necessary.

Although the calculation of the average price has to be done, it does mean the issuing is much more straightforward than with FIFO and LIFO.

AVCO STOCK ISSUING VALUES

NARRATIVE	Quantity of Boxes	Price per Box	Value of Boxes	Explanations
		£	£	
Opening Balance	20	10	200	Average price now is
Add March Receipts	20	12	240	£440 ÷ 40 = £11 per box.
	—	—	—	The March issues are at
Balance	40	–	440	this price.
less March Issues	22	11	242	
	—	—	—	
Balance	18	11	198	
Add April Receipts	20	13	260	The new average price is
	—	—	—	£458 ÷ 38 = £12·05. The
Balance	38	–	458	April issues will be at
less April Issues	17	12·05	205	this price.
	—	—	—	
Balance	21	12·05	253	
Add May Receipts	20	14	280	The new average price now
	—	—	—	is £533 ÷ 41 = £13. The
Balance	41		533	May issues will be at this
less May Issues	25	13	325	price.
	—	—	—	
Balance	16	£13	£208	

Fig. 16.

You should now complete the remaining month for yourself. The June AVCO closing stock valuation is: £226.

The only question remaining is "Which system to choose?" In reality almost nobody uses LIFO. This is because in times of rising prices (such as now with inflation) it gives, as in our example, higher costs and therefore lower profits. No company wants to understate profits to the public and most tax authorities won't allow it for taxation computations either – because it gives lower taxable profits and therefore less tax revenue.

Most businesses use FIFO or AVCO and there is not much to choose between them; except to say that in times of rapidly fluctuating prices AVCO tends to smooth out rapid changes in direct material costs. The most important point is that *once a system is adopted it should be consistently used.* In this way costs from one period to another can be fairly compared. If a business used FIFO one month and AVCO the next the comparisons would be meaningless. Indeed, consistency of method is a guiding principle of all accounts work – financial and costing.

Now work through the questions in section B at the end of the chapter.

DETERMINING OVERHEAD COSTS

If you have just done the first two parts of the chapter and are feeling tired, leave this until tomorrow. It's not that difficult; but *it is very important indeed that you understand it properly and fully.* So I strongly recommend you start this section when fresh.

There is no problem in determining the total overheads of a business for a given period (e.g. the total overheads for last year, or last month). It is really only a matter of searching in the accounts department to find out what was spent on factory indirect expenses and office costs. Similarly the total *expected* overheads for a future period can be estimated, taking into account price and wage increases and so on.

In Chapter 2 the importance of the product-by-product approach of cost accounting was emphasised – and an example given (Fig. 7) of what could be learned from dividing up costs between products. At that stage it was just assumed to be possible to do so. We already know that for direct labour and direct materials it is (in principle) always possible to know on which product the cost is, or will be, incurred. You can go and see on which product the people are working and into which one the materials go.

With overhead costs this is often *not possible, in principle.* Take administration costs – is one expected to measure how much time the Managing Director spends thinking about each product? Are the transport people expected to note down the proportion of each delivery van's load space that is used for each product? Does someone follow the works manager around, noting down the time he or she spends on sorting out production problems relating to each type of product made? Clearly all these things are quite out of the question. The more so when you consider that most manufacturing businesses make several products which go through three or four production departments. Under these circumstances, it would be impossible to *individually* measure and allocate to a particular item the individual costs which make up overheads.

There is a way to get over this difficulty:

(A) Overhead costs are always for a given period of time (e.g. one month, one year) whether estimated or actual for that time.

(B) In the same period of time there is only so much PRODUCTIVE CAPACITY available, i.e. only so many hours in which the men and machines will be working in the factory. Again this may be estimated, or be a record of the time actually worked.

(C) In that time the firm must use the PRODUCTIVE CAPACITY to make products to sell, and therefore get revenue to pay for all the costs and (hopefully) make some profit.

So there is now a fair way of allocating the overhead costs to products: TOTAL OVERHEAD COSTS ARE ALLOCATED BETWEEN ITEMS PRODUCED IN PROPORTION TO THE AMOUNT OF PRODUCTIVE CAPACITY USED UP IN MAKING EACH ITEM; i.e., if you use up one third of your production time making a bike, you must allocate one third of your overheads as part of the bike's cost. And if you predict (i.e. estimate) the bike *will* take one third of your future production time; you must include one third of your overheads as part of the bike's *estimated* product cost.

For example, imagine a month's total overheads for a domestic appliance factory to be £80,000 and in that month 500 production hours were available. Assume the output and time taken was as follows:

OUTPUT	TIME TAKEN	% OF PRODUCTION TIME AVAILABLE
		%
400 Washing Machines	150	30
500 Fridges	100	20
250 Tumble Dryers	75	15
1,000 Freezers	175	35
	500 hours	100%

As the 400 washing machines took up 30% of our productive capacity they are charged with 30% of the overhead costs incurred in the month:

WASHING MACHINE OVERHEADS = 30% × £80,000 = £24,000

$$\text{OVERHEAD COST PER MACHINE} = \frac{£24,000}{400 \text{ machines}} = £60$$

With the fridges the overhead cost = 20% × £80,000 = £16,000

$$\text{Overhead cost per fridge} = \frac{£16,000}{500 \text{ fridges}} = £32$$

With the Tumble Dryers the overhead cost = 15% × £80,000 = £12,000

$$\text{Overhead cost per dryer} = \frac{£12,000}{250 \text{ dryers}} = £48$$

With the Freezers the overhead cost = 35% × £80,000 = £28,000

$$\text{Overhead cost per freezer} = \frac{£28,000}{1,000 \text{ freezers}} = £28$$

Our total overheads of £80,000 have been allocated as costs to the products as follows:

	£
Washing Machines	24,000
Fridges	16,000
Tumble Dryers	12,000
Freezers	28,000
Total Overheads	£80,000

In cost accountant's jargon we say the overheads have been RE-COVERED by charging them as part of the cost of a product. Meaning as long as we sell all the items produced, for more than their total cost each, we will *recover* from customers as part of the selling price the overhead costs incurred. For example, imagine one Fridge's direct labour cost was £20 and direct material cost was £27. We calculated its overhead cost to be £32. Therefore the absorption product cost of one fridge is:

	£
Direct Labour	20
Direct Material	27
Overheads	32
Total Cost	£79

As long as the 500 fridges are all sold for more than £79 each we shall *recover* all of the costs of making the fridges, and in particular recover the fridge overhead costs, i.e. 500 × £32 = £16,000.

This is an easy example of overhead calculation to ensure the basis of

the method is clear – namely "allocate overheads to a product in proportion to the productive capacity used up in making it".

In reality this can be slightly more complicated because most firms
have several production departments and so several separate productive
capacities are involved. Under these circumstances the principles remain
the same; but the detail of the calculations is different.

OVERHEAD RECOVERY RATES

Take a firm with three production departments that makes wooden builders' supplies such as doors, windows, cupboards, as an example. And
instead of finding out what the overheads *were*; this time we shall pretend
we are estimating *what they will be* in the future. The basic data we start
with is:

NEXT YEAR'S ESTIMATED TOTAL OVERHEADS = £450,000
NEXT YEAR'S ESTIMATED PRODUCTIVE CAPACITY IN THE THREE PRODUCTION DEPARTMENTS:

    SAWING DEPT: 5,000 machine hours
    SHAPING DEPT: 7,500 machine hours
    ASSEMBLY DEPT: 10,000 direct labour (i.e. man) hours

Fig. 17.

NOTE: Capacity to produce things is usually a matter of the number of
hours available. However there can be two SORTS of production hours.
If a machine does most of the work (for example a power saw in the
sawing department, or a computer in a data processing department)
then it is the number of hours the *machine* works for, that defines how
much capacity is available. So if the department works for 40 hours
per week and has 3 machines, the productive capacity for that week is
40 hours × 3 machines = 120 *machine hours*. If, on the other hand, the
work is principally done by individual workers (in our example assembling the pre-shaped wooden parts to make a window, say, or painting
a house, or mending a car) it is the number of man-hours (i.e. direct
labour hours) that defines productive capacity. A department working
for 40 hours per week, with 5 people assembling wooden parts, therefore has productive capacity of: 40 hours × 5 men = 200 *direct labour
hours*.

Returning to our data in Fig. 17, we have three productive capacities
and only one total overhead figure. The next step is to divide up the total
overheads into 3 so that each department has a certain overhead amount
allocated to it – which must be recovered by being included as part of the
costs of the things made in that department.

Imagine that the £450,000 is to be divided up between the three departments as follows:

Sawing	Shaping	Assembly	TOTAL
200,000	150,000	100,000	£450,000

Fig. 18.

This means that (for example) everything made in the Sawing department will have an absorption cost which will be made up of

: Direct Labour cost of making it
: Direct Material cost of making it
: An overhead cost which will be the same percentage of £200,000 that the time taken to make it is of the total productive capacity of 5,000 sawing machine hours.

Take some wood being sawn up to make a batch of 100 doors, where the Direct Labour cost is estimated to be £400, and the direct material cost (the wood itself) to be £900. It is further estimated the wood will take 50 machine hours to saw up. 50 hours is 1% of the total 5,000 machine hours available in the sawing department. The cost of the sawn (but not yet shaped or assembled batch of doors) would be estimated to be:

	£
Direct Labour	400
Direct Materials	900
Overheads £200,000 × 1%	2,000
Estimated Absorption product cost of sawn batch of 100 doors =	£3,300

Fig. 19.

Now rather than have to decide what percentage of the productive capacity is taken up by each product made, it is easier to *work out in advance the amount of overhead that has to be charged for each hour of productive capacity used.*

In our example the sawing department has £200,000 of overheads to recover in a year (i.e. to charge as part of the cost of what it makes) and it has 5,000 hours of productive capacity in which to make things. So £200,000 ÷ 5,000 HOURS = £40 which equals the amount of overhead that has to be charged as a cost of using one hour's productive capacity.

Now the product cost calculation is a bit easier:

		£
Direct Labour	=	400
Direct Materials	=	900
Overhead = 50 hours at		
£40 per hour	=	2,000
Cost of sawn Doors		£3,300

Fig. 20.

So for businesses with several production departments this type of "overheads per hour of productive capacity" calculation is always done. The overheads are still being charged in proportion to the productive capacity used of course – it is just that the amount to be charged as overhead per hour is worked out in advance.

The amount to be charged as overhead cost, for each hour of productive capacity used up is called the "OVERHEAD RECOVERY RATE" (ORR).

The *overhead recovery rates* for the Shaping and Assembly departments will be worked out in exactly the same way: i.e. divide their overhead allocation by their productive capacities. Check with the data in Figs. 17 and 18 and you will see,

Shaping Dept   Overhead share = £150,000

         Productive capacity   =   7,500 machine hours

Therefore the Shaping Dept's ORR = $\dfrac{150,000}{7,500}$ = £20 per machine hour

Assembly Dept   Overhead share = £100,000

         Productive capacity   =   10,000 direct labour hours

Therefore the Assembly Dept's ORR = $\dfrac{100,000}{10,000}$ = £10 per direct labour hour.

Fig. 21.

EXAMPLE SUMMARY SO FAR

This business intends to spend a total of £450,000 on overhead costs in the forthcoming year. It intends to make things in the sawing department for 5,000 machine hours, in the shaping department for 7,500 machine hours and in the assembly department for 10,000 direct labour hours. As well as the direct material and direct labour costs of the things it makes; it *must include in the product costs the following amounts to cover the overheads*:

£

For each sawing hour taken up making a product   = 40
For each shaping hour taken up making a product = 20
For each assembly hour taken up making a product = 10

THE PURPOSE OF THE OVERHEAD COST ESTIMATES

The business is now in a position to ensure that it RECOVERS its total overhead costs in its selling prices. It can ensure this because IT CAN NOW ESTIMATE SELLING PRICES BASED ON THE ESTIMATED FULL ABSORPTION COST OF MAKING ITS PRODUCTS. Refer to Fig. 20, the estimated cost of the batch of so far only sawn doors is £3,300; let's extend the estimate: they will take 10 machine hours to shape in the shaping department and will incur £100 of direct labour cost there, but no more direct materials will be needed.

		£
Estimated Costs in the Shaping Department:	Direct Labour	100
	Direct Materials	–
	Overheads: 10 hours at £20 per machine hour	200
Estimated Shaping dept cost of batch		£300

Fig. 22.

In the assembly dept where pay rates are £3 per hour it will take 30 hours to assemble them and £40 worth of direct material will be used when they are painted. So the assembly dept cost of the batch will be:

		£
Estimated costs in Assembly dept:	Direct labour 30 hours at £3 per hour:	90
	Direct materials:	40
	Overheads: 30 hours at £10 per direct labour hour:	300
Estimated assembly cost of batch		£430

Fig. 23.

TOTAL ESTIMATED COST OF BATCH OF 100 DOORS:

		£
Sawing dept	(Fig. 20)	3,300
Shaping dept	(Fig. 22)	300
Assembly dept	(Fig. 23)	430
Total Cost for 100 doors =		£4,030

Fig. 24.

Therefore the estimated absorption cost per door = £4,030 ÷ 100 = £40·30 EACH. Therefore these doors must be sold for more than £40·30p each if the business is to RECOVER the costs it has incurred in making them.

OVERHEADS SECTION SUMMARY SO FAR

Firms must set selling prices which will recover all of the costs they incur in making their products. This means *EITHER* actual costs must be measured before a selling price is set *OR* estimated costs must be calculated before a firm agrees to make and sell a product for a given price. The direct costs are in principle easy to actually measure or to estimate. The overhead costs are estimated by working out (A) what the overheads *will* be in total, (B) how much production time there *will be*, (C) calculating the overhead cost per hour of production time, and (D) ensuring *for each hour of production time* used in making a product it has included in its product cost *one hour's worth of overhead costs*. And the name for 1 hour's worth of overhead costs is the OVERHEAD RECOVERY RATE – which must always be expressed as being *per machine hour* or *per direct labour hour* or *per some-particular-sort-of-productive-capacity* hour.

Finally the main point of all this estimating of absorption product costs is to SET A SELLING PRICE.

FURTHER POINTS ON OVERHEADS

Our wooden builders' supplies example took us through four stages (fig 25) when we calculated the overhead recovery rates for its three production departments. You need to know clearly and in principle what they were, and also to understand the way in which judgments rather than facts are involved in each stage.

CONSIDER EACH STAGE IN PRACTICE

STAGE 1 How easy is it to estimate the overhead costs in advance? In some businesses it's quite easy. In a solicitor's office for example, next year's rent may be fixed in the lease, the office wages agreed, the electricity and heating bills easy to predict. In this case the solicitor's estimated overheads are likely to prove very close to his actual ones. In a large business however the problems are much more fearsome. Take a car factory. It consists of acres and acres of enormous sheds, thousands of people, vast store-rooms, enormous amounts of energy are needed to work machines and heat buildings, and there are hundreds of different

	IN PRINCIPLE	In our example shown as:
STAGE 1	Estimate total overheads for a future period	£450,000 is estimated total for next year
STAGE 2	Allocate these total overheads between the production departments	£200,000 to Sawing Dept £150,000 to Shaping Dept £100,000 to Assembly Dept £450,000
STAGE 3	Estimate the productive capacity of each department for the same future period	Next year's productive capacities: Sawing Dept: 5,000 machine hours Shaping Dept: 7,500 machine hours Assembly Dept: 10,000 direct labour hours
STAGE 4	Divide the Stage 3 estimate into the Stage 2 estimate to give the overhead recovery rate, i.e. to give the amount that needs to be charged in the product cost, as overheads, for every hour of time taken making the product.	SAWING Dept: £200,000 ÷ 5,000 m/c hrs = ORR £40/mc hr. SHAPING Dept: £150,000 ÷ 7,500 m/c hrs = ORR £20/mc hr. ASSEMBLY DEPT: £100,000 ÷ 10,000 direct labour hours = ORR £10/dir. lab. hr.

Fig. 25.

departments and offices. Trying to accurately estimate the cost of it all is an enormous problem. Unforeseen charges, such as an oil-price increase, can add millions to overhead costs. If the wage settlement is for a 12% increase, where 9% was budgeted, the same happens.

So in many businesses the estimate of total overheads may be difficult to get really accurate, when compared with the actual costs later incurred.

If total overheads are *under-estimated*, the overhead recovery rate will be lower than the *actual overhead cost per hour*. This means the actual profit per item will be lower than the estimated profit – or even that a loss is made where a profit was expected; for example:

	£		£
Estimated Total Overheads	100,000	*Actual Overheads*	120,000
Total Direct Labour	50,000		50,000
Total Direct Material	60,000		60,000
Estimated Total Cost	210,000	Actual Total Cost	230,000
less SALES REVENUE	225,000		225,000
BUDGETED PROFIT	£15,000	ACTUAL LOSS	£(5,000)

Fig. 26.

Therefore businesses must very carefully check each month that their actual and predicted total overhead costs are in line. If they are not then the estimated costs must be adjusted so that predictions of future costs are accurate.

If total overhead estimates are too high, this can be equally serious for a business, because it will price its products too highly – and therefore lose sales to competitors whose prices are lower.

STAGE 2 The allocation of total overheads between production departments. In many ways this is the most important part of the overhead-setting process for cost accountants to understand. Some overheads will clearly *have* to be allocated to a particular department. For example the cost of the machinery used in the shaping department in our previous example, *must* be allocated to that department. Similarly the rent-cost of that department's floor area *must* be allocated to it.

However there are many overhead items which are not obviously allocatable to one production department rather than another. For instance Indirect Labour, Administration, Sales and distribution, Indirect material costs, are all part of the overheads which have to be divided up between the production departments. All create problems in doing so because they are not particularly "attached" to any particular one. The storemen (indirect labour) may issue materials to all the production departments: the works engineer (indirect labour) may fix machines in production, mend the roof in the stores, service the fork lift trucks, all in one day: the cleaning materials (indirect materials) will be used all over the buildings, not just in the production departments: and so on. But the decisions about how much of each to allocate to each production department are crucial because *the amount allocated to each production department affects the cost of things made there.*

Take the Sawing department as an example. Its share of the total overheads was £200,000, and it had 5,000 machine hours, so the overhead cost of a product taking one hour to saw was £40 (£200,000 ÷ 5,000 m/c hours). If the total overheads had been allocated differently (say Sawing Dept £100,000; Shaping Dept £200,000; Assembly Dept £150,000 – still totalling £450,000) then the overhead cost of 1 hour's production time in the Sawing department is £100,000 ÷ 5,000 m/c hours = £20. If the business were selling some sawn (unshaped or assembled) items – for example sawn planks for finishing by another firm – then this different allocation would be of major importance (see Fig. 27).

SAWN PLANKS PER TON

1st Allocation	£	2nd Allocation	£
Direct Labour	50	Direct Labour	50
Direct Materials	400	Direct Materials	400
OVERHEADS		OVERHEADS	
25 sawing m/c hours @ £40/hr	1,000	25 sawing m/c hours @ £20/hr	500
TOTAL COST	£1,450	TOTAL COST	£950

Fig. 27.

If we want to make a profit of £100 per ton then the two selling prices will be very different. Under the first allocation we must quote a price of £1,550 to the customer, under the second, £1,050; easily the difference between getting the business and not getting it.

Of course under the second allocation things made in the other two departments will come out *more* expensive:

Shaping and Assembly Dept Overhead Recovery Rates on Allocation 2:
Sawing Dept: £100,000 ÷ 5,000 m/c hrs = £20 per m/c hr.
Shaping Dept: £200,000 ÷ 7,500 m/c hrs = £26·66 per m/c hr. (Previously £20 per m/c hr.)
Assembly Dept: £150,000 ÷ 10,000 D.L. hrs = £15 per D.L. hr. (Previously £10 per D.L. hr.)

Fig. 28.

WHAT GUIDES FIRMS' ALLOCATION CHOICES?

Why choose the first rather than second allocation – why not choose a third or fourth or fifth? Well, every firm would start by allocating those costs which *had* to be allocated because the costs were for things *only* used in a particular department. Of the £450,000 total overheads in our example these might be:

	Sawing £	Shaping £	Assembly £	
Machine Costs	30,000	25,000	10,000	TOTAL
Rent	20,000	22,000	16,000	SO FAR
Foremen	10,000	8,000	12,000	ALLOCATED
Heating and light	11,000	13,000	9,000	
	£71,000	£68,000	£47,000	£186,000

Fig. 29.

This leaves a total of £450,000 *minus* £186,000 = £264,000 not yet allocated. Imagine this total broken down as follows:

	£
Works Engineer	30,000
Stores Rent	40,000
Cleaners and	
Storemens wages	25,000
Works Management	21,000
Sales and	
Distribution	72,000
Administration	67,000
Financial	9,000
	£264,000

Fig. 30.

Well, the works engineer would probably spend most of his time on the machinery in the Sawing and Shaping Dept so it might be allocated as shown below in Fig. 31.

	Sawing	Shaping	Assembly	TOTAL
	£	£	£	£
Works Engineer	15,000	15,000	—	30,000
Stores Area Rent	15,000	10,000	15,000	40,000
Cleaners and				
Storemens Wages	10,000	5,000	10,000	25,000
Works Management	3,000	6,000	12,000	21,000
Sales and				
Distribution	20,000	20,000	32,000	72,000
Administration	10,000	27,000	30,000	67,000
Financial	3,000	5,000	1,000	9,000
	£76,000	£88,000	£100,000	£264,000

Fig. 31.

For the *stores rent* it is usual to find out how much of the stores area is used for each department's materials. In our example most room will be taken up by un-sawn wood. It probably wouldn't be fair to put *all* this onto the sawing department as the others all *use* the wood after it has been sawn. So a *judgment* has to be made, my guess is shown in Fig. 31.

The *Cleaners' and Storemen's Wages* (indirect labour) again must be a matter of *judgment*. Obviously the time the cleaners spend in each production department is an important guide to their allocation. But they spend time cleaning the stores and offices as well. Similarly the storemen's wages will probably be allocated in the same way the stores rent was. But again they may spend most of their *time* issuing to the assembly dept such items as screws, handles and hinges. In this case perhaps the assembly dept has to have a larger share of this overhead cost. My *judgment* is shown in Fig. 31.

Works Management costs will probably be shared equally unless one department takes up much more management time than another. For instance it is possible the assembly department requires most management effort. Again my judgment is in Fig. 31.

Sales and Distribution costs are another uncertain area. One could say only assembled goods are sold, so therefore that department should bear the costs. However, everything assembled is also sawn and shaped first. So it can equally be argued the cost should be spread out between all these departments. Also it is quite possible that sawn-only or sawn-and-shaped-only, goods are sold. The shaping department may also do some work on materials supplied by customers. In all these instances the departments are benefiting from the sales and distribution effort. So again a *judgment* has to be made.

Much the same considerations apply to *financial* and *administration* costs. Every firm is different and the only way to allocate these costs is to make a fair judgment in the light of the way that firm operates.

For instance, if most of the financial costs are for borrowing money to buy machinery for the shaping department, this department would have to bear those costs. However you must understand that, because much of the *Stage 2* allocation of overheads to production departments is a matter of judgment, two similar firms could easily make different allocations.

The results of *my judgments* are all in Fig. 31. Now we would show the overheads allocated to each department as:

	Sawing	Shaping	Assembly	TOTAL
From Fig. 29.	£	£	£	£
The obviously allocatable overheads	71,000	68,000	47,000	186,000
From Fig. 31.				
The overheads allocated on a basis of assessment and judgment	76,000	88,000	100,000	264,000
	£147,000	£156,000	£147,000	£450,000

Fig. 32.

So now we have a third set of overhead recovery rates possible!
How can we tell when the judgments made are broadly correct?

ULTIMATELY MARKET FORCES GOVERN OVERHEAD ALLOCATION. If we could
charge customers with prices based on overheads at a (1st Allocation)
£40 per machine hour for sawn wood; and were only able to charge
prices based on overheads of £10 per direct labour hour for assembled
items – we would use this first allocation.

If, on the other hand, overheads of £20 per machine hour for sawn
wood gave us a selling price that was as high as the market could take,
and, meanwhile, we could also charge prices for assembly and shaping
based on overhead costs of £15 per D.L. hour and £26·66 per shaping
machine hour, we would use allocation 2.

So in real life one's best judgment is used, followed by a check on how
selling prices come out using that judgment. If they are impossible to
maintain some re-allocation is done.

This would be done within the broad principle that every product
must be able to bear a *reasonable* amount of overhead charge though.
It would not be worth making products which could hardly have any
overhead cost allocated to them before they became unprofitable or
unsaleable.

However, as already mentioned in material costing in choosing FIFO
or AVCO: *Once a basis of allocation is decided upon it should be consistently
used.* In this way the *changes* in costs are meaningful and so help managers
understand what is happening in their businesses.

So far we have discussed the problems and points involved with Stage 1
and Stage 2 of the principles involved in setting ORR's. Now to Stage 3.
Refer to Fig. 25 if your memory needs refreshing.

STAGE 3 The estimated productive capacity. Again you must be clear
that this is a prediction that may or may not turn out to be true.
A business working a machine for 40 hours per week might expect to
have 40 × 52 weeks = 2,080 machine hours capacity in a year. In
reality it won't have. There are holidays; machine-breakdowns, strikes,
power-cuts, all of which will reduce the hours available to make things.
Most firms allow at least 25% for these stoppages. In this example
we might predict 2,080 × 75% = 1,560 hours as our productive capacity.

If this is too high and we don't manage 1,560 hours work on the
machine next year, then we won't recover all our overheads, for instance
if we plan as follows:

	£
Overhead Allocation	23,400
Productive Capacity	1,560 hours
ORR/machine hour	£15

Fig. 33.

and only work for 1,200 hours, we shall only recover in selling prices: 1,200 × 15 = £18,000 of overheads. Meanwhile we have spent £23,400, so the under-recovery is:

	£
Overhead Cost	23,400
Overheads recovered	18,000
Overhead expenses not recovered in selling prices, technically "UNDER RECOVERED"	£5,400

Fig. 34.

This would mean, of course, that profits are £5,400 lower than expected.

Managements must therefore constantly check to ensure they *are* producing goods for as many hours as they planned to when they calculated the ORR. If they are not, costs will be different from those predicted and profits will be lower.

If on the other hand the machine worked for 1,750 hours when only 1,560 had been planned, the opposite would be true:

	£
Overhead Cost	23,400
Overheads recovered 1,750 × £15	26,250
Over Recovery of Overheads =	£2,850

Fig. 35.

which would mean profits £2,850 higher than expected.

Firms always hope to have neither over nor under recovery; because this means their costs are accurately predicted – which is the point of the whole exercise. While an over-recovery is a nice surprise, it may mean valuable business has been lost because costs are *apparently* too high. Using our previous example:

Predicted ORR = £23,400 ÷ 1,560 hours = £15 per machine hour (Fig. 33).
Actual Overhead cost per hour = £23,400 ÷ 1,750 hours =
£13·38 per machine hour (Fig. 35).

If we lost a sale because something that took 70 hours to make on the machine was priced too highly – our predicted cost information would have let us down; for example:

Predicted Cost		£	Actual Cost		£
Direct Labour	=	200	Direct Labour		200
Direct Materials	=	300	Direct Materials		300
Overheads 70 × £15	=	1,050	70 × £13·38		936
Estimated TOTAL COST		£1,550	Actual TOTAL COST		£1,436

Fig. 36.

If the customer would only pay £1,500 we might decide not to take the business – which had we only kept our ORR constantly up to date, we would probably have accepted.

STAGE 4 Merely a division sum – apart from checking it has been done accurately there are no problems here!

OVERHEADS SUMMARY

(A) Overhead costs are given to products in proportion to the amount of productive capacity used up making them.

(B) In practice the main use of this technique is to produce *estimated* absorption product costs on which to base selling prices.

(C) Therefore total overheads for a forthcoming period must be estimated.

(D) Therefore total productive capacity for the same forthcoming period must be estimated, for each production department.

(E) Where firms have more than one production department, and therefore more than one type of productive capacity, total overheads must be allocated between the production departments.

(F) By dividing (D) into (E) the predicted amount chargeable as overheads for 1 hour of production time in each department is found.

(G) As there is always an element of uncertainty in predicting the future, the estimates made in (C) and (D) must be *constantly compared with what actually happens*; adjusted where necessary, and the (F) calculation re-done.

(H) It must be clearly understood that the allocations made in (E) are partly a matter of *judgment*. And the consequences of different judgments will be different costs shown for using an hour of production time in a given department. Ultimately managements choose an allocation that gives fair costs in relation to selling prices the market will bear – BUT THEN THEY MUST STICK TO THAT ALLOCATION SO COST-CHANGES ARE MEANINGFUL AND INFORMATIVE.

(I) The overhead cost of using an hour of productive capacity in a department will therefore be affected by

(i) The amount spent in total on overheads.

(ii) The way they are allocated between departments.

(iii) The amount of productive capacity in that department.

IMPORTANT NOTES

One way to make things more cheaply is to add extra productive capacity without adding any more to the total overheads. To begin with imagine the following situation:

		£
Overhead Allocation	=	20,000
Production Hours on Machines	=	1,000
Therefore Overhead Cost per hour =		£20

Fig. 37.

If another machine is purchased the position could be:

		£
Overhead Allocation	=	20,000
Production Hours on Machines	=	2,000
Therefore Overhead Cost per Hour =		£10

Fig. 38.

If a product cost £70 in Direct Labour, £155 in direct materials and took 30 machine hours to make, its cost before and after adding the extra productive capacity would be:

Before		After	
	£		£
Direct Labour	70	Direct Labour	70
Direct Materials	155	Direct Materials	155
Overheads 30 hours		Overheads 30 hours	
× £20 per m/c hour =	600	× £10 per m/c hour =	300
Total Cost	£825		£525

Fig. 39.

If we want a profit of £140; before we bought the extra machine we had to sell for £965; but after buying it we can sell for £665 – cheaper than our previous cost! This procedure of adding extra capacity without adding extra overhead is called DILUTING THE OVERHEADS (i.e. spreading them out over more production hours to make it cheaper per hour).

I hope you realise what stops this process going on indefinitely – (apart from not having any more room in the factory). Although the product can be sold for £665 (instead of £965) after dilution; there are twice as many production hours to fill, so twice the number of customers is needed! They may not be easy to find. As I write, almost every manufacturing business in the UK has spare productive capacity, i.e. cannot find enough customers. Nevertheless diluting overheads is an important way to remain price-competitive, it is a matter of not going too far – in fact a matter of *judgment*!

RETAIL CONTACT WITH OVERHEAD RECOVERY RATES

In case you are thinking that you will never come into contact with an overhead recovery rate because you never go into a factory, it may surprise you to learn that as an ordinary retail customer you sometimes meet them.

Anyone who has had a car serviced, or has seen someone else's garage bill, has certainly seen a type of ORR. A typical garage bill could look like this:

Roland Simmons Blue Pentangle Garage	
To: Servicing Mr Riddle's Luton Flyer Special:	
Parts Total	£47·32
Labour: 5 hrs @ £15	£75·00
TOTAL	£122·32

Look closely at the labour charge. The mechanic is not paid £15 per hour. This £15 is in fact part ORR, part Direct Labour charge and part profit charge. It probably breaks down something like this:

	£			
ORR	10·50 per Direct Labour Hour			
Direct Labour	3·00 per	,,	,,	,,
Profit	1·50 per	,,	,,	,,
Total Hourly Charge to Customer =	£15·00			

Fig. 40.

i.e., for one production hour (one hour of mechanic's time = 1 Direct Labour hour) a garage business charges a *combined* hourly rate, (a) to recover overheads, (b) to recover direct labour costs, and (c) to provide some profit. This is a good example of how a business will modify the basic cost accounting approach to suit its particular needs. The important thing is to *understand* the modifications in terms of the basics being learned now.

Most professional firms such as solicitors and accountants have similar hourly rates for their "Direct Labourers" – not that the Partners would like to be considered as such! A solicitor might charge £20 per hour for giving advice – which could break down as follows:

	£
ORR per Direct Labour hour (1 hour of solicitor's work)	12
Direct Labour cost (i.e. solicitor's wages per hour)	6
Partners' Profit	2
Total Hourly Charge	£20

Fig. 41.

OTHER VARIOUS POINTS ABOUT OVERHEAD RECOVERY

1. Occasionally, firms *whose productive capacity is in Direct Labour hours*, use a different method of calculating the overhead costs of a product. In principle it is the same as always of course (i.e. allocate overheads in proportion to productive capacity used) but the method is different. This way is to calculate the relationship between total overheads and direct labour costs: e.g.

Total Direct Labour Costs: £25,000 = 100%
Total Overheads: £100,000
Relationship: Overheads are 400% of Direct Labour costs.

If a product cost is estimated giving Direct Labour costs of £300 and Direct Material costs £400, the overheads would be the Direct Labour cost multiplied by the percentage that overheads are of Direct Labour:

Overheads = £300 × 400% = £1,200.

So the product cost =

		£
Direct Labour		300
Direct Materials		400
Overhead £300 × 400%	=	1,200
Product Cost	=	£1,900

Fig. 42.

This method relies on the following logical sequence:

(A) Direct Labour hours are the measure of productive capacity.
(B) Direct Labour hours available are proportional to Direct Labour wages.
(C) Therefore £1 of Direct Labour wages represents a unit of productive capacity.
(D) If overheads need to be allocated per unit of productive capacity they can be allocated per £1 of Direct Labour cost instead:
  Therefore when we read of an ORR of "Direct Labour × 400%": this is really saying, "For every £1 of D.L. cost incurred, a set amount of productive capacity has been used, which costs in overheads £4.

2. Referring to Chapter 2: for stock valuation purposes the *Cost of Production* must be used (i.e. Prime Cost + Factory Indirect Expenses). If an overhead recovery rate is used which includes Office Costs as well (such as mainly used in this chapter) the valuation of finished-goods-stock in year-end financial accounts will have to be adjusted downwards. This need not concern you for costing purposes, except to say that some businesses use an overhead recovery rate *which only includes Factory Overheads*. In this way their stock of finished goods is always valued at Cost of Production. However in this case the *Factory* Absorption Cost so produced is *not* a complete guide to setting a selling price. As the Office costs have still to be included before a full *Total* Absorption Cost is found, not until this is done can the entire cost of the product be known, and a selling price set.

The golden rule is that each business will organise its cost accounts (if it has them at all!) in a way that it finds most convenient. One business may use a total overhead recovery rate such as generally illustrated here. Another may use a Factory overhead recovery rate, and then later adjust the factory cost of a product upwards, to take account of the office costs.

The important point is that the method chosen should be consistently used so that everyone in the particular business *knows* what is meant when "product cost" is being talked about.

CHAPTER SUMMARY

The main components of an *absorption product cost* are Direct Labour, Direct Materials and Overheads. These components can be calculated from predicted data (be estimated) or from actual data (be the actual costs incurred). Direct labour and material costs are measurable, overhead costs are given in proportion to the production time used up making the item.

The components together give either the estimated or the actual absorption cost of a product. The estimated cost is used principally to set selling prices based on "cost plus so-much". The actual costs are used to check if the intended profits are being made, and if not, to reveal in which component expenses differ from those predicted.

Most businesses have a normal or basic marketing plan. This might be to make and sell 50,000 fridges per year, for instance. The *normal* selling prices of the fridges would be based upon their absorption product cost, plus so-much for profit.

The overhead component of an absorption cost (in a business with several products made in a variety of production departments) partly reflects how the management have chosen to allocate the overheads to the various production departments.

You should now work on the questions in Section C at the end of the chapter.

Having completed the work in the first three chapters you are in a strong position to go onto the next stage of the book. This deals with *costing systems*. These are the various ways firms organise the components of cost to economically produce product costs, in a way suitable for the particular product made. For instance, a paper-mill will use a *costing system* that is quite different from one used by a house-builder. The *components* of cost will be the same; but they will be organised by the costing system differently. If you are clear about the components, understanding the systems is quite straightforward. If you are *not* quite clear about any aspect of this chapter; *don't go on until you are.*

SELF-ASSESSMENT QUESTIONS

SECTION A

1. Northgate Ltd are concerned whether they are paying wages to their employees in the most appropriate way for their business. You are asked to produce a report showing the remuneration of each employee, for each of the following wage methods:

(i) Hourly rate
(ii) Basic piece rate per unit produced

Data: Name of Employee	VOWLES	SHIBLI	DAVIDSON
Units produced	135	100	110
Time taken in hours	40	38	36
Rate per hour	£5·00	£4·20	£4·80
Rate per unit	£1·60	£2·00	£1·92

* 2. A factory made 35,000 cartons of cornflakes in one week. Its wage-bill for *all* workers was £8,000 and 30% of this total was for Indirect Labour. What is the Direct Labour cost per carton of cornflakes?

* 3. A factory making LP records has 4 people working the machines stamping out the discs. Their clock cards for week 25 were:

HOURS:	MON	TUES	WED	THURS	FRI
Mr Collins	7	7	—	7	7
Mr Heath	8	8	10	8	8
Mr Gill	6	6	6	6	7
Mrs Bache	8	8	8	8	8

They are all paid £3·50 per hour.

(i) How much did each earn in week 25?
(ii) What was the Direct Labour cost per day in week 25?
(iii) What was the Direct Labour cost in total in week 25?
(iv) If 2,000 records were made what was the Direct Labour cost per record to the nearest penny?

4. In a newly opened biscuit factory in which it had been agreed the production workers would move around as necessary, the time sheets of four production workers revealed the following information for one week:

Hours in Departments:	*Baking*	*Mixing*	*Packing*	*Grading*
Mr Sherriff	4	14	16	6
Mr Brunsdon	20	15		5
Mr Dillingham		35	5	
Mr Stone	5	5	5	5

Mr Sherriff is paid £2 per hour. Mr Brunsdon is paid £3 per hour. Mr Dillingham is paid £3·25 per hour and Mr Stone £3·50.

  (i) How much is each person paid this week?
  (ii) What is the Direct Labour cost in each department?
  (iii) If 4,000 kilos of ingredients were mixed, what is the Direct Labour cost per kilo of mixing the ingredients?

SECTION B

* 5. (A) A business made 35 inflatable life-rafts last week and issued £9,500 of materials to production for the purpose. Of this total £500 were indirect materials and £2,000 of direct materials were left over for the next week's production. What is the Direct Material cost per life-raft?

  (B) In the same week the Factory Wages totalled £4,500. Of this total Works management, foremen and storemen were paid £1,000. What is the Direct Labour cost per life-raft?

  (C) What is the prime cost per life-raft?

* 6. The following stock records were compiled by Mr Parker, the storeman in charge of bicycle chains which are used in the production of the best selling road-runner bike: there was no opening stock.

January 15:	Received:	400 @ £3 each
January 19:	Received:	150 @ £2 each
January 23:	Issued:	200
February 7:	Received:	300 @ £2·50 each
February 14:	Issued:	340
February 22:	Issued:	210
March 10:	Received:	330 @ £3·20 each
March 14:	Received:	150 @ £4 each
March 20:	Issued:	370
April 9:	Issued:	150

All the materials issued each month were used in production in that month.

(A) Calculate the Direct Material cost of chains used in production each month (January, February, March, April) using

  (i) the FIFO issuing method.
  (ii) the LIFO issuing method.
  (iii) the AVCO issuing method.

(B) What is the closing stock valuation in April under (i) FIFO (ii) LIFO (iii) AVCO issuing methods?

7. A wholesaler sells Video recorders to shops for £240 each. They buy them in at various prices, and for September to November the stock records showed:

> Opening Stock 1 September: 90 videos cost £110 each.
> Received 10 September: 50 videos Cost Price £120 each.
> Issued and Sold 20 September: 80 videos.
> Received 7 October: 120 videos cost £130 each.
> Issued and Sold 14 October: 90 videos.
> Received 21 October: 70 videos cost £125 each.
> Sold 7 November: 130 videos.

(i) Calculate the "gross margin" (i.e. the difference between the cost of the videos and the selling price) made in total on each batch sold, using (A) the FIFO stock issuing method, (B) the AVCO method.

(ii) What is the closing stock value using each method?

SECTION C

* 8. Overheads for the next four week period are estimated to be £22,000. The firm has only one production department which employs 18 production people who assemble electrical components into radios and cassette recorders. They work 40 hours per week; but only actually assemble goods for 36 hours. The rest of the time is preparation and cleaning work.

(i) What type of hours best indicates this firm's productive capacity?

(ii) What would the next period's ORR be?

(iii) If the firm *actually* spent £24,000 on overhead expenses what would the under-recovery of overheads be (A) IN TOTAL and (B) PER HOUR?

(iv) If it takes 4 hours to assemble a cassette recorder, the production workers are paid £3 per hour and the direct materials cost £8: how much was the estimated absorption cost of one cassette recorder?

(v) How much was the actual cost?

* 9. Poorl, Shire, Reef and Co. are solicitors. Their overhead costs for next year are estimated to be:

Office Rent	£2,500
Secretaries' Wages	£5,000
Rates	£1,200
Heat and Light	£600
Stationery	£500
Post and Telephone	£1,850
Motor Expenses	£1,450

The three partners each intend to work for 48 weeks in the year. Whilst they will be in the office for 45 hours each week, they estimate they will only be working on clients' behalf for 37 of those hours.

(i) What is the ORR per partner hour?

(ii) If the partners wished to have a combined rate to include their own salaries as well as the overheads – assuming each partner wanted a salary of £15,000 per year – how much per hour would the combined rate have to be?

(iii) If the partners actually worked on clients' behalf for 40 hours each week: (A) what would be the total OVER RECOVERY of overheads in the year? (B) How much extra salary would the partners have earned if they used the combined rate you calculated in (ii)?

10. Mammoth Appliances make all sorts of domestic appliances. Their next year's overheads are estimated to be £1,560,000. They have three production departments: Metal Cutting; Enamelling; Final Assembly. The metal-cutting department has 10 machines which work 35 hours each week. The enamelling department employs 14 enamel-sprayers who each work 38 hours. Final assembly consists of 28 assemblers who work 40 hours. The firm intends to operate for 47 of the 52 weeks next year.

(i) What type of hours in each department best represents its productive capacity?

(ii) How much productive capacity is each department estimated to have next year?

(iii) Of the total overheads those solely incurred by each department are:

Metal Cutting	Enamelling	Final Assembly	TOTAL
£340,000	£210,000	£187,000	£737,000

Which leaves £823,000 worth to be allocated. Of this sum 25% are allocated to Metal Cutting, 35% to Enamelling and 40% to Final Assembly.

(A) What is the total overhead allocation of each department?

(B) What is the overhead recovery rate of each department?

(iv) A batch of fridges is planned to take 40 hours of production time in the metal cutting department: 12 hours of enamelling production time and 55 hours of final assembly time. (A) What is the estimated overhead cost of the batch in each department?

(v) If the metal cutting department actually worked 36 hours each week (A) how much would the over-recovery of overheads be? (B) What effect would this have on the firm's profit?

(vi) If the final assembly actually worked only 38 hours each week (A) what would the under-recovery of overheads be? (B) What effect would this have on the firm's profit?

(vii) If two more machines were added to the metal cutting department, and overheads remained the same, so there was now a total of 12 machines working 35 hours per week (A) what would the new ORR for that department be? (B) What would the Metal Cutting department overhead cost of the batch of fridges in (iv) above now be?

11. Two firms make the same type of precision engineered products and both have total overhead costs of £375,000 per year. The first firm allocates these as follows: Casting Dept 40%, Machining Dept 35%, Polishing Dept 25%. The second allocates 30% to Casting, 50% to Machining and 20% to Polishing. For both firms the productive capacities of the departments are: Casting 7,000 machine hours; Machining 10,000 machine hours; Polishing 5,000 Direct Labour hours.

(i) What is the overhead recovery rate for each department in firm one?

(ii) What is the overhead recovery rate for each department in firm two?

(iii) If an item took 5 hours to cast, 20 hours to machine and 8 hours to polish; what would its overhead cost be in (A) Firm one and (B) Firm two?

12. The Rational Food Firm has estimated its overhead costs as follows:

		£
Production Dept 1:	Rent	1,000
	Rates	300
	Heat	400
	Machinery costs	500
Production Dept 2:	Rent	400
	Rates	100
	Heat	500
	Machinery costs	700
Production Dept 3:	Rent	2,000
	Rates	600
	Heat	700
	Machinery costs	300

OTHER DEPARTMENTS

	£
Cost of Works Engineers	1,200
Cost of Stores Department	1,700
Cost of Works Management	500
Sales and Distribution Costs	3,000
Other Office Costs	2,100

The management of Rational Food find out the following facts which they decide to use as a basis of allocation of the other departments overheads:

: The works engineer spends $\frac{1}{4}$ of his time in each production department, $\frac{1}{4}$ of his time is spent servicing the delivery trucks.
: On average out of every 100 items issued by the stores 60 go to department 1, 15 go to department 2 and 25 go to department 3.
: The works management spends $\frac{1}{2}$ of its time in production department 1: $\frac{1}{10}$ of its time in department 2 and the rest in department 3.
: Sales and Distribution costs: each department makes products which are sold direct to customers. The quantities of products sold by each department are in the ratio $3:2:1$.
: The other administration departments consider they spend an equal amount of time managing and controlling each production department.

(A) What is each production department's *total* overhead allocation?
(B) If department 1 has 200 hours of productive capacity, department 2 has 300 hours, and department 3 has 280 hours; calculate each department's overhead recovery rate per hour of productive capacity.
(C) What other basis of apportionment could be used to allocate (i) Stores Costs (ii) Sales and Distribution Costs?

13. If a business had, in a year, Total Overheads of £42,000, in that time produced for 12,000 Direct Labour hours, and paid wages of £3 per hour, (A) What would the overhead rate be as a percentage of the Direct Labour cost per hour? (B) What would the absorption cost be of a product which took: 7 hours of Direct Labour to make: £300 of Direct Materials? (Remember to calculate *all three components!*)

14. A small engineering company with two production departments, Machine Shop and Assembly has prepared the following budget for next year:

Products	GEARS	SHAFTS	COWLS
Production-units	28,000	20,000	12,000
Material cost per unit	£18	£14	£17
Production times – per unit of production:			
Labour Hours – Assembly shop	3	10	2
Machine Hours – Machine shop	4	3	2

	Machine Shop	Assembly
Factory Overhead Costs	£1,225,000	£770,000

Required: (i) Calculate the overhead recovery rate per labour hour for the Assembly shop, and per machine hour for the Machine shop. (ii) Calculate the overhead cost of producing one of each of the products.

15. Receipts and issues of a stock item for word processor manufacture are:

Date	Units purchased	Purchase Price (each) £	Units Issued
April 4	400	14·00	
6	300	16·00	
10			200
15			360
17	160	13·00	
26			200

You are required to draw up a stores schedule to record the transactions using (1) the "First-in, First-out" method and (2) the "average cost" method when pricing issues.

16. Michael has been trading for a year dealing in one product. The figures of receipts and sales are:

Receipts		Sales	
February	56 @ £20 each	March	22 for £32 each
May	24 @ £20 each	June	30 for £32 each
September	28 @ £22 each	November	20 for £33 each

Required:

(A) Draw up a clear schedule showing the profit made and closing stock values if (i) FIFO and (ii) LIFO stock valuation methods are used.

CHAPTER 4

JOB AND PROCESS COSTING SYSTEMS

CHAPTER OBJECTIVES

Having studied this chapter you should be able to:

* CALCULATE SIMPLE JOB COSTS

* CALCULATE SIMPLE PROCESS COSTS

* DECIDE WHETHER A JOB OR PROCESS COSTING SYSTEM IS A SUITABLE COSTING METHOD FOR A GIVEN PRODUCT.

THE STORY SO FAR

When *all* of the costs a business incurs are spread evenly, or fairly, over the items produced – the cost per item so calculated is called an ABSORPTION cost. Generally an absorption cost is calculated by finding out its three components: the Direct Labour Component: the Direct Material component: and the Overhead component. These three added together give the absorption cost of the item. ("Item" could be fridge, car, soap, dry cleaning service, solicitor's advice, dentist's services, and so on). Chapter 3 dealt with how people "find out" the three components in practice. This chapter deals with how they are "added together" in practice. The general term for the *methods* used to "add together" the components of cost is a COSTING SYSTEM.

ABSORPTION COSTING SYSTEMS

In practice these fall into three categories:

(a) JOB COSTING SYSTEMS
(b) PROCESS COSTING SYSTEMS and
(c) STANDARD COSTING SYSTEMS.

This chapter deals with (a) and (b) and Chapter 8 with (c). They are all absorption costing systems because (even though Standard Costing is much more complicated than job or process costing) they all produce a product cost which includes a fair share of *all* the costs a business incurs. Job and Process costing systems are very widely used in business – whether manufacturing or service industries, so a thorough knowledge of them is important.

JOB COSTING

The essence of job costing is that an *individual* product is the focus of the costing system. Some items are worth *individual* attention – others are not. For instance, if you wanted your house painted, it would be worth a painter's while coming and looking at it, and giving you a price based on his assessment of the work to be done on your particular house. But what about the manufacturer of the paint itself? I.C.I. produce hundreds of thousands of tins of paint a week – it would be completely stupid to pay someone to examine each individual tin and calcualte *separately for each tin* what it cost to make. You would need nearly as many costing clerks as you made tins of paint!

Now consider what the general characteristics are of a product which is worth individual attention: first it must be of a *reasonably high value*, otherwise the wages cost of the person giving the attention will be too high in relation to the value of the product.

Second the products (or batches of product) must be *different*, i.e. must be "one-off" non-standard ones. If they were not different from one another they would not need *individual* attention; because having calculated the cost of one, it would be unnecessary to repeat the exercise.

Typical high value non-standard products are: buildings, ships, handmade suits, house painting work, electrical installations (e.g. re-wiring an old house), central heating installations, air-conditioning installations, solicitor's advice, accountant's advice (extremely valuable!), printing a batch of travel brochures, printing a firm's notepaper.

So items such as these, worth individual attention, with the general characteristics of being high-value and non-standard, will be costed using a JOB COSTING system. By "costed" is meant:

(A) The system will be used to calculate the *estimated* cost of the product, and

(B) It will be used to calculate the *actual* cost of a product.

The estimated cost will be used as a basis for setting the selling prices. The actual cost will be used to check if the job went as planned *and to reveal where the differences are if it did not.*

CALCULATING A JOB COST

In fact most of the examples in Chapter 3 followed a job-costing type format, so it won't strike you as very new.

Suppose you wanted the electricity board to come and install some

JOB 140 Re-wiring at No 7 Hall Road			
DIRECT LABOUR: 2 men × 8 hrs × 3 days = 48 hrs @ £3 per hr	ESTIMATE £144	ACTUAL	VARIANCE
DIRECT MATERIALS: 300 yds cable @ £1 per yd 10 switches @ £4 per switch	£340		
OVERHEADS: 48 D.L. hrs × £5 per hr	£240		
TOTAL COST	724		
PROFIT	76		
SELLING PRICE	£800		

Fig. 43.

new wiring in your house. They would send round a person to find out exactly what needed doing. The amount of time it would take would be estimated (say 2 men for 8 hours a day for 3 days). The necessary amount of cable and switches would be noted (say 300 yards of cable and 10 switches). I hope you don't need telling that in work of this type the overheads would be calculated per DIRECT LABOUR HOUR (say the ORR is £5 per D.L. hour).

Back at the office a job-number would be given to this work (Job 140 say) and the estimated cost would be worked out on a JOB CARD as shown in Fig. 43 above.

The electricity board would then send you a letter saying the work would cost you £800. Imagine that you accept and the work is done. The actual time spent and the actual cost of the materials used would be recorded, and filled in on the *actual column* on the job card. Assume the actual figures were:

Direct Labour: 52 hours taken
Direct Materials: 330 yards of cable used; but only 9 switches.

The *actual* job cost can now be calculated:

		£	£
Actual direct labour:	52 × £3 =		156

Actual direct materials: 330 × £1 = 330
                   plus   9 × £4 =   36   366

Actual Overheads: 52 × £5 =   £260

These figures would be filled in on the job card *and the differences between actual and estimated costs highlighted in the variance column*, as shown below in Fig. 44. (The figures in brackets show where *costs were higher than estimate* or *profits lower than estimate*):

Job 140			
	Estimate	Actual	Variance
DIRECT LABOUR	144	156	(12)
DIRECT MATERIALS	340	366	(26)
OVERHEADS	240	260	(20)
TOTAL COST	724	782	(58)
PROFIT	76	18	(58)
SELLING PRICE	800	800	—

Fig. 44.

The management of this business would now have some useful information about (i) why the firm's profit was lower than expected; (ii) the amount of cable needed for future estimates of this type; (iii) the amount of time this sort of job really takes. This information can be made use of in the future to ensure estimates are more accurate, and so help managers run the business efficiently.

That is a simple example to get us started. Costs can vary from estimate for other reasons too. The wages may *actually* be £3·25 per hour, the cable may *actually* cost £1·10 per yard, the overhead recovery rate may *actually* need to be £5·50 per direct labour hour. The benefits of comparing actual costs with estimates will apply even more in these cases. You will be surprised how easy it is in a large organisation to have estimators using data which is no longer accurate.

HERE IS A MORE COMPLICATED EXAMPLE

Job 59 is the manufacture of a special piece of furniture. It will be made in 2 departments: Frame-making and Upholstering. You find out the following information. It will take a frame-maker four days at 8 hours per day to make the frame. He will use wood and screws costing £110, and he is paid £5 per hour. The overhead recovery rate is £8 per direct labour hour in this department. In the upholstering department £250 of materials will be used to cover the frame and it will take 3 days working 7 hours per day by 2 people being paid £4 per hour to complete the work. Overheads in this department are recovered per direct labour hour at a rate of £6.

The estimated cost of Job 59 is:

	FRAMING DEPARTMENT	£	£
Direct Labour:	4 days × 8 hours = 32 hours		
	@ £5	= 160	
Direct Materials:		= 110	
Overheads:	32 hours @ £8	= 256	
	Framing Dept total cost	=	526
	UPHOLSTERY DEPARTMENT		
Direct Labour:	2 people × 3 days × 7 hours		
	= 42 hours @ £4	= 168	
Direct Materials:		= 250	
Overheads:	42 hours @ £6	= 252	
	Upholstery Dept total	=	670
	Total Estimated Cost	=	1,196
	Profit 10%		120
	Selling Price		£1,316

We submit the price to the customer who accepts it. As we do the job we record the actual data which turns out to be:

Framing Dept: Hours worked: 27
                   Wages per hour: £5·50
                   Direct Materials: £115
                   Overhead rate is unchanged.

Upholstery Dept: 49 hours are worked,
                   Wages per hour   £3·80
                   Direct Materials £225
                   The estimators should have
                   used the new
                   ORR of £6·50 per hour in the
                   estimate.

The actual cost of the job now is:

			£	£
Framing Dept:	Direct Labour:	27 × £5·50	= 148·50	
	Direct Materials		= 115	
	Overheads: 27 × 8		= 216	
	Framing Dept Total			= 479·50
Upholstery Dept:	Direct Labour:	49 × 3·80	= 186·20	
	Direct Materials		= 225·00	
	Overheads: 49 × 6·50		= 318·50	
	Upholstery Dept Total		=	729·70
	Actual Job Cost			£1,209·20

The variances can now be worked out:

FRAMING DEPT

	Estimate	Actual	Variances
Direct Labour	160	148·50	11·50
Direct Materials	110	115	(5·00)
Overheads	256	216	40
Dept Total	526	479·5	46·5

UPHOLSTERY DEPT

Direct Labour	168	186·20	(18·20)
Direct Materials	250	225	25
Overheads	252	318·50	(66·50)
Dept Total	670	729·70	(59·70)
Total Cost	1,196	1,209·20	(13·20)
Profit	120	106·80	(13·20)
Selling Price	1,316	1,316	—

Fig. 45.

Again the management have learned a lot of useful information about the business. This type of job takes longer to upholster than was thought; but less long to frame. There may be reasons that need investigating, and lessons to be learned. The costing system has (A) directed management's attention to problems and (B) shown up savings that could perhaps be made use of in other areas, once it is known *why* the savings occurred. (In our example once it is known *why* we saved 5 D.L. hours in the framing department and *why* we saved on direct materials).

So that's job costing done. Now you should work through the questions in Section A at the end of this chapter.

PROCESS COSTING

There are many products which are not worth costing on an *individual* basis. A packet of washing powder, a tin of paint, a jar of jam, a paper clip, a golf ball, a gallon of petrol, a packet of sweets, a bottle of milk and hundreds more like these. Even some services are like this in principle: dry cleaning, for example or an automatic car wash. With this type of product or service, costs are found by: (i) measuring TOTAL COSTS OVER A PERIOD OF TIME and (ii) measuring TOTAL OUTPUT OVER THE SAME PERIOD OF TIME. As a quick example take the production of Washing Powder for a week:

Total Cost (D.L., D.M., and O.H.)	= £25,000
Total Output	= 50,000 KILOS

Cost per kilo   = £25,000 ÷ 50,000

Therefore Unit Cost = £0·5 per kilo.

Fig. 46.

So with process costing it is fundamentally a matter of measuring (A) the costs fed into the process for a given time; and (B) the output from the process in that time. In principle, then, process costing is quite straight-forward. Costs are *found* in exactly the same way as described in Chapter 3, whether they are used for job-costing or process costing. The *focus* of process costing is not the individual unit of product though. It is the *total costs* incurred in a particular period of time that is concentrated upon – together with the *total output* from the process in the same time. Thereafter the unit cost of an item of product is found by division as shown in Fig. 46 above.

Here is another example: an oil refinery incurs the following costs in April in its petrol-making plant:

Direct Materials: 450,000 barrels of crude oil at £20 per barrel.
Direct Labour: 30 people worked 160 hours and they are paid £4 per hour.
Overheads: Total overheads for April were £2,000,000.

The output from the refinery was 20,250,000 gallons. What is the cost per gallon?

Costs incurred in the process:

			£
Direct Labour:	30 people × 160 hrs × £4		19,200
Direct Materials:	450,000 barrels × £20		9,000,000
Overheads:			2,000,000
Total process cost for April			£11,019,200

$$\text{Unit Cost per gallon of petrol} = \frac{£11,019,200}{20,250,000}$$

$$= £0\cdot55p \text{ (rounded up)}.$$

Fig. 47.

No attempt is made to measure the time it took for any particular gallon to be refined. It is just a matter of measuring the totals of cost and output, and then doing a division sum to find the unit cost. In fact with process costing the unit cost is an *average cost per unit*.

So we can formulate some general principles which will guide you when deciding if a product should be costed using a process costing system:

1. The products must be identical (or the average cost will be meaningless)

2. The products must be of low value. (If they are not then an average method will not be informative enough.) All Jaguar XJS sports cars are identical; but you wouldn't want to control their costs by building 1,000, then averaging what you spent on 1,000 cars. So much money is involved in any one car that it needs to be costed in a more individual manner – which is where Standard Costing applies. (See Chapter 8.)

At this point you may be considering that this is all very straightforward and too good to be true. And of course there is a catch. This catch is frequently brought up in examinations, and often never occurs anywhere else.

The difficulty is based upon the fact that there may be different quantities of half-finished product in the process at the beginning and the end of the cost-measuring period. Diagrammatically Fig. 48 could be the case with our oil-refinery, look at it now.

In terms of quantities, we poured in 350,000 barrels of crude oil in April and got out 450,000 barrels of refined petrol. This was only possible because the process already contained some 300,000 barrels on 1 April. We find out the quantities actually used to give the April output of petrol quite easily:

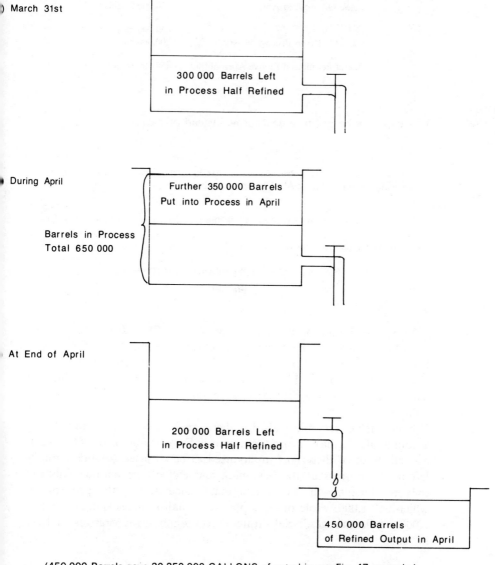

March 31st

300 000 Barrels Left
in Process Half Refined

During April

Further 350 000 Barrels
Put into Process in April

Barrels in Process
Total 650 000

At End of April

200 000 Barrels Left
in Process Half Refined

450 000 Barrels
of Refined Output in April

(450,000 Barrels gave 20,250,000 GALLONS of petrol in our Fig. 47 example.)

Fig. 48.

: Opening Stock in Process	300,000 barrels
: *Add* Oil input in April	350,000 barrels
	650,000 barrels
: *less* Oil left in Process 30 April	200,000 barrels
Therefore oil used to give April output	= 450,000 barrels

This can now be put into cost terms instead of barrels:

		£
Cost of Direct Materials in Process: March 31st 300,000 barrels @ £20 =		6,000,000
Add Materials input during April 350,000 barrels @ £20	=	7,000,000
		13,000,000
Less Cost of Materials left in process: April 30th 200,000 barrels @ £20 =		4,000,000
Cost of Materials used to give April output	=	£9,000,000

(Proof: £9,000,000 ÷ £20 per barrel = 450,000 barrels.)

Fig. 49.

You should now be clear that the costs INPUT during the period must be adjusted for the opening and closing amount left in the process before the correct cost of the period's output can be known. As long as you are clear, go on. If you are not, then go over this example, get help from your friends, but do be sure you understand this point before going on.

Now it is not just materials that there are various opening and closing amounts of. To make a product involves Direct Labour and Overheads as well. Both of these cost inputs need to be adjusted for the amounts left in the process at the beginning and end of the period. This can only be done by an "equivalent unit" calculation – the principle of which is; "1,000 whole oranges plus 4,000 half-oranges is equivalent to 3,000 whole oranges." Substitute Direct Labour for oranges and we have:

"If £6,000 of Direct Labour completed the D.L. content of 1,000 items and *half* completed the D.L. content of 4,000 items, the £6,000 has paid for the equivalent D.L. cost of 3,000 complete items." Because 1,000 actually complete items *plus* 4,000 half complete items equals the equivalent of 3,000 complete ones. Do not go on until this point is completely understood.

Now it is possible to calculate the D.L. cost of one item:

£6,000 ÷ 3,000 *equivalently* complete items = D.L. cost of £2 for one. Therefore D.L. cost of the 1,000 *actually complete items* = 1,000 × £2 = £2,000. Therefore the D.L. cost *left in the process* at the end of the period = £6,000 minus £2,000 = £4,000. Don't go on until this part is clear.

Now to apply these points to an entire problem and all three components of cost. Take the manufacture of golf balls as an example. Suppose in the first month we start up the plant (i.e. we have no opening amounts left in the process) we input the following costs:

	£
Direct Labour	2,300
Direct Materials	3,900
Overheads	5,000
Total monthly costs input =	£11,200

Fig. 50.

At the end of the first month we have the following information which has been recorded by the production department:

(A) Number of Golf Balls produced = 42,000 balls.

(B) Information about partly-completed golf balls:

   (i) There are 5,000 which have only had half of the necessary direct labour spent on them.

   (ii) There are 10,000 which have only $\frac{1}{5}$ of the direct materials necessary.

   (iii) Overheads are apportioned on the basis of direct materials used (i.e. overhead costs are given to a golf ball as material costs build up, e.g. if a ball is $\frac{1}{5}$ complete for materials it is $\frac{1}{5}$ complete for overheads. If it is fully complete for materials it is fully complete for overheads, and so on).

So, what has each of the cost components input in the month ACTUALLY PAID FOR? Taking one at a time:

Direct Labour: Cost Input = £2,300. This paid for 42,000 complete balls *plus* 5,000 $\frac{1}{2}$ complete balls. That is it paid for THE EQUIVALENT OF: 42,000 + 2,500 (5,000 × $\frac{1}{2}$) = 44,500 Direct Labour – complete golf balls.

Direct Materials: Cost Input = £3,900. This paid for 42,000 complete balls *plus* 10,000 $\frac{1}{5}$ complete balls. That is it paid for THE EQUIVALENT OF: 42,000 + 2,000 (10,000 × $\frac{1}{5}$) = 44,000 Direct Materials – complete golf balls.

Overheads: Cost Input = £5,000. As overheads are allocated in proportion to materials, the number of balls complete for Direct Materials will also be complete for their share of overheads. So this overhead input of £5,000 paid for THE EQUIVALENT OF 44,000 Overhead – complete golf balls.

We can now easily calculate the cost of the *actually* complete golf balls, *and the costs remaining in the process at the end of month 1*:

DIRECT LABOUR

Cost of 1 equivalently-complete ball for Direct Labour = $\dfrac{£2,300}{44,500 \text{ balls}}$

Therefore cost of 42,000 *actually* complete balls for Direct Labour =
$$\frac{2,300}{44,500} \times 42,000 = £2,171$$

Therefore the amount of D.L. cost left in the process = 2,300 − 2,171 = £129

DIRECT MATERIALS

Cost of 1 equivalently-complete ball for Direct Materials = $\dfrac{£3,900}{44,000 \text{ balls}}$

Therefore cost of 42,000 *actually* complete balls for Direct Materials =
$$\frac{3,900}{44,000} \times 42,000 = £3,723$$

Therefore the amount of D.M. cost left in the process = 3,900 − 3,723 = £177

OVERHEADS

Cost of 1 equivalently-complete ball for overheads = $\dfrac{£5,000}{44,000 \text{ balls}}$

Therefore Cost of 42,000 *actually* complete balls for overheads =
$$\frac{5,000}{44,000} \times 42,000 = £4,773$$

Therefore the amount of O/H cost left in the process = 5,000 − 4,773 = £227

So in a summarised form the results of the process for month 1 are:

	Costs Input		Cost of Output produced		Closing Cost of Work in Progress
	£		£		£
Direct Labour:	2,300	=	2,171	+	129
Direct Materials:	3,900	=	3,723	+	177
Overheads	5,000	=	4,773	+	227
	£11,200	=	£10,667	+	£533

Fig. 51.

Unit Cost of one ball produced in month 1 = 10,667 ÷ 42,000 = £0·254 each.

NOTE: A new term has been introduced: "Work in Progress". This just means the "stock" of partly finished items. The value of the partly completed golf balls left in the process at the end of month 1 is the "Closing work in progress".

In month 2 the costs input for the new month are added to the (now) opening work in progress to give a new total of costs in the process at the end of month 2. For example:

	Month 2 costs Input	+	Opening W.I.P.	=	Month 2 Total Costs in process
	£		£		£
Direct Labour	3,400	+	129	=	3,529
Direct Materials	4,600	+	177	=	4,777
Overheads	5,800	+	227	=	6,027

Fig. 52.

The new equivalent-unit calculations at the end of month 2 would now be applied to the new monthly totals, that is to Direct Labour £3,529, Direct Materials £4,777, Overheads £6,027.

Make sure you are absolutely clear about the way the equivalent unit calculations were done before going any further with this section. If you are, then you understand the basics of process costing. From now on it is really just practice and slightly more complicated examples.

The main new thing to get used to is that within a business one process often links up to another to make the final product. Take a Bakery as an example. The flour and yeast are *mixed*, then the dough so mixed is *baked*, then the baked bread is *wrapped*. So there are three processes to consider. With drink products like beer there are several processes, e.g. brewing and bottling. Taking a brewery as our next example, using the two processes mentioned, imagine you were given the following information for August:

		£
Brewing Dept: Opening Work in Progress:	Direct Labour:	1,200
	Direct Materials:	2,700
	Overheads:	1,800
Costs Input in the Period:	Direct Labour:	13,000
	Direct Materials:	21,000
	Overheads:	16,500

Fig. 53.

Output

At the end of August 40,000 gallons of beer are ready for bottling. However, still being brewed are 10,000 gallons of beer which are 75% complete for materials and 50% complete for Direct Labour costs. Overheads are per Direct Labour hour in this department.

Question Part 1:

What is the cost of the 40,000 gallons transferred to the Bottling Dept and what is the value of the closing Work in Progress?

Solution to Part 1

Direct labour total cost in process = W.I.P. 1,200 + Input 13,000 = £14,200.

Equivalent units this paid for = 40,000 gallons + 50% × 10,000 gallons =
$$45,000 \text{ gallons}$$

D.L. Cost of 40,000 actually completed units = $\frac{£14,200}{45,000}$ × 40,000 = £12,622

D.L. Left in process as closing W.I.P. = £14,200 − 12,622 = £1,578

Direct Materials total cost in process = W.I.P. 2,700 + Input 21,000 = £23,700

Equivalent units this paid for = 40,000 gallons + 75% × 10,000 gallons =
$$47,500 \text{ gallons}$$

D.M. Cost of 40,000 actually completed units = $\frac{£23,700}{47,500}$ × 40,000 = £19,958

D.M. Left in process as closing W.I.P. = 23,700 − 19,958 = £3,742

As the overheads are allocated on the basis of direct labour hours, the equivalent units for Direct Labour will also apply to the overhead costs.

Total Overhead cost in the process = W.I.P. 1,800 + Input 16,500 = £18,300

Equivalent units this paid for (D.L. units apply) = 45,000 gallons

Overhead cost of 40,000 actually completed units = $\frac{18,300}{45,000}$ × 40,000 = £16,267

Overhead cost left in process as closing W.I.P. = 18,300 − 16,267 = £2,033

So the 40,000 gallons transferred to the bottling dept cost:

		£
	D.L.	12,622
	D.M.	19,958
	O/H	16,267
Total cost of 40,000 Brewed gallons		£48,847

Unit cost per gallon brewed = 48,847 ÷ 40,000 = £1·22 per gallon.

Fig. 54.

		£
Closing Work in Progress =	D.L.	1,578
	D.M.	3,742
	O/H	2,033
		£7,353

Fig. 55.

Question Part II

You are given the following information about the bottling department for September. (There is no opening or closing work in progress as everything brewed is bottled):

	£	
Direct Materials: Bottles and labels:	8,000	
Direct Materials: (From Brewing Dept 40,000 gallons):	48,847:	(See calculations in Part I above)
Total D.M. Cost	£56,847	

(*Note* when a product is transferred from process 1 to process 2 its total cost is always included as DIRECT MATERIALS in process 2.)

Direct Labour:	£9,000

Overheads:	£16,000

Output = 78,000 half-gallon flagons.

What is the cost of a half gallon flagon of beer?

Solution Part II

		£
Costs Incurred in the period:	Direct Labour:	9,000
	Direct Materials:	56,847
	Overheads:	16,000
	Total	£81,847

Output in the period: 78,000 flagons
Cost per flagon: 81,847 ÷ 78,000 = £1·05

SUMMARY

This part of the chapter has taken you through the principles of process costing. Of course you will find more complicated examples as you progress further in the subject. However if you understand these basics properly you will easily master the complications to come.

Of course you can have estimated and actual process costs. Estimated process costs are easy to calculate once the data is known, because you needn't worry about opening and closing W.I.P. Take our brewing example for instance. We would merely need to estimate the costs of D.L., D.M. and O/H for a given output.

Say we estimated our unit costs for brewing, on the basis of 20,000 gallons taking 2 weeks to brew would be:

		£
Direct Labour:		6,000
Direct Materials:		10,000
Overheads:		8,000
Total		£24,000

$$\text{Unit Cost } \frac{£24,000}{20,000 \text{ gallons}} = £1 \cdot 20 \text{ per gallon}$$

This figure can then be used for comparison with our actual unit cost already calculated (£1·22, see Fig. 54). If there was a large discrepancy between the actual and estimated unit costs, the reasons could be further identified by working out the unit costs of the components, actual and estimated. For example:

Brewing Costs:	Estimate per Unit		Actual Per Unit		Variance per Unit
Direct Labour	$\frac{£6,000}{20,000}$ =	0·30	$\frac{£12,622}{40,000}$ =	0·315	(0·015)
Direct Materials	$\frac{£10,000}{20,000}$ =	0·50	$\frac{19,958}{40,000}$ =	0·50	—
Overheads	$\frac{£8,000}{20,000}$ =	0·40	$\frac{16,267}{40,000}$ =	0·405	(0·005)
TOTAL Unit Cost		£1·20		£1·22	£(0·02)

Fig. 56.

Managers would now know that it was in Direct Labour and Overhead Costs, rather than direct materials, that the problems of higher-than estimated-cost lay.

SUMMARY OF PROCESS COSTING CALCULATIONS

FOR EACH COMPONENT OF COST:
(A) Add opening work in progress to the costs input in the period to give total costs in the process, e.g. O.W.I.P. £2,000 + Input £5,000 = £7,000.
(B) Calculate the *equivalent units* this total cost had produced, e.g. 1,500 complete + 500 ½ complete + 1,000 ¼ complete = EQUIVALENT OF 1,500 + 100 + 250 = 1,850 complete.
(C) Calculate the cost of ONE equivalent unit. That is A ÷ B:
$$\frac{7,000}{1,850} = £3 \cdot 78.$$

(D) Find cost of units *actually* transferred out of the process: That is (C) × number actually complete: 3·78 × 1,500 = £5,670.

(E) Closing work in progress is A − D:7,000 − 5,670 = £1,330.

You should now be able to work through the questions in Part B at the end of the chapter.

Even if you find process costing a bit complicated, don't worry. In practice it is not usually too complicated even though in exams it can be. The great thing to remember is that both job and process costs are ABSORPTION costs.

BOOK SUMMARY SO FAR

Chapter 1 explained and illustrated that there were at least two answers to the question "What does it cost?" And the one given depends upon what the answer will be used for. If we want to know what an extra one will cost, or what we will save if we make one less, the *marginal cost* is the right answer. If we want to set a selling price for our normal intended output, then the *absorption cost* – i.e. one that includes a share of all of the costs a business incurs – must be the answer supplied. If you can't really recall all this RE-READ CHAPTER ONE IMMEDIATELY.

Chapter 2 then explained the cost-accounting classification which is used to divide up *all the expenses a business incurs* into headings suitable for costing purposes. Chapter 3 then explained how this classification is divided into three main components (Direct Labour, Direct Materials and Overheads) and how these components of cost were measured and given to the items produced. This chapter has dealt with two commonly used methods (costing systems) which are used to "add together" the components of cost to arrive at the *absorption cost* of certain types of product or service.

This finishes our work on absorption costs for the time being. The next two chapters deal with aspects of Marginal costs. However, there are some important general points to be made before continuing – that you need to be absolutely clear about: namely: *What will alter the absorption cost of a product?*

1. *How much you pay for each unit of what you use* will alter the cost of an item: e.g. if 1 hour of Direct Labour costs £6, the items will cost more than if that hour only cost £4. Similarly a car made of steel costing £400 per tonne will be less expensive than one made of steel costing £600 per tonne. If the rent of your factory is £27,000 per year, your output will cost more than if the rent was £17,000 per year.

2. *How much of each resource you use* will affect the cost of an item. If you use 300 kilos of steel to make the car-body then it will cost more than if you used only 250 kilos. If it takes 15 gallons to paint a house, it will cost less to paint than one needing 20 gallons to do.

3. *FINALLY and most importantly* THE SPEED WITH WHICH THE ITEMS ARE MADE will affect their cost. This is because the overhead costs usually may be regarded as providing the structure of the business: the factory, the machines, the offices, the vehicles, the telephones, the sales-team, production controller and so on. Most of them will be incurred *whether anything is actually being made or not.* If a day's overheads are £1,000 and we make 400 items the overhead cost per item will be £2·50. If we make 500 in a day the overhead cost per item will be £2·00 – so the cost of it will be that much cheaper. Direct Labour costs per unit are similarly diluted if more are made in a given time.

If the word PRODUCTIVITY has any meaning at all, it means the cost savings that can be made by making an item faster, and therefore more cheaply. Which in turn means its selling price can be more competitive and a profit still be made.

SELF-ASSESSMENT QUESTIONS

SECTION A

* 1. The Ace Dress Company hopes to receive an order for a special batch of uniforms for the Lord Mayor's Show. They are required to give an estimated price. The specification for the batch is as follows:

> Materials required: 35 yards red serge @ £20 per yard,
> 15 yards gold and silver braid @ £18 per yard.

You calculate it will take the dress-makers 31 hours to cut out and sew the batch. The overhead recovery rate is per Direct Labour hour and is £15. The manager wants to make a 15% profit on the cost of the job. The dressmakers are paid £3·50 per hour. Calculate the estimated cost and selling price.

* 2. (A) Star Machine and Engineering specialise in development work for the automobile industry. Jaguar cars, who are developing a new engine, ask them to quote a price for making a special "one-off" cylinder head.

As junior estimator you are given the following information by the salesman who deals with Jaguar's business and asked to work out a selling price based on a profit of 5% on cost:

Materials: A 100-kilo ingot of high-strength Titanium Steel will be required which is in stock valued at £2,500.

Direct Labour: A skilled draughtsman will be working on the job for 18 hours, and the lathe and machine operators for a total of 20 hours. The draughtsman is paid £7 per hour; the lathe operators £5.

Machine time: the work was on the machine for a total of 60 hours.

The overhead recovery rates are as follows:
Drawing Department: Per Direct Labour hour: £26.
Lathe and Machine Departments: Per Machine hour: £46.

(B) We are lucky enough to obtain the job. The actual manufacture of the cylinder head works out as follows:

Materials: The stock ingot had been used by the time the Jaguar job was started; so another had to be purchased costing £28 per kilo. But a 95-kilo ingot was in fact calculated to be large enough so one weighing this amount was used.

Direct Labour: The draughtsman in fact worked 16 hours on the drawings; but it took 24 hours of machine operators time to set up the machinery.

Machine time: The job was actually on the machines for a total of 58 hours.

Actual pay-rates and overhead recovery rates were as estimated.
Produce a full job-cost statement showing Estimated and Actual costs and profits.

3. Jack Jones is a plumber. Hitherto he has roughly estimated job costs; but now he wants to do things more clearly, and properly record the results. He has been charging £10 per hour for labour and overheads of which he pays himself £6 – leaving £4 per hour over for paying overheads. At the end of the year he is concerned that he has a bank overdraft and asks you to explain what has happened. Your investigations reveal:

He worked for 47 weeks at 38 hours per week last year. His costs were his own wages, plus the following overheads:

Office expenses	£3,000
Advertising	£1,500
Van expenses	£3,200
Accountants fees	£700
Insurances	£1,200

How much per hour should Jack Jones have charged for Labour and Overheads combined? What was the loss he made on Job 92 last year, on which he worked for 72 hours?

4. Geoff Boyd is a builder specialising in alterations to houses. He is asked to quote for the following work on Mr Cunningham's house:

(A) Installing Central Heating system
(B) Re-modelling the Bathroom.

Work (A) will take Geoff 40 hours. The boiler, pipes and radiators will cost £1,300.

(B) will take 60 hours. The new bath and basin will cost £300 and the tiles £240.

Geoff pays his workmen £5 per hour and charges overheads at 80% of the Direct Labour cost on a job. As there are always extra materials required such as clips, joints and so on which cannot be known in advance, Geoff always includes an extra 10% of the material costs as "sundry materials" in all his cost estimates.

Produce the estimated cost of the work on Mr Cunningham's home. What is the selling price to be quoted to Mr Cunningham if Geoff wants to make 20% profit?

5. Superprint specialises in advertising brochures for the travel industry. Guinea Holidays ask for a quotation for their Winter Holiday brochure, the specification of which is as follows:

No of A4 pages: 128
Paper Type: Worcester No 2 quality
Binding Method: Stapled spine
Quantity required: 250,000 copies

The job will be done in 3 departments: Platemaking, Printing, Binding. The Superprint estimators hold the following information which they use to make up quotations:

Platemaking Department: 128 pages requires 16 plates to be made. 1 plate costs £45 in Direct Materials and takes 2 direct labour hours to make. Platemakers are paid £8 per hour. The ORR is £15 per Direct Labour Hour.

Printing Department: Worcester No 2 quality paper costs £650 per tonne. A 128 page brochure will use 1 tonne of paper for every 5,000 brochures printed. Ink will cost £40 for every 1,000 128 page brochures printed. The machine time used will be 1 hour for each 2,000 brochures printed.

The overhead recovery rate is per Machine hour *and includes the Direct Labour cost*. It is £320 per machine hour.

Binding Department: Materials used in the Binding Dept cost £20 per 1,000 copies bound. The binding will take 35 hours on the machine and the combined Direct Labour and Overhead Recovery Rate per machine hour is £90.

Produce the estimated cost of the Guinea Holidays Brochure. What is the selling price if a 12% profit on cost is required?

6. The Acme Company carries out work on a job basis. You have been given the following details for carrying out a job for a new customer.

Direct materials – 7.50 kilos @ £40.00 per kilo

Direct wages

Department	Hours	Rate per hour
Machine Shop	20	£5·00
Assembly Dept.	10	£4·00
Packing Shop	2	£3·00

Annual Budget for Overheads

Department	Hours	Overheads
Machine Shop	1,000	10,100
Assembly Dept.	1,500	4,500
Packing Shop.	800	5,200

Profit – 25% of total cost in the required mark up.

You are required to:
(A) Calculate the overhead recovery rates for each department.
(B) Calculate the price of the job using departmental rates.

7. Harry Wells is a decorator. He has been asked to quote for decorating a hall, staircase and landing in a prosperous neighbourhood where he knows a high standard of work will be required.

He can get a trade discount of 25% on his materials and he expects that his overhead expenses will be as follows:

Van expenses	£3,000
Office costs	£2,000
Overalls, rags, detergent, etc	£2,500
Accountancy fees	£1,000

He expects to work 35 hours per week on 42 weeks of the year and thinks that £10 per hour is a fair rate for himself. His mate is not so skilled and Harry feels that £8 per hour is a fairer charge.

This job is likely to take 14 rolls of wallpaper at a list price of £6 per roll, 10 litres of gloss paint at £3 per litre and 30 litres of emulsion paint at £2 per litre. Harry and his mate expect to work on the house for three 8-hour days.

(i) Produce Harry's quotation, to allow him a 10% profit on sales.

In the event, the job proved to be much more difficult than expected. Not only was the old paper more difficult to strip than Harry had thought but the customer proved to be very demanding indeed. Further, Harry's mate went down with flu after working for only 12 hours, leaving Harry to work alone for 40 hours. The job also took 15 rolls of paper, 12 litres of gloss and 35 litres of emulsion paint.

(ii) Produce Harry's job cost statement, comparing actual and estimated costs assuming that he has estimated his overhead costs correctly.

8. EE Ltd is a knitwear manufacturer who is about to introduce a new range of men's sweaters.

The first production runs will be small, to test the market for the new designs – and the company hopes to make in larger quantities later.

The options are to use a traditional machine which has an output of 10 sweaters per hour and costs £40 per hour to run, or an electronically operated machine with an output of 40 sweaters per hour, but costing £120 per hour to run.

Set-up times are 10 hours on the traditional machine but only 6 hours on the electronic machine.

Prepare a job cost each of three production runs: 100, 500, and 1,000 sweaters.

When you have read Chapter 5, come back to this question and calculate the point at which it pays EE Ltd to use the electronic machine instead of the traditional one.

SECTION B

9. Which of the two costing systems, Job and Process would you recommend is used for each of the following products of services? (A) Resurfacing a drive up to a house, (B) Making and bottling lemonade in commercial quantities, (C) Re-roofing a house, (D) Manufacturing roof tiles, (E) Professional advice from an Accountant, (F) Consulting your vet about a sick animal, (G) Manufacturing frozen peas, (H) Installing air-conditioning in an office, (I) Making instant coffee powder, (J) Servicing and repairing a car, (K) Making a made-to-measure suit at an expensive tailor, (L) Milling flour, (M) Refining sugar, (N) Quarrying sand and gravel.

* 10. The following actual costs were incurred in Process 2 for January in a plant making polythene sheets:

Opening Work in Progress

	£
Direct Labour	1,200
Direct Materials	10,800
Overheads	1,000

Costs input in January: £
Cost of items transferred from Process 1
  (Treated as Direct Materials in Process 2);   38,000
Extra Direct Materials added in Process 2:   21,000
Direct Labour   5,520
Overheads   4,880
                                                ───────

4,000 kilos of polythene are completed at the end of Process 2.
400 kilos of polythene are partly completed as follows:
100% of their Direct Materials are in the process.
Only 50% of their Direct Labour has been input.
Only 50% of their Overheads have been input.

(A) What is the total cost (split between D.L., D.M. and Overheads) input into the process by the end of January?
(B) What is the total cost of the 4,000 finished kilos of polythene?
(C) What is the unit cost of a finished kilo?
(D) What is the closing work in progress figure (split between D.L., D.M. and Overheads)?

11. The Sensational Software Dress Co. specialises in ready to wear clothes produced in large numbers. Their factory uses a process costing system. For July the following information is available from the cutting department:

	Opening Work in Progress	Input in July
	£	£
Direct Labour	250	1,700
Direct Materials	1,700	350
Overheads	900	370

At the end of July 1,500 dresses have been cut out and sent to the stitching department. 500 dresses have been half completed for Direct Labour and one third completed for Direct Materials. 400 dresses are one quarter complete for Direct Labour and one eighth complete for Direct Materials. The overhead recovery rate is per Direct Labour hour.

(A) What is the total cost input into the process by the end of July? (Split between D.L., D.M. and O/H).
(B) What is the cost of the 1,500 completely cut dresses, in total, *and* per dress?
(C) What is the closing work in progress value (split between D.L., D.M. and O/H)?

12. Tennis ball manufacture is in two stages, Moulding and Covering. A process costing system is used and at the end of day 1 the Moulding department gave the following information:

Total Costs (including opening WIP) input into the process:

Direct Labour	£15,700
Direct Materials	£12,900
Overheads	£14,600

There were 68,000 completed tennis balls and 12,000 which had only one quarter of their raw material content and had three quarters of their direct labour content completed. The overhead recovery rate is per machine hour and the 12,000 part completed balls are only half machined.

(A) What is the cost of the 68,000 balls transferred to the Covering Dept at the end of day 1?

(B) What is the closing work in progress of the moulding dept?

In the Covering Department the following total costs are in the process at the end of day 2 NOT INCLUDING the cost of the 68,000 moulded balls (transferred at the start of day 2) which you should also include, using your answer to (A):

Direct Labour	£7,100
Direct Materials	£4,000 plus answer to part A.
Overheads	£5,600

The covering department tell you that at the end of day 2: 72,000 balls were completed, and 3,000 remained half completed for Direct Labour and 80% complete for Direct Materials. Overheads are recovered per Direct Labour hour in this department.

(C) What is the total cost of the 72,000 completed tennis balls?

(D) What is the unit cost per ball?

(E) What is the closing work in progress figure of the covering department?

13. The following details are given for Marina plc which manufactures one product from a single process.

Opening Work-in-Progress	6,400 UNITS	
		£
Direct Materials	100% complete	28,000
Direct Wages	75% complete	13,000
Production Overhead	60% complete	26,000
October Input		
October costs		
Direct Materials		192,000
Direct Wages		118,250
Production Overhead		236,500
Closing Work in Progress	5,000 UNITS	
Direct Materials	100% complete	
Direct Wages	50% complete	
Production Overhead	50% complete	

59,000 units were completed in October.

Prepare a production cost statement showing:

(*i*) the total cost of production of the finished units.

(*ii*) the valuation of closing work-in-progress.

CHAPTER 5

MARGINAL COSTING – PART 1

CHAPTER OBJECTIVES

Having studied this chapter you should be able to:

* EXPLAIN THE MEANING OF THE TERM "MARGINAL COST" AND THE BASIS OF MARGINAL COSTING THEORY

* ILLUSTRATE THE MAIN USES OF A MARGINAL COST TO A BUSINESS

* CALCULATE THE MARGINAL COST OF ONE ITEM

* RELATE THE MARGINAL COSTING CLASSIFICATION OF A BUSINESS'S EXPENSES TO THE BASIC COST CLASSIFICATION AND THE PROFIT AND LOSS ACCOUNT CLASSIFICATION

* CALCULATE BREAK EVEN POINTS

* EXPLAIN THE IMPORTANCE OF THE TERM "CONTRIBUTION" TO MARGINAL COSTING THEORY

* UNDERSTAND THE ASSUMPTIONS UNDERLYING MARGINAL COSTING THEORY AND COMMENT UPON THEIR VALIDITY

WHAT IS A MARGINAL COST?

Assuming you have re-read Chapter 1 as advised at the end of the previous chapter, you should be clear that the marginal cost of an item essentially means "the extra cost incurred by making one more". In more detail, we need to qualify this slightly by adding "In a given length of time (e.g. one week) the marginal cost of an item is the extra cost incurred by making one more."

For example assume a business makes wheelbarrows and nothing else. Each week they intend to make 400 of them. The workforce is paid by the week, not by the barrow, and Direct Labour costs for a week are £1,700. The Direct Material cost of 400 Barrows is £2,100 and a week's overheads which are chiefly rent, rates and office staff wages total £1,900.

Total costs for 1 week therefore are:

	£
DL	1,700
+ DM	2,100
+ O/H	1,900
	£5,700

Fig. 57.

If in fact 405 barrows are made one week (because there has been a particularly good production run for example) how much will the five extra barrows cost? Direct Labour costs will not go up. Overheads will not go up. Only Direct Materials will go up: D.M. Cost of 1 barrow = 2,100 ÷ 400 = £5·25. So the five extra barrows *made that week* will cost an extra £5·25 each. In this example the *marginal cost* of a barrow is £5·25. Obviously you can't make 5 extra barrows without using 5 extra lots of direct materials!

It is quite possible for elements of Direct Labour and of overheads to be included in the marginal cost. For example if the workforce were paid a shared bonus of £0·50 for each barrow produced, the marginal cost per barrow would be £5·25 + £0·50 = £5.75.

If the power needed to weld a barrow together (included in overheads for the base load of 400) cost £0·15 per barrow, then the marginal cost per barrow would be

	£	
	5·25	Direct Material
+	0·50	Direct Labour
+	0·15	Overhead
=	£5·90	

Fig. 58.

Nothing too difficult so far. To state in general terms what we have illustrated above, it is clear that:

(A) Some costs will be volume of output – sensitive. That is the amount spent on them will go up when output goes up, and go down when output goes down. Most obviously Direct Materials is one of these.

(B) Some costs will be incurred anyway, *regardless of output volume* (assuming there is a business in existence). Most obviously Rent. Rates, non-bonus related wages, are examples of these.

MARGINAL COSTING THEORY

In theory marginal costing assumes every cost can be placed either in category A or B, and there are special jargon words for each category. Output – volume – sensitive costs such as Direct Materials are called "VARIABLE" costs. This means the cost incurred will "vary in relation to output volume". (The terms "marginal cost" and "variable cost" are interchangeable).

Those costs that are incurred anyway regardless of output volume (assuming the business is still functioning that is) are called "FIXED" costs. This is a most unfortunate and misleading term; but one we are all stuck with. FIXED costs can ALTER. In this special marginal costing sense "FIXED" does not mean cannot alter: only "will not alter as a direct result of making one more item". The Rent and Rates can and do go up! They don't go up however as a result of making one more wheelbarrow – only as a result (in the case of rates) of the local authority spending more of our money for us than before!

So remember that in Marginal Costing the terms "Fixed Costs" and "Variable Costs" have specialised meanings.

Our wheelbarrow company's total costs for making 400 wheelbarrows in one week (see Fig. 57) can therefore be split into the two categories: (A) the Volume sensitive costs – the *variable costs* and (B) the costs incurred regardless of how many are made – the *fixed costs*. Assuming as before the power used to weld each barrow is £0·15, the Bonus per barrow is £0·50 and the Direct Materials are totally variable, then the costs of making the normal output of 400 barrows could be shown as follows:

	Total Cost	Fixed Costs	Variable Costs
	£	£	£
Direct Labour	1,700	1,500	200
Direct Materials	2,100	—	2,100
Overheads	1,900	1,840	60
	£5,700	£3,340	£2,360

Fig. 59.

The marginal (or variable) costs for 400 barrows = £2,360. The variable costs per barrow = £2,360 ÷ 400 = £5·90 (which agrees with our illustration in Fig. 58 of course).

In fact we now have a new classification of costs. In Chapter 2, Fig. 6 we saw how the Profit and Loss classification of costs related to the basic cost classification. Figure 59 above showed how the basic cost classification splits into Fixed and Variable Costs. So for our wheelbarrow company we have three possible analyses (I have made up typical profit and loss account headings):

Profit and Loss		Basic Cost Classification		Marginal Costing Classification	
	£		£		£
Wages	2,200	Direct Labour	1,700	VARIABLE	
Materials	2,400	Direct Materials	2,100	COSTS	2,360
Insurances	50				
Vehicles	300	FACTORY INDIRECT		FIXED COSTS	3,340
Heat and		EXPENSES			
Electricity	200	+ OFFICE COSTS			
Rates	100	i.e. OVERHEADS =	1,900		
Rent	300				
Depreciation	150				
	£5,700		£5,700		£5,700

Fig. 60.

REVENUE STATEMENTS IN MARGINAL COSTING FORMAT

If we intend to sell our wheelbarrows for £20 each it is obvious our profit will be (if we sell 400):

			£
Revenue 400 × £20	=		8,000
less Costs			5,700
			£2,300

It is usual however, if a marginal costing layout is being used, to expand this statement as follows:

		£
Revenue: 400 wheelbarrows at £20:		8,000
less Variable Costs: 400 wheelbarrows at £5·90:		2,360
equals CONTRIBUTION:		5,640
less Fixed Costs:		3,340
equals PROFIT:		£2,300

Fig. 61.

The costs are taken from the revenue IN TWO STAGES: first the marginal (or variable) cost is subtracted which leaves *the amount of revenue left over after the variable costs are paid for.* This is called the CONTRIBUTION. (Revenue *less* variable costs = Contribution).

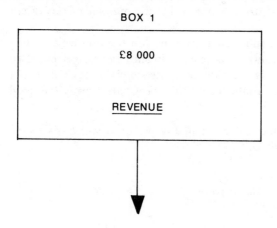

BOX 1

£8 000

REVENUE

First Pays For:

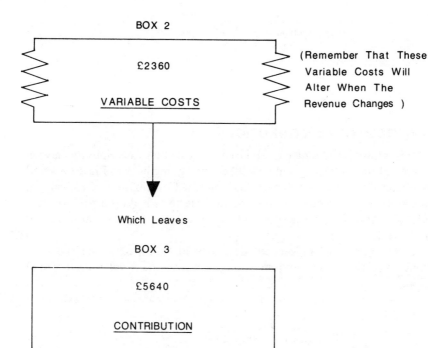

BOX 2

£2360

VARIABLE COSTS

(Remember That These Variable Costs Will Alter When The Revenue Changes)

Which Leaves

BOX 3

£5640

CONTRIBUTION

Diagrammatically, box 1 above represents the revenue from the 400 wheelbarrows. The marginal costing system supposes it is first used to pay for the variable costs incurred in making 400 barrows (in the diagram, the Revenue box is divided up first into box 2). Whatever is left after this determines the "size" of box 3; i.e. the amount of CONTRIBUTION.

Next the fixed costs are subtracted from the contribution which leaves the profit. (Contribution *less* fixed costs = Profit.) People get muddled by contribution: but it is (as you can see) quite simply what remains out of the revenue when the variable costs have been taken away (i.e. paid for).

We could also re-do the statement in Fig. 61 on a *unit* basis to the contribution line for instance:

		£
Unit Revenue	=	20·00
less Unit Variable Cost	=	5·90
Unit Contribution		£14.10

		£
TOTAL CONTRIBUTION = £14·10 × 400 units =		5,640
less Fixed Costs	=	3,340
PROFIT		£2,300

Fig. 62.

THE ROLE OF CONTRIBUTION

It is important to understand the central role that Contribution plays in marginal costing theory and how it behaves: going back to Fig. 61 we sold 400 wheelbarrows for £20 each and made a Contribution of £5,640 (i.e. the amount of revenue left *after* the variable costs had been paid for, was £5,640). After fixed costs of £3,340 had been paid for, a profit of £2,300 remained.

If 405 barrows had been made and sold that week, then the Revenue, Variable costs, and most importantly, the *Contribution* would change:

		£
Revenue = 405 × £20	=	8,100·00
less Variable Costs 405 × £5·90	=	2,389·50
CONTRIBUTION		£5,710·50

But the fixed costs will NOT alter because 5 extra barrows have been made that week. So the profit is:

	£
CONTRIBUTION	5,710·50
less Fixed Costs	3,340·00
= Profit	£2,370·50

Interestingly the Contribution went up by £70·50:

		£
Contribution from 405 Barrows	=	5,710·50
less Contribution from 400 Barrows	=	5,640·00
Extra Contribution		£70·50

And so did the profit:

		£
Profit on 405 Barrows	=	2,370·50
Profit on 400 Barrows	=	2,300·00
Extra Profit		£70·50

In other words because the fixed element of the costs will not alter as revenue alters, Contribution and Profit move up and down BY EQUAL AMOUNTS, i.e. EXTRA CONTRIBUTION = EXTRA PROFIT.

On a unit basis the profit and contribution relationship is even clearer. Check Fig. 62, the unit contribution from one barrow is £14·10. (Unit Revenue *minus* Unit Variable Cost = Unit Contribution: 20 − 5·90 = £14·10.) Now the relevant contributions for each sales level are easily found:

Contribution from 400 Barrows:		£
£14·10 × 400	=	5,640
less Fixed Costs	=	3,340
Profit		£2,300

Contribution from 405 Barrows:		£
£14·10 × 405	=	5,710
less Fixed Costs	=	3,340
Profit		£2,370·50

Fig. 63.

In fact the difference in contribution (and therefore profit) can be found even more easily:

Extra Contribution from 5 extra barrows = 5 × £14·10 = £70·50

And we know, now, that if contribution goes up by £70·50 so will profit.

Here is another example: What will the profit be if we only make and sell 370 wheelbarrows in the week?

Long Way of Answering (a full Marginal Costing Statement):

		£
Revenue 370 barrows × £20	=	7,400
less Variable Costs 370 Barrows × £5·90	=	2,183
CONTRIBUTION		5,217
less Fixed Costs		3,340
Profit		£1,877

Fig. 64.

Quick Way of Answering

Profit at 400 wheelbarrows was	£2,300
less Contribution lost = 30 barrows × £14·10 (30 barrows × unit contribution) =	£423
New Profit	£1,877

Fig. 65.

Because we know profit and contribution will alter by equal amounts *once the contribution change is known* the *profit change is known*. Because EXTRA CONTRIBUTION = EXTRA PROFIT, of course *less* contribution = *less* profit too!

This section must be thoroughly understood. Do not go on until you are certain you grasp it. If you think you are sure, do the quick questions in Section A at the end of this chapter, now, to be sure that you have got it clear.

CONTRIBUTION/SALES RATIOS

Before going on to the *uses* of marginal costing, there is one more piece of jargon you must be familiar with. Marginal costing requires the student to learn first how all the bits of the theory work, before applying it to a business problem. However this is the last piece to get hold of.

We have dealt with the relationship between contribution and profit in the last section. (Contribution and profit alter by equal amounts). This section deals with the relationship between CONTRIBUTION AND SALES. Take a simple example first:

		Percentage relationship
	£	%
Sales revenue:	1,000	100
less Variable Costs:	600	60
= Contribution:	£400	40

Fig. 66.

If sales revenue goes up to £1,200 (because we sell more items) then we can expect the variable costs to go up in total by the same amount, i.e. by $\frac{1}{5}$. (Remember that variable costs are output-sensitive, when the number sold goes up so does the total variable cost.) So now the example would be:

		Percentage relationship
	£	%
Sales revenue	1,200	100
less Variable Costs		
$(600 + \frac{1}{5} \times 600) =$	720	60
CONTRIBUTION	£480	40

Fig. 67.

Although the revenue has changed *the proportion of that revenue that is left over as Contribution* remains the same, i.e. 40%.

The relationship is known as the CONTRIBUTION/SALES RATIO. The contribution/sales ratio *means* "the percentage of sales revenue that will be left over as contribution". In our example therefore the C/S ratio = 40%.

WARNING Some people call the contribution/sales ratio the PROFIT/ VOLUME ratio (P/V Ratio). In my view this is a misleading term but it means *exactly the same thing*. In this book the term C/S ratio will be used throughout. If you see P/V ratio (in an exam question for instance) it means C/S ratio.

So what is the C/S ratio of our wheelbarrow firm?

		Relationship
	£	%
Selling Price per wheelbarrow	20·00	100
Variable Cost per wheelbarrow	5·90	29·5
Contribution per wheelbarrow	£14·10	70·5

So the C/S ratio is 70·5%. Using the total figures from Fig. 61 the relationship still holds good:

	£	%
Sales Revenue 400 × 20	8,000	100
less Variable Cost 400 × 5·90	2,360	
CONTRIBUTION	£5,640	70·5

(Proof: 8,000 × 70·5% = 5,640, check it on your calculator!)

So one use of this C/S ratio would be to make it easy to calculate what the extra contribution would be from extra sales. Question: If we sell 5 more barrows what will the extra contribution be? *Answer:* C/S Ratio = 70·5% (i.e. of any extra sales revenue 70·5% will be left over as contribution when the variable costs have been paid for). Extra revenue = 5 barrows at £20 = £100. So Extra Contribution = 100 × 70·5% = £70·50. It's true, check with Fig. 63 where we worked it out the long way. And of course the extra contribution is extra profit – so we know that the profit will go up by £70·50 as well.

Now do the quick questions in Section B at the end of the chapter to be sure you have grasped what the C/S ratio is, before going on.

THE USES OF MARGINAL COSTING

All very interesting so far; but what does marginal costing help a business to do? So far we know two things: In a given period (i) the *extra* cost of making one more item will be its marginal (variable) cost (ii) the profit made will be proportional to the contribution. What use can businesses make of this information?

At this starting stage we will consider three distinct uses that can be made of the information, to help managers run their businesses (which is the point of all cost accounts remember):

(i) To help decide whether to take an order at a special price.
(ii) To help decide between alternative marketing strategies.
(iii) To calculate break-even sales (i.e. the sales level where a business makes neither a profit nor a loss).

Dealing with each in turn:

1. DECIDING UPON A SPECIAL PRICE FOR A CUSTOMER

We make radio sets, and the present sales and revenues for the next six months are:

	£
Direct Labour	25,000
Direct Materials	45,000
Prime Cost	70,000
Indirect Labour	10,000
Indirect Materials	4,000
Machinery Costs	8,000
Building Establishment Costs	15,000
Cost of Production	107,000
Sales and Distribution	16,000
Administration	9,000
Finance	2,000
Sundry	1,000
Total Cost	£135,000

Fig. 68.

We intend to make 5,000 sets in the six months and to sell them for £30 each. *We have enough spare capacity to make 6,000 sets if necessary.*

The *absorption cost* per set is £135,000 ÷ 5,000 = £27. The profit we are hoping for is:

Revenue 5,000 × £30 =	£150,000
less Total Cost =	£135,000
	£15,000

Task

Along comes a well-known chain of electrical discount stores we have not previously dealt with and says to us "We like your radios: we want to place an order for 800 of them; but we will only be prepared to pay £22 a set. Will you do us a deal?"

At first glance it would be a silly thing to do because the price being offered is below the £27 absorption cost. However, (after the fine training provided by Foundation Cost Accounting) you realise that: (A) We have spare capacity to make *extra* radios in the six months coming, (B) More importantly you realise that the *cost of the extra radios will only be their marginal cost.*

Method

So clearly the thing to do is to find out what the marginal cost of a radio is: You investigate and find out the following: *Direct Labour* is 10% variable because of a bonus element in wages. *Direct Materials* are completely variable. *Indirect Labour* will share in the bonus scheme so it is also 10% variable. All the other costs are fixed (i.e. will not go up as a direct result of making 800 more radios in the period).

(1) Analyse the costs for the base load of 5,000 radios between Fixed and Variable Costs:

	Total	Fixed	Variable
	£	£	£
Direct Labour	25,000	22,500	2,500
Direct Material	45,000	—	45,000
Indirect Labour	10,000	9,000	1,000
Indirect Material	4,000	4,000	—
Machinery Costs	8,000	8,000	—
Building and Establishment	15,000	15,000	—
Sales and Distribution	16,000	16,000	—
Administration	9,000	9,000	—
Finance	2,000	2,000	—
Sundry	1,000	1,000	—
Total	£135,000	£86,500	£48,500

Fig. 69.

(2) Now the variable costs for the normal output of 5,000 radios are known (£48,500) the variable (marginal) cost of ONE radio $= \dfrac{£48,500}{5,000}$

$$= £9{\cdot}70$$

(3) The extra order can now be evaluated using the marginal costing-type layout you have already learned:

		£
Extra Revenue = 800 sets × £22	=	17,600
less Extra Variable Costs: 800 sets × £9·70	=	7,760
Extra Contribution		£9,840

Fig. 70.

There are no extra fixed costs so the extra Contribution is all extra profit. *SO THE ORDER IS WORTH TAKING.* Again using the Marginal Costing layout we can clearly show the "before" and "after" position:

WITHOUT EXTRA ORDER		WITH EXTRA ORDER		
	£		£	£
Revenue £30 × 5,000 sets	= 150,000	*Revenue:* £30 × 5,000 =	150,000	
less Variable Costs	= 48,500	*Plus* £22 × 800 =	17,600	
Contribution	101,500			167,600
		less Variable Costs:		
		5,800 × £9·70 =		56,260
less Fixed Costs	86,500			
		Contribution		111,340
		less Fixed Costs =		86,500
Profit	£15,000	Profit		£24,840

Fig. 71.

The Extra Profit $= 24,840 - 15,000 = £9,840$

which is the extra contribution from the extra order – see Fig. 70.

That illustrates the first basic use of marginal costs; to evaluate orders at special prices. Make sure you understand it before going on to the second use. As an exercise: what is the C/S ratio of (A) the basic 5,000 sets and (B) the extra order?

$A = 67.67\%$
$B = 74.23\%$

2. DECIDING BETWEEN ALTERNATIVE MARKETING STRATEGIES

In the radio set example just used, the basic marketing strategy was to make 5,000 sets in six months and to sell them for £30 each, the hoped-for profit being £15,000. We actually have capacity to make 6,000 sets in the six months though, which is why the extra order was considered.

It is perfectly possible that the managers might want to consider alternative basic pricing policies though, to see if more profit could be made. For instance one manager might suggest (A) reducing the price per set to £27 and therefore (B) aim to sell all 6,000 sets that could be made.

Assuming the marginal cost per unit is known (£9·70, see Fig. 70), the marginal costing layout makes it very easy and quick to see if this is a good alternative:

	£
Revenue = 6,000 sets × £27	= 162,000
less Variable Cost 6,000 sets × £9·70	= 58,200
Contribution	£103,800

$c/s = 64\%$

Fig. 72.

If you have taken in the fact that "extra contribution = extra profit" you already know whether this alternative is more profitable. Look at the "Without Extra Order" part of Fig. 71. This shows the contribution and profit made on our original marketing strategy and the contribution was £101,500. As the contribution under this new strategy is £103,800 the extra contribution will be extra profit:

	Old Strategy	New Strategy	Difference
	£	£	£
CONTRIBUTION	101,500	103,800	+ 2,300
less FIXED COSTS	86,500	86,500	—
PROFIT	£15,000	£17,300	+ £2,300

Fig. 73.

Interestingly enough this would not be a good alternative to the original plan *and* extra order, as another glance at Fig. 71, this time at the "With Extra Order" column would show! Remember that we would be using up all our capacity under this new basic plan, so we would not be able to accept any "one-off" special orders.

Another manager might suggest that the price could be pushed up to £34 and 4,000 sets still be sold. This idea could also be quickly evaluated:

	£
Revenue 4,000 sets × £34	= 136,000
less Variable Costs 4,000 sets × £9·70	= 38,800
Contribution	£97,200

Fig. 74.

And you should already know that this is *not* a good idea because the contribution is lower than all the other alternatives. The profit would be:

	£
Contribution	97,200
less Fixed Costs	86,500
Profit	£10,700

This illustrates the second use of marginal costing: to enable a quick evaluation of alternative marketing strategies to be made. And something for you to work out: What are the two new C/S ratios of the two alternative marketing strategies evaluated?

3. FINDING BREAK EVEN POINTS

This is the third use of marginal costing which will be dealt with in this chapter. All businesses try to make profits, and as far as the people working in them are concerned, the gloom which descends over a loss-making company has to be experienced to be believed. Even a small profit does wonders for everyone's feelings, after a loss has been made. Therefore the break-even point, the point at which a firm is no longer in danger of making a loss *in the period under review*, is an important point to reach. So managers need to know where it is, and when they have reached it.

To recapitulate, Marginal Costing theory works like this: *In a given time* the bigger the amount of Contribution (i.e. what is left over from revenue after the variable costs have been paid) the bigger the profit, because the fixed costs do *not* go up as Contribution goes up. Diagramatically:

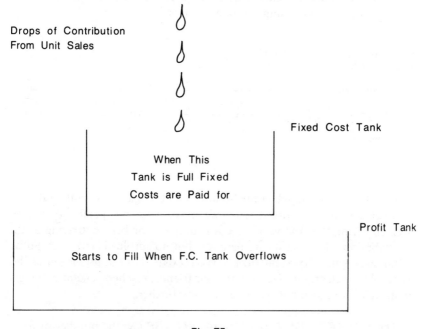

Drops of Contribution
From Unit Sales

Fixed Cost Tank

When This
Tank is Full Fixed
Costs are Paid for

Profit Tank

Starts to Fill When F.C. Tank Overflows

Fig. 75.

This diagram well illustrates why extra contribution is extra profit in a given period. If the fixed cost tank is full, the extra drops of contribution run straight into the profit tank, the more contribution the more profit.

Now, what if there is ONLY ENOUGH CONTRIBUTION TO JUST FILL THE FIXED COST TANK? Variable costs have been paid for already before contribution is arrived at – and there is just enough contribution to pay for fixed costs? Under these circumstances a business has made neither a profit nor a loss, in fact it has BROKEN EVEN because its revenue has just met its costs with nothing over. For instance:

	£			£
Revenue	1,000	————————— TOTAL REVENUE	1,000
less Variable Costs	600		equals	
	——		TOTAL COSTS	£1,000
CONTRIBUTION	400			
less Fixed Costs	400			
PROFITS	—			

Fig. 76.

More importantly we can say: Break even happens when CONTRIBUTION = FIXED COSTS. Using the same figures:

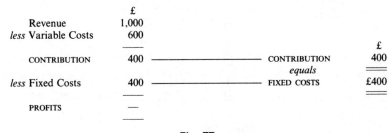

	£			£
Revenue	1,000			
less Variable Costs	600			
	——			400
CONTRIBUTION	400	————————— CONTRIBUTION	400
			equals	
less Fixed Costs	400	————————— FIXED COSTS	£400
PROFITS	—			

Fig. 77.

If there is only enough contribution to fill the fixed cost tank and none to overflow into the profit tank, we make neither a profit nor a loss. Remembering that the variable costs are paid for before arriving at the contribution, all the costs are paid for; but no surplus is left over. So we break even when CONTRIBUTION = FIXED COSTS. Do not go on unless this is absolutely clear. Go over it with your friends, teachers, enemies, but get it straight in your mind before going any further.

The *BREAK EVEN POINT* means *EITHER* (A) the number of *items* needed to be sold so that the business breaks even *OR* (B) The amount of *revenue* needed so that the business breaks even. (Stable selling prices are assumed for any break even calculation.)

So how do we find out this magic point? In fact it is very easy provided you have taken in the first part of the chapter and can remember what UNIT CONTRIBUTION is. If you can't, read no further until you have revised Fig. 62 and its accompanying text.

A. TO FIND THE BREAK EVEN POINT IN ITEMS NEEDED TO BE SOLD

Break even occurs when the contribution is just enough to "fill the fixed cost tank". So providing we know the level of fixed costs, we know the amount of contribution needed to break even. If contribution equals fixed costs to break even – FIXED COSTS *must equal contribution required to break even*! For example if your business has fixed costs each week of £400, you know it *must generate £400 contribution each week to break even.*

Using a new example, a business sells dresses for £25 each. The marginal (variable) cost per dress is £15. So the unit contribution is:

	£
Unit Revenue	25
less Unit Variable Cost	15
Unit Contribution	£10

Fig. 78.

Assume the fixed costs are £3,600 for one month. What is the break even point in items needed to be sold? Consider these steps:

(A) Fixed Costs for one month are £3,600
(B) Therefore we need contribution of £3,600 to break even.
(C) Unit contribution = £10.
(D) Therefore we break even when we have enough £10s to pay for £3,600 of fixed cost.
(E) So 3,600 ÷ 10 = Number of unit contributions needed to break even = 360.
(F) One unit contribution can only come from one unit being sold. So if 360 unit contributions are needed to break even: 360 UNIT SALES are needed to break even, i.e. the Break Even point is 360 units.

dresses

PROOF

		£
Revenue 360 × £25	=	9,000
less Variable Cost 360 × £15	=	5,400
Contribution		3,600
less Fixed Costs		3,600
Profit		—

B/E

Fig. 79.

These steps can now be summarised as a formula:

$$\text{Break Even point in Units} = \frac{\text{FIXED COSTS}}{\text{UNIT CONTRIBUTION}}$$

Another example. We make a really expensive range of furniture. Fixed costs are £54,750 per year, selling price per unit is £750, and variable costs per unit are £500. The Unit Contribution is:

	£
Unit Revenue	750
less Unit Variable Cost	500
Unit contribution	250

$$\text{Break even point} = \frac{\text{Fixed Cost 54,750}}{\text{Unit Contribution 250}} = 219 \text{ units}$$

PROOF

		£
Revenue 219 × £750	=	164,250
less Variable Cost 219 × £500	=	109,500
Contribution		54,750
less Fixed Costs		54,750
Profit		—

Fig. 80.

B. TO FIND BREAK EVEN POINTS IN REVENUE

Obviously if you know the unit selling price, it is easy to find the break even revenue. The proof in Figs. 79 and 80 showed that Break even revenue was £9,000 per month for the dresses and £164,250 per year for the furniture, i.e. Break even revenue must be B/E units × Unit selling price. In practical business you would always know what the unit prices were, but frequently in examinations they don't tell you them. Consider the following information relating to a business selling bread. For the next six months their projected costs and revenues are as follows:

	£
Revenue	100,000
less Variable Costs	60,000
Contribution	40,000
less Fixed Costs	25,000
Profit	£15,000

Fig. 81.

How do we find the break even revenue now? We can't find the unit contribution because we don't know how many units there are. So we can't find the break even point in units and multiply it by the unit selling price (as we did in the proofs above) to find the break even revenue. So what to do?

All those who remember what the Contribution/Sales ratio is read on. All those who do not, go back to that section of the chapter and revise it now.

In the example above (Fig. 81) the C/S ratio is:

	£	%
Revenue	100,000	100
less Variable Costs	60,000	60
Contribution	£40,000	40

Fig. 82.

This ratio is really telling us something very important:

For every £1 of revenue £0·40 will be contribution

Now finding the break even revenue is possible using essentially the same procedures as before:

(1) Contribution from £1 of revenue = £0·40.

(2) Therefore we break even when there are enough £0·40ps to pay for the £25,000 fixed costs.

(3) 25,000 ÷ £0·40 = 62,500. This shows (A) the number of £0·40ps needed to break even *AND*

(4) As £0·40 of contribution must come from £1 of sales it shows that 62,500 lots of £1 are needed *as revenue* to break even. That is £62,500 = Break Even point in revenue.

PROOF

	£	%
Revenue	62,500	100
less Variable Costs		
60% × £62,500	37,500	
Contribution	25,000	40
less Fixed Costs	25,000	
Profit	—	

Fig. 83.

These steps can be summarised then:

To find the Break Even point in Revenue (when units are not known):

(i) *Find Contribution per £1 of Revenue* (use the C/S ratio to do this).

(ii) Break Even Revenue $= \dfrac{\text{Fixed costs}}{\text{Contribution per £1 of Revenue}}$

Another example:

The fast food company sells hamburgers and has the following projected costs and revenues for the forthcoming 3 months:

	£
Sales	3,690,000
less Variable Costs	1,660,500
Contribution	2,029,500
less Fixed Costs	1,650,000
Profit	£379,500

Fig. 84.

(i) Find the C/S Ratio (i.e. contribution £2,029,500 as a percentage of Sales £3,690,000) = 55%. Therefore Contribution per £1 of sales = £0·55.

(ii) Break Even Revenue $= \dfrac{\text{Fixed Costs £1,650,000}}{\text{Contribution per £1 of sales £0·55}}$

$= £3,000,000$

PROOF

	£	%
Revenue	3,000,000	100
less Variable Costs £3,000,000 × 45%	1,350,000	45
Contribution	1,650,000	55
less Fixed Costs	1,650,000	
Profit	—	

Fig. 85.

And that's how to find break even points.

SUMMARISING EXAMPLE

In the following example all of the aspects of marginal costing dealt with in this chapter are illustrated so that you have another chance to see how the various concepts relate to a single enterprise:

The estimated costs for the Hardwick Book Co., which manufactures and writes books, are as follows for the forthcoming 6 months:

	£
Direct Labour	130,000
Direct Materials	270,000
Indirect Labour	40,000
Indirect Materials	25,000
Machinery Costs	62,000
Building Establishment Costs	36,000
Sales and Distribution	65,000
Administration	27,500
Finance	3,500
Sundry	1,000
TOTAL COSTS	£660,000

Fig. 86.

The estimated output and revenues will be as follows for the same 6 month period:

Books produced:	200,000 copies
Selling price per book:	£4 each

You have been asked a number of questions and you realise the marginal cost must be found to answer them. In fact the first question is from the sales director:

Q.1. "We have enough production time to make 250,000 books if necessary, how much would the extra books cost to make?"

Your researches reveal the following information about the estimated costs:

Direct Labour is 15% variable as a result of bonus payments. Direct Materials are 100% variable. Indirect Labour is 15% variable. Power costs (included in Building and Establishment expense) of £6,000 are 100% variable. 10% of Sales and Distribution expenses are variable.

The total costs for the 6 months can now be analysed into their fixed and variable components:

	Total	Fixed	Variable
	£	£	£
Direct Labour	130,000	110,500	19,500
Direct Materials	270,000	—	270,000
Indirect Labour	40,000	34,000	6,000
Indirect Material	25,000	25,000	—
Machinery Cost	62,000	62,000	—
Building & Establishment Costs	36,000	30,000	6,000
Sales & Distribution	65,000	58,500	6,500
Administration	27,500	27,500	—
Finance	3,500	3,500	—
Sundry	1,000	1,000	—
TOTAL	660,000	£352,000	£308,000

Fig. 87.

Therefore if £308,000 is the variable cost for 200,000 books, the UNIT VARIABLE COST (marginal cost) per book =

$$\frac{£308,000}{200,000 \text{ books}} = £1{\cdot}54 \text{ Variable Cost per Book}$$

Fig. 88.

So the answer to the sales director's question is that *any extra books* over 200,000 will cost £1·54 each.

Q.2. The Managing Director wants to know, "If extra books were sold at the normal price, how much extra profit would be made for every £1,000 of extra sales?"

This is where the C/S ratio can be best used. Lets put the original plan into Marginal Costing format:

		£
Revenue 200,000 books × £4	=	800,000
less Variable Costs 200,000 books × £1·54	=	308,000
Contribution	=	492,000
less Fixed Costs	=	352,000
Profit		£140,000

Fig. 89.

The C/S Ratio is Contribution as a percentage of Sales. So 492,000 = 61·5% of £800,000. This means *that for every £1 of Sales, £0·615 will be contribution.* So for an extra £1,000 of Sales, £615 will be extra contribution AND THEREFORE EXTRA PROFIT. That's the M.D.'s question answered.

Q.3. The Marketing Director thinks that if the book prices were reduced to £3·50 each, 250,000 books could be sold – which we can make in the period under review. She wants to know, "Would it be worth it from a profit point of view?"

		£
Revenue 250,000 × £3·50	=	875,000
less Variable Cost 250,000 × £1·54	=	385,000
Contribution	=	£490,000

Fig. 90.

You need go no further. The contribution is £2,000 lower than in our original plan (Fig. 89). Therefore the profit will be £2,000 lower. (Proof £490,000 less Fixed Costs £352,000 = Profit £138,000. The original profit was £140,000).

Q.4. The Chairman, who wants to ensure the business is prepared to withstand hard times in the market-place, as well as take advantage of good times, asks "What is the break-even point, how many books do we have to sell to avoid making a loss?"

	£
Unit Selling Price	4
less Unit Variable Cost	1·54
Unit Contribution	£2·46

$$\text{Break Even point in units} = \frac{\text{Fixed Costs £352,000}}{\text{Unit Contribution £2·46}}$$

$$= \quad 143,090 \text{ Books (round up)}$$

Fig. 91.

NOTE: If we *did not know the unit contribution* the break even point *in Sales Revenue* can easily be found because we know the C/S ratio is 61·5%. Which means that for every £1 of Revenue £0·615 is contribution. Therefore:

$$\text{Break Even in Revenue} = \frac{\text{Fixed Costs £352,000}}{\text{Contribution per £1 of Revenue £0·615}}$$

$$= \quad £572,360 \text{ (rounded up)}$$

PROOF

143,090 B/E books × £4 per Book = £572,360 = Break Even Revenue.

Q.5. The production director wants to know, "How much per book do the basic 200,000 books cost?" You explain to him that ON AN ABSORPTION COST BASIS the cost per book is,

$$\frac{\text{TOTAL COST £660,000}}{\text{BOOKS MADE 200,000}} = £3\cdot30 = \text{ABSORPTION COST PER BOOK BASED ON 200,000 BOOKS}$$

"That's what I thought," he said, "so why does the sales manager want to take this special order from Giant Chain Stores Ltd for 35,000 extra books at only £2 each?"

You produce the following statement to show him:

Narrative	Basic Output	Narrative	Extra Order	Basic Output + Extra Order
	£		£	£
Revenue 200,000 × £4	800,000	Revenue 35,000 × £2	70,000	870,000
less		*less*		
Variable Costs		V.C. 35,000 × £1·54	53,900	361,900
200,000 × £1·54	308,000			
CONTRIBUTION	492,000	CONTRIBUTION	16,100	508,100
less Fixed Costs	352,000	*less* Fixed Costs	—	352,000
PROFIT	£140,000	PROFIT	£16,100	£156,100

Fig. 92.

NOTE: Of course it must be remembered that better still would be to sell the extra 35,000 books at the normal £4 price! In other words the main task of a business is TO MAKE ITS APSORPTION COST-BASED MARKETING PLAN WORK (in our example to sell 200,000 Books at £4 each). Selling at marginal cost based prices will improve profits *once the basic plan is well on the way to being achieved*. If *all* the books the firm could make were to be sold at £2 each, the firm would run out of capacity before making enough contribution to make a profit:

				£
Revenue	250,000 × £2	=	500,000
less Variable Cost	250,000 × £1·54	=	385,000
	Contribution		115,000
	less Fixed Costs		352,000
	Loss		£(237,000)

Fig. 93.

Therefore selling at marginal-cost based prices must be done with care, and must not be allowed to deflect people's attention from the main task, i.e. Making the absorption-cost-based marketing plan work.

You should now be able to work through the questions in section C at the end of the chapter. There are some important general points to be aware of as well, which are mentioned in the remaining part of the chapter.

GENERAL POINTS ABOUT MARGINAL COSTING THEORY

If marginal costing is to work in practice then the conditions that the theory assumes to exist, must actually occur. So you need to know what these theoretical assumptions are. If a real situation does not conform to the theoretical one, then marginal costing won't be much use to the management of that business.

THEORETICAL ASSUMPTIONS OF MARGINAL COSTING

1. That variable costs *can* be identified in a business. In practice it may be quite hard to identify variable costs sufficiently precisely to make clear-cut decisions. Especially in enormous factories, where there are complicated bonus-systems, rules on attendance of various ancillary workers if the factory is open (e.g. Firemen, Nurses, Security men, and so forth). Under these circumstances the variable cost of an extra Sunday shift may be completely different from the variable cost of producing extra items on a week-day evening's overtime. Allied to this is the assumption that fixed costs *are predictable*; of course they are not necessarily. A sudden breakdown can mean engineers working hours of overtime and a big bill for spare parts. These are all fixed costs; but hardly predictable ones. Fixed costs do change remember.

2. That variable costs will go up and down *exactly proportionately* with output. In practice if fewer items are made then raw materials prices may go up – because bulk-buying discounts are lost, for example. Equally if electricity is a major item in variable cost (which in steel-making or aluminium making it is) then if more of it is used there can be peak-loading penalties which greatly increase the price of the electricity.

3. The assumption of price-stability. In our example we have assumed that *prices remained stable throughout the period being examined.* In practice prices change quite quickly and this needs to be remembered. If petrol costs go up – then delivery costs go up, for instance. If direct material prices go up, so do the unit variable costs.

Points 2 and 3 can be illustrated in graph form. I'm not very keen on graphs to illustrate accounting points; because real businessmen understand figures, not pretty diagrams.

Teaching accounting students to draw graphs is a waste of time because they will never use them *in business*. If you want to draw a graph – and occasionally mis-guided examiners ask for them – you plot costs against output as follows:

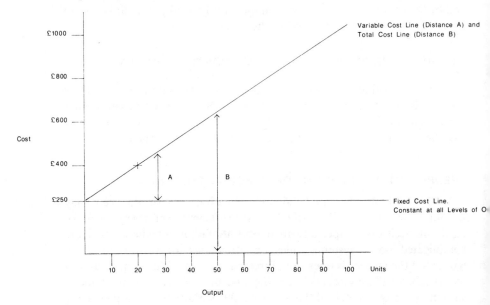

Fig. 94.

At 20 units the x on the variable cost line shows total costs to be £400, being Fixed Costs £250 and Variable Costs 400 − 250 = £150.

Points 2 and 3 are saying that this graph won't be true if *prices* change in the period. For instance if the rates go up by £50 the fixed costs will no longer be £250; but £300.

4. The assumption that all fixed costs provide the same amount of productive capacity. Absolutely theoretically, a business could be working 7 days a week, 24 hours a day, 365 days a year. (In which case the marginal cost of one more item would be the cost of a whole new factory!) When in our questions we talked of "Spare Capacity" we meant there was room in the existing set up, without having to build a whole new one, to make extra items in the time under review. Now the fixed costs, by and large, represent the cost of production facilities used – machines, buildings, sales force and so forth. In practice **it is very unlikely indeed that all these separate facilities will have exactly the same amount of spare unused capacity.**

Take the works manager – whose salary will be a fixed cost. If a night-shift were to be added, then a night-manager would be needed. The spare capacity of works management was, in fact, NIL. Similarly the sales-force might be fully stretched at normal output, and extra items to be sold might need more staff to be taken on. Also extra output may mean that a particular machine becomes too busy, and another one needs to be purchased.

All these things happen in reality, and they all mean that fixed costs will not, in reality, remain unchanged over changes in output. Because some aspects of production (i.e. some elements of fixed cost) have *less* spare capacity than others, *extra fixed costs will in reality be incurred as output is increased.*

The truth of this has led some people to talk of "Step-Variable Costs". This is meant to describe elements of productive capacity and therefore of fixed costs, which do not (in a particular case) have very much spare capacity; so that when output is increased past a certain limit, more fixed cost has to be incurred. My objections to this name are that they are not step-*variable* costs at all; but step-FIXED costs.

In practice therefore, the cost accountant needs to be aware of the output levels at which these "fixed cost steps" occur.

5. Finally there is the assumption of *a constant level of production efficiency*. At the end of chapter 4 we went through the factors that affected the absorption cost of a product. The third of which (and in my view most important) was the speed with which the items are made. In marginal costing theory it is assumed this remains unchanged. But anyone in industry, or commerce, will tell you that this just is not the case. As output goes up or down, efficiency of output (i.e. speed of output and quality of it) changes.

Take variable costs for example. About 10% of most direct materials in the engineering industry are wasted for one reason or another, e.g. off-cuts of sheetmetal, quality control rejections of finished goods, metal swarf from boring holes, and so on. If production levels alter, so will material waste levels, they may go up or down; but you can bet they won't be the same. And if these things alter, so will the unit variable costs from one level of output to another.

ASSUMPTION SUMMARY

These practical points do not invalidate the principles of marginal costing. The firm which is recovering all its overheads between Monday and Friday will certainly be able to produce goods in Saturday overtime at a marginal cost which is lower than the normal absorption cost. However the practical realities mean that care must be taken by the cost accountant to ensure that any marginal-cost-based information produced for managers as far as possible predicts what will *really* happen. To do this requires an understanding of where the theoretical assumptions of marginal costing may not completely co-incide with reality.

MARGINAL COSTING AND SELLING PRICES

There are two practical problems with setting selling prices based on the "can we take this extra order at a lower price" technique explained in this chapter.

1. There are often TIMING problems. Businesses often take orders well in advance of delivery. The printing of mail-order catalogues and advertising brochures is often ordered months ahead of delivery for instance. Say someone comes into your office and offers you business based on a marginal cost type selling price THREE MONTHS before delivery. Meanwhile you had not yet achieved your absorption-cost based sales for three-months-hence. What to do? Do you refuse the order, in which case you might lose valuable contribution and have machines standing idle? Or accept the order, in which case you may have to turn down full priced business offered later? A manager's job is not an easy one. Suffice it to emphasise here; in practical business, orders do *not* come along neatly timed: first the absorption-cost-based business; then the marginal-cost-based work.

2. If word gets out among your normal customers (who pay £4 per book for example) that you are willing to sell the books for £2; then *everyone* will want them at £2. In other words you can easily destroy your normal markets by selling at marginal-cost-based prices. So businesses must be very careful how they go about such deals. "Own Brand" goods in Supermarkets are an example of how manufacturers protect their normal brands. The Giant Supermarket Co.'s Baked Beans will be made by a company that also makes its own (more expensive) beans. Bowater-Scott make their (very good) Scotties tissues, as well as making tissues under "own brand" labels for various supermarkets. The perceived difference between a Giant Supermarket Co. tissue and a Scottie, is enough to protect Bowater-Scott's normal business from being eroded by a cheaper product.

Exporting is another way of ensuring goods sold at marginal-cost-based prices do not ruin the absorption-cost-based market. U.K. customers often have no idea what price is paid for cars exported to India, or Italy or Germany – so they don't put pressure on the manufacturer to lower U.K. prices in line.

This is called "Market Segmentation" and it occasionally breaks down.

For instance in the U.K. in 1982/83 the ability to personally import cars from the E.E.C. countries (where selling prices are much cheaper) has started to erode the normal selling price structure for cars.

If you haven't already done so, now work through the Section C questions.

MARGINAL COSTING AND SHOPS

The most common application of marginal costing in day-to-day business life is in retail shops – whatever their size. Retail (i.e. ordinary) shops ONLY use marginal costing based techniques.

Imagine a shop that opens up one day and nobody at all comes in to buy anything. The shop will incur all its fixed costs: the staff will all be there, the heating will be on, the rates will still be paid and the rent, the costs of the machinery and tills and signs and advertising will still be paid.

If nobody enters a shop one day the only costs that will NOT be incurred are the variable costs. For a shop the only significant variable cost is the cost of buying-in whatever the shop sells. Although this cost will be saved as no stock will have been used up, more importantly no sales revenue and NO CONTRIBUTION will have been gained.

The following example illustrates this point for a shop which buys jackets for 30 each from its suppliers sells them for 75 each to its customers, and incurs fixed costs of 1,600 each day:

	Day 1 (no customers)		Day 2 (50 customers)	
Revenue	(0 × 75) =	0	(50 × 75) =	3,750
less: Variable				
costs (0 × 30) =		0	(50) × 30) =	1,500
equals Contribution:		0		2,250
less: Fixed Costs		1,600		1,600
equals Profit (loss)		(1,600)		650

It is never worth a shop's while trying to work out the absorption cost of selling a jacket (or a packet of peas or a box of soap powder). The only thing that matters to a shop is GETTING THE MAXIMUM CON-TRIBUTION EVERY DAY. Shop managements are totally concerned with *contribution per square metre per day*. A shop has only so much space, if one item takes up a metre of shelf space it means another item cannot be sold there. So it isn't just a matter of mark-up (i.e. buy for 30 sell for 75, mark-up 45). It is a matter of HOW MANY mark-ups are gained in a day from that space, compared with how much would be earned from another product in it. For instance jackets and handbags:

Jackets: mark-up (unit contribution)	=	45
Sales per day in units	=	50
Space taken up in square metres	=	4
Contribution per metre per day	=	$\dfrac{45 \times 50}{4} = 562$

Handbags: mark-up (unit contribution)	=	15
Sales per day in units	=	100
Space taken up in square metres	=	2
Contribution per metre per day	=	$\dfrac{15 \times 100}{2} = 750$

The shop will do better to devote two of the jacket's metres of space to selling handbags. Of course fewer jackets will be sold; but even if NO jackets were sold, the daily contribution will be higher.

That is why the SPEED with which things sell is so vital to shops, at least as important to them as the mark-up on each individual sale. It further explains why shops are often keen to remain open as much as possible (e.g. on Sundays) because extra opening gives a shop the chance to make extra contribution.

EXAM TECHNIQUE NOTES

1. In exam questions there are often certain assumptions to be made. Unless told to the contrary you should always assume Direct Materials are 100% variable. Direct labour costs are more tricky. You are quite likely to be told how to treat them; but if you are not you should assume they *are variable*. Unless told to the contrary (or given a hint in code such as "incurred for every item made" or "sales commission payable per item" or some such) *you should assume all other costs are fixed*.

2. Quite often information is temptingly presented by examiners in ABSORPTION COST form, as starting data for a marginal cost question. For instance:

"The cost of one radio is made up as follows:

	£
Direct Labour	8
Materials	15
Fixed Costs	10
Total Cost	33
Selling Price	36
Profit per Unit	£3

These costs are based on the normal output of 1,000 radios per month."

You will then be asked to do a lot of marginal cost based calculations, e.g. "Would it be better to sell the maximum capacity of 1,200 radios at £30 each?" This is where you need to be aware of the fact that the *fixed costs per unit figure is only true for 1,000 radios.* All you need to do to calculate the fixed costs is:

$$\text{Fixed Costs} = £10 \text{ per unit} \times 1,000 \text{ units} = £10,000$$

Now you know this figure you can forget fixed costs PER UNIT for the rest of the question, and just use the fixed costs in total, as is normal in marginal costing statements. Similarly ignore the profit per unit figure which will only be true for 1,000 items as was the fixed cost per unit figure.

ANSWER: Alternative plan:

		£	
Revenue 1,200 at £30	=	36,000	
less V.C. 1,200 at £23	=	27,600	– (DL and DM
			are assumed
CONTRIBUTION		8,400	to be variable)
less Fixed Costs		10,000	
LOSS		£(1,600)	

No it would not be better to sell the maximum capacity at £30 each.

Of course the new fixed cost figure *per unit* would no longer be $\dfrac{£10,000}{1,000 \text{ units}} = £10$; but would be $\dfrac{£10,000}{1,200 \text{ units}} = £8.33$

The absorption cost at 1,000 units is *only true* at 1,000 units. At 1,200 units the absorption cost is different *because the fixed costs are being spread over more output.* The examiner is tempting you to use an absorption cost as a marginal one; don't fall into the trap!

SELF-ASSESSMENT QUESTIONS

SECTION A

* 1. Tyres sell for £27 each. The variable cost per tyre is £9. (A) What is the Unit Contribution? (B) Fixed Costs for 2 months are £54,000. We hope to sell 3,800 tyres in this time. What is the total contribution we aim to make, and the total profit? (C) Using the "quick way" of answering (see Fig. 65 in Chapter 5) what will be the profit if we sell (i) 3,600 tyres? (ii) 4,000 tyres? (iii) 3,400 tyres?

2. We make washing machines and sell them for £136 cash to retail shops. The total variable costs for March were £23,200. Fixed Costs for this period were £18,000. We made and sold 340 machines in this time. (A) What is the Unit Variable Cost? (B) What is the unit contribution? (C) What is the Profit? (use a full layout for this (C) answer); (D) What would be the contribution in total if we made and sold (i) 330 machines (ii) 360 machines? (E) Using the "quick method" what would the profit be at (i) 350 machines and (ii) 320 machines made and sold?

SECTION B

* 3. If total sales were £6,200 for one month and variable costs were £2,790. (A) What is the contribution? (B) What is the Contribution/Sales ratio (also known as P/V ratio)? (C) If sales went up by £2,000 how much would the contribution go up by?

4. A car sells for £6,000 and its unit variable cost (marginal cost) is £1,500 (A) What is the C/S ratio? (B) If 300 cars were made and sold in September what would the total contribution be?

5. If the price of the cars is raised to £6,300 and the variable cost remains the same at £1,500 (A) What is the new unit contribution? (B) What is the new C/S ratio (the nearest 1%)? (C) If after the price rise only 280 cars were sold what would the total contribution be? (D) Would it be more profitable (i.e. which has the most contribution) to sell 300 cars at £6,000 (your answer in 4B) or 280 cars at £6,300 (your answer in 5C)?

SECTION C

* 6. The following costs are estimated for 1 months production of Alvi-speed gear-boxes by the G. Riddle Fast Car Co.:

	£
Direct & Indirect Labour: 20% variable:	4,000
Direct & Indirect Materials: £300 Fixed, £6,700 Variable:	7,000
Rent:	2,000
Machine Costs:	4,000
Sales and Distribution: 10% Variable:	1,000
Finance Costs:	2,000
TOTAL COSTS	£20,000

A normal months production is 50 gear boxes, which sell for £500 each. However, 65 boxes could be made in a month. Two alternative plans are under discussion.

(i) Reduce the price to £450 and sell all 65 that could be made.
(ii) Raise the price to £600 but sell only 40 boxes.

(A) What is the marginal (variable) cost per gear box?
(B) Which is the most profitable plan; normal, plan (i) or plan (ii)?
(C) What is the C/S ratio for each of the three alternatives?
(D) What is the break even point in units for each alternative?

* 7. Next years budget for the Fashion Dress Co. is as follows:

	£	£
Revenue Dress Sales (£10 each)		1,000,000
Costs		
Direct Materials (100% variable)	250,000	
Direct Labour (20% variable)	150,000	
Overheads		
Variable Overhead	70,000	
Fixed Overhead	480,000	
Total Cost		950,000
PROFIT		£50,000

(A) What is the unit variable cost per dress?
(B) What is the contribution per unit?
(C) If maximum capacity is 150,000 dresses;
    (i) Would an extra order, at £4 per dress, for 20,000 dresses be profitable?
    (ii) Would it be a worthwhile alternative to reduce the selling price to £9 per dress and so sell all 150,000 dresses that could be made?
(D) What is the C/S ratio under the original budget, and under alternative C(ii)?
(E) What is the break even revenue under the original budget and under alternative C(ii)?

8. The following estimated costs relate to the production of racing bicycles for May:

	£
Labour 45% variable	3,000
Materials 60% variable	4,000
Machinery Costs	1,200
Establishment costs (5% variable)	400
Selling Expenses (10% variable)	550
Finance Expenses	350
Administration Expenses	200
	£9,700

These costs are based upon making 225 bikes and selling them for £45 each. Maximum capacity is 240 bikes per month.

(A) Is it worth taking an extra order of 10 bikes at £14 per bike?
(B) Is it worth taking an extra order of 10 bikes at £25 per bike?
(C) What is the break even point in bikes for the company?
(D) What is the C/S ratio?

9. A company making cider has the following costs for each 6 monthly production cycle *at the normal production level of 150,000 gallons.*

| Fixed Costs: | £320,000 |
| Variable Costs: | £200,000 |

The cider sells for £4 per gallon.

By spending a further £20,000 on machinery costs per 6 months, the production level could be raised to 190,000 gallons, still at a selling price of £4 per gallon.

(A) Produce two marginal cost statements showing Revenues, Variable Costs, Contribution, Fixed Costs, and Profit, comparing these two output possibilities.
(B) What is the break even point in revenue at normal output (150,000 gallons) and at the new level of production of 190,000 gallons?
(C) If a special Christmas-pack of cider were produced, it would require extra packaging costs per gallon of £0·60. No more could be charged for each gallon, though sales would be expected to rise as a result.
  (i) What would the new unit variable cost per gallon be and the new unit contribution per gallon?
  (ii) What would the new break even sales in units be?
  (iii) What would be the number of Christmas-pack gallons needed to be sold *to make as much profit as the normal-pack 150,000 gallons made?* (Hint for answer to C(iii). How much contribution did the normal 150,000 gallons make? This is the key to answering C(iii)).

10. The absorption cost per bicycle is £50, made up of Direct Materials £18, Direct Labour £10 and Overheads £22, and 1,700 bikes are made each month:

(A) If overheads per unit are all fixed costs apart from £2 energy costs; and Direct Labour is 15% variable,
  (i) What is the marginal cost per unit?
  (ii) What are total fixed costs for one month?

(iii) If selling prices are £55 each what is the break even point in units?

(iv) Would it be better to make 2,000 bikes and sell them for £48 each?

11. The directors of Global Ltd are reviewing the profitability of the Company's four products and considering the potential effect of alternative courses of action for varying the product mix.

The Company Accountant has given them the following information on which to formulate their decisions.

		PRODUCT			
	Totals	A	B	C	D
	£	£	£	£	£
Sales	125,200	20,000	36,000	25,200	44,000
Cost of goods sold	88,548	9,500	14,112	27,936	37,000
Gross profit/(Loss)	36,652	10,500	21,888	(2,736)	7,000
Operating expenses	24,024	3,980	5,952	5,652	8,440
Net Profit/(Loss)	12,628	6,520	15,936	(8,388)	(1,440)
Units sold		1,000	1,200	1,800	2,000
Sales price per unit		£20	£30	£14	£22
Variable cost of goods sold per unit		£5	£6	£13	£12
Variable operating expenses per unit.		£2·34	£2·50	£2·00	£2·40

Requirements:

Each of the following proposals is to be considered independently. State any assumptions you make regarding Fixed Costs.

(A) Determine the effect on net profit if product C is discontinued.

(B) Determine the total effect on net profit if product C is discontinued and a consequent loss of customers causes a decrease of 200 units in sales of product B.

(C) Determine the effect on net profit if the sale price of C is increased to £16 with a decrease in the number of units sold to 1,500.

(D) The plant in which C is produced can be utilised to produce a new product, X. The total variable costs and expenses per unit of X are £16·10 and 1,600 units can be sold at £19 each. Determine the total effect on net profit if X is introduced and C is discontinued.

CHAPTER 6

MORE THINGS TO DO WITH MARGINAL COSTING

CHAPTER OBJECTIVES

Having studied this chapter you should be able to:

* EXPLAIN HOW A BUSINESS' COST-STRUCTURE AFFECTS ITS ABILITY TO WITHSTAND DOWNTURNS IN TRADE

* CALCULATE MARGINS OF SAFETY

* DEDUCE MARGINAL-COST INFORMATION FROM CHANGES IN TOTAL REVENUES AND TOTAL COSTS FROM ONE PERIOD TO ANOTHER

* CALCULATE MOST-PROFITABLE SALES MIXES WHEN A FACTOR OF PRODUCTION IS LIMITED

* EXPLAIN THE CONSEQUENCES OF MAKE OR BUY DECISIONS ON A BUSINESS' TOTAL COSTS

COST STRUCTURE

The balance, at normal output, between the levels of fixed and variable costs within total costs, can have profound effects on the profitability of a business *when trading conditions change.*

By definition, variable costs automatically decrease as output drops – they are output volume sensitive. Equally, fixed costs are insensitive to output volume changes – in as much as they will not automatically decrease when output drops. In fact fixed costs can usually only be decreased *by management action.* If half of the factory is unused because business is slack, the rent will not be reduced by half automatically. To reduce fixed costs the management will have to sub-let the unused half, or sub-let all of it and move to smaller premises.

The problem with reducing fixed costs is that they broadly represent the cost of providing the productive capacity of the business. After any wasteful expenditure has been cut, further fixed cost reduction means a dismantling of the business to some extent. This is often a painful, lengthy and difficult process for everyone concerned. And from the cost point of view "lengthy" is the operative word. Incidentally it needs to be said that many organisations are incapable of identifying their wasteful expenditure – hence the existence of management consultants – and there is usually lots of it to cut before the output capacity of the business is seriously affected by fixed cost reductions.

It follows from all these points that if a business:

  (i) at normal output has a large proportion of fixed costs within total costs and,

 (ii) experiences a drop in sales and therefore output . . .

it will have NO automatic reduction in expenditure on its large-proportion of fixed costs. Therefore it will experience a drop in revenue; *but a smaller drop in costs.* Therefore it will have its profits enormously affected by a drop in demand. For example:

Firmly Fixed Company

	Normal Output			15% Reduced Output	
	£	£		£	£
Revenue		100,000			85,000
Variable Costs	20,000			17,000	
Fixed Costs	70,000			70,000	
less Total Costs		90,000			87,000
Profit		£10,000		Loss	£(2,000)

Fig. 96.

When revenue drops 15% only the variable costs automatically reduce (20,000 less 15% = 17,000). Therefore the business makes losses, unless the management reduce fixed costs. Which, as emphasised, is usually a lengthy process, so this business will make losses for some time while the fixed cost reduction is going on.

Contrast Firmly Fixed Co. with the Variety Variable Co. below:

Variety Variable Company

	Normal Output		15% Reduced Output	
	£	£	£	£
Revenue		100,000		85,000
Variable Costs	70,000		59,500	
Fixed Costs	20,000		20,000	
less Total Costs		90,000		79,500
Profit		£10,000	Profit	£5,500

Fig. 97.

This time when revenue drops 15% the reduction in costs is large because a large proportion of costs are variable. Therefore the profits do not disappear.

It should be clear now that the following general rules apply:

(A) Firms with mainly fixed costs will be highly vulnerable to downturns in trade.

(B) Firms with mainly variable costs will be far less vulnerable to downturns.

Equally firms with mainly fixed costs AND SPARE CAPACITY, will benefit from increases in revenue much more than firms with mainly variable costs:

	Firmly Fixed at 10% Increase in Output			Variety Variable at 10% Increase in Output		
	£	£		£	£
Revenue		110,000	Revenue		110,000
Variable Costs	22,000		Variable Costs	77,000	
Fixed Costs	70,000		Fixed Costs	20,000	
Total Costs		92,000	Total Costs		97,000
PROFIT		£18,000			£13,000

Fig. 98.

In this instance Firmly Fixed has recorded an 80% increase in profit for only a 10% increase in revenue.

To summarise then, similar firms with different cost structures will be very differently affected by changes in demand for their products. A firm's *cost-structure* will govern how its profits will react to changes in demand. Therefore managers need to bear this in mind when deciding (for example) how to go about increasing output. The section in this chapter on Make or Buy decisions will further expand this point.

In reality which businesses *do* have mainly fixed costs? Well, Airlines, Railways, Hotels, Mines, are all good examples. Once an airline's flying schedule is agreed, *all* its costs are fixed. An aircraft with two passengers costs just as much to fly the Atlantic as one with 300 people on board. If Break Even for an airline is to have 100 people on board all its trans-atlantic flights and it only gets 85 people – you know what happens to profits. And in reality that is why such businesses plunge into and out of profit so quickly. If the airline has 110 people on board each flight – you know what happens to profits too.

MARGINS OF SAFETY

Low profits are not as good as high profits; but losses are a disaster. Every firm has a sales target it wants to reach, at which it willmake profits. Break even points are calculated so managers know when the crucial no-loss stage is reached.

However, it is equally useful to know, in advance, *how far above break even the sales target is.* This distance (measured in money or units) is called the *Margin of Safety*:

	Budgeted Revenue/or units
less	Break Even Revenue/or units
=	Margin of Safety Revenue/or units

Fig. 99.

Take the two following similarly profitable products, only one of which the firm will invest in making and selling, which are budgeted as follows:

	Product A	C/S Ratio	Product B	C/S Ratio
	£	%	£	%
Revenue	75,000	100	75,000	100
less Variable Costs	25,000	33	45,000	60
Contribution	50,000	67	30,000	40
less Fixed Costs	40,000		20,000	
Profit	£10,000		£10,000	

Fig. 100.

Break Even for Product A in Revenue $= \dfrac{40,000}{0\cdot67} = £59,701$

Break Even for Product B in Revenue $= \dfrac{20,000}{0\cdot40} = £50,000$

Margin of Safety		Product A	Product B
		£	£
	Budgeted Revenue	75,000	75,000
less	B/E Revenue	59,701	50,000
	Margin of Safety	£15,299	£25,000

Fig. 101.

Therefore Product B has a greater margin of safety, i.e. Product B's sales forecast can be more wrong before it really hits trouble (i.e. makes losses).

It should be clear to you that (for similar budgeted profits) the product, or business, with the lower fixed costs will always have the higher margin of safety. In other words margin of safety and cost structure are of course linked.

It is usually impossible to accurately predict sales, especially of a new product. So the margin of safety is a very important aspect to consider when launching a new product. If there is a low margin of safety then falling short on sales by a small amount will mean the project makes losses. Under which circumstances, the managers should come up with a better idea!

If Products A and B above were sold for £10 each, then their B/E in units, Budgeted Sales in units, and margins of safety in units are:

		A	B
	Budget Sales	7,500 units	7,500 units
less	B/E Units	5,970	5,000
	Margin of Safety in Units	1,530 units	2,500 units

Fig. 102.

This can be a quite important aspect; because what if As were sold for £10 each and Bs for £500 each? Then the margins of safety in *UNITS* would be:

		A	B
	Budgeted Sales in Units	7,500	150
less	B/E in Units	5,970	100
	Margin of Safety in Units	1,530	50

Fig. 103.

This is valuable information of course. B has the greater margin of safety in *REVENUE*; but lower *in units*. The question for managers then becomes one of "Is it easier to sell 7,500 As or 150 Bs?" The figures help to concentrate the minds of the decision makers! If it was decided to make and sell Bs then everyone would know that a shortfall from target of (say) 10 units would be far more serious than a 10 unit shortfall in As sales target.

DEDUCING MARGINAL COST INFORMATION

Examiners are quite keen on this type of question, and in practice it can be useful for analysts too. The idea is to try to calculate from *gross* cost and revenue figures what the marginal cost structure of a business is. The calculations are based on the usual marginal costing theory that:

(A) Fixed costs do not change, and
(B) Changes in profits are solely due to changes in contributions – which in turn are proportional to the number of units sold.

As you should know, not all of this is strictly true in practice. Fixed costs *do* alter – economy drives reduce fixed costs, wage rises increase them, so does new machinery purchased, and so on. However the hope is that things do not alter *so much* between consecutive trading periods that the conclusions are wholly wrong.

For instance imagine the following revenues and total costs are recorded for Zoom Airlines in August and September:

	August	September
	£	£
Revenue	1,500,000	1,200,000
Total Costs	1,300,000	1,100,000
	£200,000	£100,000

Fig. 104.

The *changes* in costs, profits and revenues between the two months are:

	CHANGES
	£
Revenue	300,000
Costs	200,000
PROFITS	£100,000

Fig. 105.

Apply your theory to these figures:

Question. If fixed costs do not change; what must cost-changes be caused by? *ANSWER* Variable Cost Changes.

Question. If profits have changed and fixed costs do not change; what must have changed? *ANSWER* Contribution.

The changes can therefore be re-labelled:

	£
Revenue	300,000
Variable Costs	200,000
CONTRIBUTION	£100,000

Fig. 106.

And the C/S ratio can now be calculated, which comes to: Revenue 100%, Variable Costs 66·6% and Contribution 33·3%.

We now know all we need to know (about Zoom Airlines) to work out a full marginal costing statement for *either* month. Taking August as an example, first down to the contribution line:

	£	C/S Proportions %
August Revenue	1,500,000	100
less Variable Costs (which must be 66% × Revenue)	1,000,000	66·6
= CONTRIBUTION (which must be 33% × Revenue)	£500,000	33·3

Now for the rest of the statement. The normal equation is:

CONTRIBUTION *minus* FIXED COSTS = PROFIT

It is therefore *also true* that:

CONTRIBUTION *minus* PROFIT = FIXED COSTS

	£
Contribution for August was	500,000
Profit for August was	200,000
Therefore Fixed Costs are	£300,000

So the entire statement for August is:

		£	C/S Ratio %
	Revenue	1,500,000	100
less	Variable Costs	1,000,000	66·6
	= Contribution	500,000	33·3
less	Fixed Costs	300,000	
	Profit	£200,000	

Fig. 107.

All of which was deduced from two consecutive Revenue, Total Cost and Profit figures. In fact it *could* be deduced from sets of Revenue + Profit figures alone; because Total Cost can be deduced from these two (Revenue *minus* profit = Total Cost), or even from 2 sets of Profit and total cost figures alone (Profit *plus* Total Cost = Revenue). There must be two sets though, so the *changes* can be found and then marginal costing theory applied.

Apply the C/S ratio to the September figures and produce the September statement for yourselves.

Obviously (I hope) once the marginal costing statement is done, all the other techniques are possible. You should be able to work out for yourselves the following items:

* Zoom Airlines break-even revenue
* Zoom Airlines Margin of Safety in Revenue for: August
                                                September

Remember the key to this technique is to remember that (i) Cost-changes are Variable Cost changes (ii) Profit Changes are contribution changes. Therefore taken together the Revenue Change, Cost Change and Profit Change, from one period to the next, give you the relationship between Revenues, Variable Costs and Contributions. Then the C/S ratio can be calculated. Then it can be used to break down the total cost figure into Variable and Fixed Costs, and then the full range of marginal costing based techniques can be used.

MAXIMUM PROFITS WHEN RESOURCES ARE LIMITED

Sometimes, particularly in exams, a particular factor of production can be limited in quantity, so that the business cannot make as many items as it would wish. For example a shortage of raw materials or of skilled labour, or of machine capacity, may mean although there are orders for 1,000 cars, only 800 can be made that week. If the business only has *one* product, there is no management decision necessary other than to try and find extra supplies of the shortage item, and to decide which customers to supply.

However if there are two or three products *and* there is a shortage of (say) raw materials used by all three; there *is* a management decision necessary about the *quantities of each to be made.* This decision will in practice rest on many factors; but to begin with we will assume the managers wish to make the *maximum profit.*

NOTE: In fact there is *always* a limiting factor in business. The most usual one being *demand.* When demand is the limiting factor (although it is not called one usually) you all know what to do. Maximum Contribution = Maximum Profit. If two alternative products were being considered, demand for one of which produced contribution of £1,000 per week, and the other £1,500; from a profit point of view the £1,500 contribution product would be the one to make. What *limits* contribution usually is demand for the product, i.e. the revenue it can attract. When demand is the limiting factor therefore, we go for the product with the highest contribution (from the revenue the product attracts) assuming common fixed costs for the alternatives.

Equally when something else is the limiting factor we still go for the highest contribution; but this time for *the highest contribution possible before we run out of the scarcity item.* (Normally we go for the highest contribution possible before we run out of demand of course.)

Under these circumstances the maximum contribution possible can only be found by calculating **how much contribution each of our products makes for every £1's worth of scarce item it uses up.**

Quick Example: We make two products, Bikes and Prams, their revenues and variable costs are as follows:

		Bikes			Prams	
		£	£		£	£
Unit Revenue:			45			25
Variable Costs:	Materials	18		Materials	7	
	Labour	5		Labour	5	
			23			12
Unit Contribution:			£22			£13

Fig. 108.

Imagine that (A) we only have £1,000 worth of steel (materials) available this week, (B) we want to make the most profit, and (C) the normal output is 50 bikes and 30 prams. (D) Fixed costs are £850 per week.

There is obviously not enough steel to make our normal output because the *materials required* are:

		£
50 Bikes × £18 of Steel	=	900
30 Prams × £7 of Steel	=	210
Steel Required		£1,110's worth

Fig. 109.

The question is "how many bikes or prams do we make for maximum profit?" We know the answer lies in making the *most contribution* before we run out of steel. Therefore we need to know which product makes the most contribution from every £1's worth of steel it uses up. That is we need to calculate the *contribution per £1 of limiting factor*:

Bikes make Contribution of £22 each:

But use up £18 of steel to make the £22 contribution:

Therefore BIKE Contribution PER £1 OF STEEL USED $= \dfrac{22}{18} = £1\cdot22$

Prams make Contribution of £13 each:

BUT use up £7 of steel to make the £13 contribution:

Therefore Pram Contribution PER £1 OF STEEL USED $= \dfrac{13}{7} = £1\cdot86$

Therefore prams make more contribution per £1 of materials than Bikes. Therefore we will make *all* the prams we can sell (30) and use the materials left over to make as many bikes as we can before running out:

		£
Materials Available		1,000
less Used up on 30 prams: 30 × £7	=	210
Materials left for Bikes		£790

Fig. 110.

It takes £18 of steel to make one bike; so the number of bikes we can make will be:

$$£790 \div 18$$

$$= 44 \text{ bikes (rounded up)}$$

The profit we will make is now easily found:

				£
Total Contribution from Prams	= 30 prams × £13 unit Contribution	=		390
Total Contribution from Bikes	= 44 bikes × £22 unit Contribution	=		968
		Total Firm's Contribution		1358
	less	Fixed Costs		850
		Profit under limiting Factor		£508

The steps necessary can be easily summarised:

To find the maximum profit under one limiting factor when there is more than one product being made:

(A) Find the Unit Contribution of each product.
(B) Find the amount of limiting factor used by each product.
(C) Divide (A) by (B) to find the Contribution per £1 of limiting factor.
(D) Make the product with the highest Contribution per £1 of limiting factor first; then use the remaining amount of the scarce item to make the product with the next highest contribution per £1 of limiting factor; then use the remaining amount of the scarce item to make the product with the next highest contribution per £1 of limiting factor; and so on until all the scarce item has been used up.
(E) D has shown how many of each product to make; using these output figures, *contribution and profits are calculated normally.*

Another example, this time more complicated because there are three products:

The Blue Pentangle axle company makes three types of rear axle, the costs of which are:

	De Dion	Slip Grip	Overland
	£	£	£
Direct Materials	42	28	38
Direct Labour			
Lathe Workers	12	18	6
Assembly Workers	6	8	2
Total Variable Cost	£60	£54	£46

Fig. 111.

Fixed costs £650,000 per year. Sales information is as follows:

> De Dion: 6,000 units selling for £100 each
> Slip grip: 10,000 units selling for £90 each
> Overland: 8,000 units selling for £80 each

There is a 25% shortfall in the amount of direct materials needed. What should be made to make maximum profit?

First find out the amount of Direct Materials available:

Total Materials Needed:	£
De Dion 6,000 units × £42 of D.M. =	252,000
Slip Grip 10,000 units × £28 of D.M. =	280,000
Overland 8,000 units × £38 of D.M. =	304,000
Total Needed	£836,000

Fig. 112.

A 25% shortfall means Materials Available are £836,000 × 75% = £627,000

Follow the steps (summarised above) to find the profit under these conditions:

(A) Unit Contribution:	De Dion	Slip grip	Overland
	£	£	£
Selling Price:	100	90	80
less Unit Variable Costs:	60	54	46
Unit Contribution:	£40	£36	£34

(B) Amount of limiting Factor			
used by each product, i.e. amount of Direct Materials:	£42	£28	£38

(C) Contribution per £1 of			
Limiting Factor $\frac{A}{B}$:	£0·95	£1·28	£0·89
Order of Profitability:	(2)	(1)	(3)

Fig. 113.

(D) Output Plan:

		£
Materials Available		627,000
less 10,000 Slip grip × £28 materials	=	280,000
Materials left	=	347,000
less 6,000 De Dion × £42 materials	=	252,000
Materials left		£95,000

$$\text{Maximum Number of Overlands possible} = \frac{95,000 : \text{Materials Available}}{38 : \text{Materials Cost of 1 Overland}}$$

$$= 2,500 \text{ Overlands}$$

(E) To find the profit made:

PRODUCT	QUANTITY ×	UNIT CONTRIBUTION	=	TOTAL CONTRIBUTIONS
		£		£
De Dion	6,000	40		240,000
Slip grip	10,000	36		360,000
Overland	2,500	34		85,000
		FIRM'S TOTAL CONTRIBUTION		685,000
		less Fixed Costs		650,000
		PROFIT		£35,000

Fig. 114.

Although it may seem a bit involved, once you have done two or three limiting factor questions, you will see that they are really pretty straightforward. However, before closing this section, there are some important general points to make about how far a real manager would follow maximum profitability when deciding on which of the products to make.

PRACTICAL USE OF LIMITING FACTOR ANALYSIS

Obviously the sales mix that would give the maximum profit NOW is of interest and importance in deciding what to make. However from a commercial point of view, the business must also consider its profits in the longer term.

For instance, how would you feel as a regular customer of an engineering business, if they suddenly refused, one month, to supply you with your regular order? This could obviously happen if there was a steel shortage and your product was ranked low in contribution-per-£1-of-steel used. Clearly you would feel let down, annoyed, and go to another company with your valuable business.

In a shortage, the prudent thing to do is to supply *all* your regular customers if you can. Only after that should limiting factor contribution be used to dictate what else is made. Remember, ultimately a business only needs two things: a good product and customers. Anyone who has been in business will tell you the customers are the most important people a business is involved with. They are considerably more vital than accountants to a business, for example!

Even giant businesses that sell to masses of individuals (e.g. breweries supermarket chains, chocolate manufacturers) abandon a product in times of shortage at their peril. It is well known in the U.K. that Brewers have made more profit on their lager sales than on other draught beers. This is because the public perceives lager as a premium drink, and is prepared to pay more for it. Occasionally, in very hot summers, brewing capacity cannot keep up with overall demand. However, brewers do not stop making the other beers and concentrate on lager only for a month. The reason they don't is that if (for instance) Whitbread were to stop making bitter-beer in August, thousands of habitual Whitbread bitter-beer drinkers would go and buy *someone elses* bitter-beer, rather than buy the Whitbread lager. You never know, they may not go back to Whitbread after the shortage is over.

A business never leaves a segment of its market "un-defended" i.e. without a product available for sale, unless it has decided to drop that product completely.

I'm not saying that limiting factor analysis might not mean, in times of shortage, *that a firm's output will lean towards* the more profitable product. No doubt it will. However, it will be careful not to overdo it, and thereby ruin its business in the longer term.

MAKE OR BUY DECISIONS

When a firm wants to expand output it can do it in two ways:

Either, (i) Expand its own production facilities, i.e. buy more machinery, employ more people, rent more factory space, in order to MAKE more items.

Or, (ii) Contract with other firms for the supply of certain components, sub-assemblies, and so forth, in order to increase output by BUYING in more items or part-items.

Put into Marginal-Costing parlance, a firm can increase output by:

Either (i) Incurring extra fixed costs (which are broadly the category of Costs incurred when more production facilities are added).

Or (ii) Incurring extra variable costs. (Which buying in components and sub-assemblies would definitely be, as they would be classed as direct materials.)

Why does it matter? Re-read the section of this chapter on cost structure if you can't remember. In terms of the strategic ability of a business to withstand downturns in trade, it matters a great deal. Fixed costs are hard and painful to get rid of, when demand drops.

Factories have to be closed, people made redundant, machines disposed of. All this takes time and is expensive. By contrast variable costs are somewhat easier to reduce. It requires a phone call to say, "Don't deliver any more items until next month please, and only half as many as usual then." Two firms in the same business making the same product have expanded to the state shown below in Fig. 115: Firm 1 by making its extra output, Firm 2 by buying it.

	Firm 1	Firm 2
	£	£
Revenue	50,000	50,000
less Variable Costs	10,000	30,000
Contribution	40,000	20,000
less Fixed Costs	35,000	15,000
Profit	£5,000	£5,000

Fig. 115.

Both are successful, profit is 10% of Turnover, not bad at all considering the U.K. average for manufacturing companies, pre-tax, is something well under 4% in 1982. But what happens if a recession bites, and both firms lose 20% of their orders? Firm 1 has no quick way to reduce fixed costs, neither has Firm 2; Firm 1's problem is that its fixed costs are such a large proportion of its total expenditure: Fig. 116 shows the consequences.

	Firm 1 less 20% of Sales	Firm 2 less 20% of Sales
	£	£
Revenue	40,000	40,000
less Variable Costs	8,000	24,000
Contribution	32,000	16,000
less Fixed Costs	35,000	15,000
Loss	£(3,000)	Profit £1,000

Fig. 116.

Firm 1's total costs dropped by only £2,000 when revenue dropped by £10,000.

Firm 2's total costs dropped by £6,000 when revenue dropped by £10,000.

Therefore, when a firm is expanding, ONE of the considerations it should bear in mind when deciding whether to expand by making more, or buying more, is the effect on its COST STRUCTURE.

This apart what will be the major influences on the management's decision? Obviously the *cost per unit* will be the most important consideration, and there will be many other things to bear in mind as well. As this is an accounting book we deal first with the cost per unit aspects of the make or buy decision.

As a preliminary, you need to be aware of two distinct situations managers can be in when considering whether to *make* extra items:

(A) When the firm has existing idle facilities that could be used to make extra output.

(B) When a "green field" site would be needed to make extra output (i.e. a wholly new factory, new labour-force, and new machinery).

Taking each in turn:

(A) WHAT ARE THE COST-IMPLICATIONS WHEN DECIDING WHETHER TO MAKE OR BUY EXTRA OUTPUT WHEN THERE ARE EXISTING IDLE FACILITIES?

To start with **beware of the ABSORPTION cost of making the extra output.** For example imagine a firm has two workshops, one of which is not being used, and existing fixed overheads are allocated as follows:

	Workshop 1 (in use)	Workshop 2 (idle)	Total Overheads
1 month's Overheads	30,000	15,000	£45,000

We are considering using workshop 2 to make 5,000 extra saw-blades per month. To do this we would employ 3 extra workshop staff costing £1,200 per month; and the Direct Materials would cost £1 per blade, so £5,000 is the projected Direct Material total each month.

The Absorption cost of *making* the 5,000 blades would therefore be:

	£
Direct Labour:	1,200
Direct Materials:	5,000
PREVIOUSLY UNRECOVERED OVERHEADS:	15,000
Total Absorption Cost of Blades	£21,200

$$\text{Absorption cost per blade} = \frac{21,200}{5,000} = £4\cdot24 \text{ each}$$

Fig. 117.

Now suppose we could sub-contract the work to another engineering firm who would charge us £3·20 per blade. Would it be better from a cost point of view to buy in the extra output, (which would cost in total £3·20 × 5,000 blades = £16,000)?

If the buying price of £3·20 and the absorption cost of £4·24 are compared, *apparently* it is better to buy. *However this comparison is quite misleading*, and is a prime example of the fallacy of using absorption costs for the wrong purposes.

The true position is best illustrated by comparing the totals the business would spend if it either made or bought the saw-blades:

Firm's Total Costs Incurred:

When Making		When Buying	
£		£	
1,200	Direct Labour	—	
5,000	Direct Materials	16,000	
15,000	EXISTING FIXED OVERHEAD INCURRED IN BOTH CASES	15,000	Difference
£21,200	TOTAL COST	£31,000	£9,800

Fig. 118.

Clearly the firm will be £9,800 worse off if it buys in the extra output. Therefore the absorption cost of making the extra output (£21,200 total, £4·24 per blade) *when existing idle facilities are being used* is no guide to the right decision.

The truth of this point relies upon the marginal costing premise that fixed costs do not disappear with output; and on the practical point that in general fixed costs are hard to reduce. Obviously given time it is possible to eliminate "unused" fixed costs, so Make or Buy decisions, like all decisions depend on the time-factor. We are really concerned with the short-medium term in these *cost* calculations. Other considerations such as cost structure, and the commercial points at the end of this section, apply in all circumstances of course.

Under case (A) the *marginal costs* of making and buying need to be compared to get the right answer. This is in fact what was done in Fig. 118 above, which could be represented, comparing the marginal costs only, like this:

Make		Buy	
£		£	
1,200	Direct Labour	—	
5,000	Direct Materials	16,000	Difference
£6,200	TOTAL MARGINAL COSTS	£16,000	£9,800

Fig. 119.

In the author's view although the *difference* is not affected, the first presentation in Fig. 118 is preferable. This is because the magnitude of the numbers involved *in itself influences peoples decisions*. For example the marginal costs *only* of a make or buy comparison could be:

Make		Buy	Difference
£15,000	Marginal Costs	£14,500	£500

Fig. 120.

But how much more careful would you be about the decision if *all* the costs involved were like this?

Make		Buy	
£		£	
15,000	Marginal Costs	14,500	
600,000	Overhead incurred anyway	600,000	Difference
£615,000	Cost Total	£614,500	£500

Fig. 121.

I suggest the decision would be considered much, much, more seriously. Think of what £600,000 worth of idle production facilities would do for the morale of the staff and the confidence of customers in the firm.

To summarise, in case (A) where there are existing idle facilities, the marginal cost comparison is the key to the relative costs of making or buying the extra output.

Quite often, of course, a certain amount of extra expenditure is incurred on fixed overheads, even when mainly existing facilities are to be used. For example a business might have an existing workshop that required new machinery before production could be increased. In this case the *extra* fixed costs would be included only on the *making* side of the comparison. Imagine that to make the 5,000 saw blades we needed to use an extra machine at a cost of £1,400 per month. The comparison statement would look like this:

Make		Buy	
£		£	
1,200	Direct Labour	—	
5,000	Direct Materials	16,000	
1,400	Extra overheads incurred by making	—	
15,000	Existing Fixed Overheads incurred in both cases	15,000	Difference
£22,600	TOTAL COSTS	£31,000	£8,400

Fig. 122.

Therefore when in Case A you are told to compare the marginal costs of making and buying, "marginal" is meant in the broadest sense: i.e. compare *all the extra costs* (whether technically "Fixed" or "Variable") of making, with *all* the extra costs of buying.

(B) WHERE MAKING EXTRA OUTPUT INVOLVES WHOLLY NEW PRODUCTION FACILITIES (A "GREEN FIELD" SITE)

Under these circumstances, where quite definitely new fixed costs will be incurred, where previously there were none, the *extra costs* incurred by making are ALL the costs of making. In other words the TOTAL COST of the extra output produced by the totally new factory, must be compared with the buying costs. As far as method is concerned, there is in principle no difference. We are still comparing the *extra costs* of making (even though all the costs of making are extra) with the costs of buying.

For instance consider the following alternatives:

(i) To build or rent a new factory, buy machinery and train staff, in order to make a new range of winter outdoor clothing.

(ii) To sub-contract this work to another garment making company.

If we made, assume that each year: the factory would cost £30,000 to rent; machinery costs would be £9,000, labour costs would be £110,000, Direct Materials would total £65,500, and other fixed overheads would total £13,500.

The factory would turn out 38,000 garments each year.

If an order were placed with another manufacturer the garments could be bought for £5 each (total cost 38,000 × £5 = £190,000). However extra warehouse staff costing £11,500 per year would be needed to handle the deliveries at our existing factory.

Total Costs Incurred by the Firm:

When Making		When Buying	
£		£	
110,000	Direct Labour	11,500	
65,500	Direct Materials	190,000	
9,000	Machinery Costs	—	
30,000	Rent	—	
13,500	Other Overheads	—	Difference
£228,000	Total Costs	£201,500	£26,500

Fig. 123.

It is clearly cheaper to buy-in the garments.

SUMMARY

The key in both cases is to ensure the comparison between the costs of making and buying extra output compare (1) *all the costs* (even if they are *all* extra) *incurred* when making with (ii) *all the costs incurred* when buying.

OTHER CONSIDERATIONS IN THE MAKE OR BUY DECISION

Before a decision was made in reality, there would be a number of other points for the alert manager to consider, besides the difference in unit costs:

Available Capital. It would probably require far more initial cash to green-field-site make, than to buy. All the costs of training, buying machinery, renting buildings and financing output, until customers at last paid, would require a large amount of cash to be available from the start. Even using existing facilities to make extra output is liable to require more money, initially, than buying. If a business buys, it receives an invoice *after* the goods have been delivered, and it probably won't pay it for 2 months after that. Therefore in terms of the cash available, buying requires less of a lump sum to be ready initially.

Possibility of Buying. Quite often it may not be possible to buy-in what you are considering selling. A totally new product (e.g. a new type of car tyre such as the Goodyear NCT or Pirelli P7) which has just been designed by your own research staff, may be incapable of manufacture except by totally new facilities only the product developer has the know-how to build.

Security. If there is anything confidential (either from a marketing or industrial secret point of view) it is far less likely to be kept confidential if two companies know about it – i.e. the principal company and the sub-contractor.

Skilled Labour. On the other hand if the product is to be made, it probably requires extra skilled labour which may not be available. Many new factories in development areas have failed because of the impossibility of attracting skilled (and therefore essential) labour to the area.

Management Skills. This is a specialised category of skilled labour of course. It needs to be realised that managing a factory is very much more difficult than buying from a supplier. If a firm has not got a suitable manager to run the expanded facilities among its existing staff, it may find it very difficult to recruit someone suitable.

Quality Control. One of the problems of buying-in items is that their quality can be unreliable. In 1982 Jaguar cars found out that over 65% of their new-car warranty claims were caused by faulty bought-in components, rather than by assembly-problems in the Jaguar factory. Therefore businesses which regularly buy-in large quantities of items need very strict quality control procedures. Of course making items can still give poor quality; however it is generally easier to build-in quality control checks *while* manufacturing the product, than *after* it has been made. Quality control is also easier to make sure of if the entire operation is controlled by the principal firm's own management; rather than by a possibly less-aware management at a sub-contractor.

Delivery Certainty. Human nature being what it is, a sub-contractor having production problems is liable to hope-against-hope that the delivery date will be met, somehow. If it isn't, the first indication to the principal may be when the goods don't arrive as expected. By which time the principal company may be vastly inconvenienced by their non-appearance. If everything is made by the principal firm, then it is likely that earlier and better information on deliveries will be available.

The Type of Product. Some products are very much easier than others to buy-in, and yet control their quality and delivery. For instance clothing is relatively easy to control in this way as Marks and Spencers and Mail Order catalogues prove. Electronic components are another example of items that it is relatively easy to buy with confidence. Most Radio, T.V. and Hi-Fi manufacturers don't make their own transistor and chip components. By contrast, it would be very difficult to develop and market a new mass-production car, if you did not also make it.

These are just some of the non-accounting considerations which are part of any "make or buy" decision managers may take. In the author's view it is essential that all accountants realise that most business decisions have a non-accounting aspect to them. The purpose of this last section has been to introduce you to some of the commercial considerations. Any accountant who understands the broader view will be a vastly more useful person to have in a business. Remember that, and try to acquire it; not enough accountants do.

SELF-ASSESSMENT QUESTIONS

1. Below are the costs and revenues of two businesses which are in competition with each other. These figures represent their normal targeted output.

Calculate (i) the C/S ratio of each firm (ii) their margins of safety (iii) what percentage the fixed costs are of total costs at normal output (iv) their expected profits at normal output and if there is (A) a 20% downturn in trade and (B) a 10% upturn.

	Teme Traders	Valley Merchants
	£	£
Sales	700,000	700,000
Variable Costs:		
Direct Materials	175,000	245,000
Direct Labour	30,000	50,000
Variable Overhead	17,500	35,000
Variable Selling Costs	52,500	60,000
Sales Commission	35,000	80,000
Fixed Costs:		
Direct Labour	40,000	55,000
Fixed Overhead	100,000	35,000
Fixed Selling Costs	110,000	30,000
Administration Costs	70,000	40,000

2. The Herefordshire railway company reported the following trading results for January and February:

	January	February
Revenue	£450,000	£400,000
Profits	£50,000	£10,000

Calculate (i) the C/S ratio of the company (ii) the fixed costs (iii) the break even revenue (iv) the margin of safety, assuming January is the targeted revenue.

3. Budgeted sales and costs for November are as follows:

Product	A	B	C	D
Budgeted Sales in units	5,000	5,000	5,000	5,000
Selling price per unit	£25	£33	£43	£56
Variable Costs:				
Materials	£9	£12	£17	£20
Labour	£8	£10	£12	£18
Overhead	£4	£5	£6	£9

Fixed costs for November total £80,000.

The supply of raw materials is limited to £200,000's worth, and all products use the same raw material.

(i) What is the most profitable sales mix? (ii) Produce a statement comparing budgeted revenues and costs with your answer in (i).

4. The Eastern Cider Co. produces four brands, the cost and revenues per barrel are as follows:

	Aged	Dry	Mellow	Bubbly
	£	£	£	£
Selling price	30	25	25	26
Direct Materials	20	12	15	10
Direct Labour	4	4	5	7

Fixed overheads amount to £7,000 for the next month and the marketing plan for that period is based on selling:

Aged 300 Barrels
Dry 400 Barrels
Mellow 200 Barrels
Bubbly 500 Barrels

Unfortunately, only 70% of the required amount of raw material is available in this month.

(A) What sales mix will give the most profitable use of materials? Produce a statement showing the expected profit.
(B) If a minimum of 50% of each product's original sales target must be made, thereafter using the remaining materials most profitably, what is the new sales mix and what will be the expected profit?

5. The Coomber Education Hi-Fi company produces a radio cassette player especially for use in schools and colleges. Their most recent model (called the "Oliver") has just been launched after a 9 month research and development period.

It is hoped that sales will be £8,000,000 per year, representing 200,000 units. At this output costs will be as follows:

Variable Costs:

	£
Direct Materials	10
Direct Labour	8
Overhead (variable)	3·75
Total Unit Variable Cost	£21·75

Fixed Costs total £3,300,000 for the year.

(i) What is the break even sales for the Oliver model?

(ii) What is its margin of safety in (A) units (B) revenue?

(iii) Produce a clear statement showing revenues, costs and profits (A) at the intended sales (B) if only 80% of the intended sales are made.

(iv) How many Olivers would have to be made and sold to produce a profit of £400,000 (to the nearest unit)?

(v) What would the selling price have to be to produce the intended profit (calculated in answer to (iii) A) if only 170,000 Olivers were made?

6. Sharput Tool Company have a certain amount of spare capacity and are considering making their own bearings, instead of buying them as they do at present. You are asked to produce a statement showing, from a purely financial point of view, the advantage or otherwise of doing so. Your enquiries reveal the following costs will be considered as bearing costs by the business:

	£
Allocation of rent for spare workshop	10,000
Cost per year of a new machine	26,000
Extra labour	40,000
Existing labour re-deployed	13,000
Materials for the bearings	39,000
Existing machinery costs	12,000

To buy the same number of bearings would cost £126,500.

7. The type 19 ladies shoe has an *absorption cost* of £7·40 per pair, made up of a £4·40 variable element and a £3 fixed overhead allocation. This absorption cost is based on making 1,000 pairs each month.

(A) What are the total fixed costs per month that are recovered in the type 19's absorption cost?
We have capacity to make 1,500 pairs. However a sub-contractor has offered to make type 19s on our behalf for only £5 per pair.

(B) Should we continue making type 19s or buy them in from the sub-contractor (assuming continuing sales of 1,000 pairs per month)?

(C) If we sold the type 19 for £10 per pair on the basis of selling 1,000 pairs; what could we reduce the selling price by, if we sold 1,500 pairs, yet still made the same profit as 1,000 pairs sold at £10 each?

8. The Celebration Company produces a single product. All units produced are sold immediately. No stocks of finished goods are carried. A budgeted profit and loss account for the next period shows:

Profit and Loss Statement

	£	£
Sales of 5,000 units		100,000
Costs:		
Direct materials	30,000	
Direct wages	20,000	
Variable production overhead	3,000	
Fixed production overhead	1,000	
Variable administration overhead	1,000	
Fixed administrative overhead	5,000	
Variable selling overhead	6,000	
Fixed selling overhead	9,000	75,000
Net Profit		25,000

You are required to:
(A) Calculate the break-even point and margin of safety;
(B) construct a graph and label the margin of safety;
(C) explain the ways the business may be able to improve profit for the period by 20 per cent;

9. Do all Ltd. manufactures three products and wishes to maximise its profit.

There is considerable information available about the products and it may be summarised as follows:

Product	Sales possible (units)	Selling price £/unit	Machine hours per unit	Variable cost £/unit
A	100	15	3	6
B	100	14	2	7
C	100	8	1	3

Machine capacity is limited to 450 hours: total fixed expenses are £1,000: ample skilled labour is available.

Prepare a plan to maximise profit.

10. Charnwood Engineering Ltd. expects its costs at a production level of 10,000 units per annum to be:

	£
Direct Materials	140,000
Direct Labour	120,000
Factory Indirect Expenses	60,000
Selling Expenses (Fixed)	10,000
Administration Expenses (Fixed)	20,000

One third of the factory indirect expenses are fixed. Selling price is £40, per unit.

(A) Calculate the Break Even point in units and pounds.
(B) Calculate the profit or loss at:
   (i) 8,000 units
   (ii) 11,500 units
(C) What would be the effect on profit if selling price was reduced to £38 and sales rose to 12,000 units.
(D) What would be the effect on profit if the selling price was raised to £43 and sales fell to 7,500 units.

11. A manufacturer of motor cycles has been operating at 80% of plant capacity. In order to utilise more capacity, the plant manager is considering making a headlight which is currently being purchased from outside suppliers for £6.10 per unit. The plant has the equipment and labour force necessary to manufacture this light, which the design engineer estimates would cost £1.40 for raw materials and £3 for direct labour. The plant overhead rate is 200% of direct labour cost. An analysis of these plant overheads has shown that they are 60% variable and 40% fixed.

Should the company make the light or continue to buy it from an outside supplier? Support your answer with appropriate computations and reasons, including any reasons other than economic which might have a bearing on such a decision.

12. Dell PLC's output consists of two products only, Major and Minor. In percentage terms these two products account for 60% and 40% of the total sales revenue of the company which is 1,500,000. The variable costs of each product expressed as a percentage of each product's sales revenue is 60% for Major and 85% for Minor. The total fixed costs of the company are £300,000.

   (i) From the above information calculate the individual contributions of each product and calculate the break-even point for Dell.
   (ii) If the total fixed costs of Dell PLC increased by 30% calculate the sales revenue needed to earn a profit of £180,000.

(iii) If the selling price and unit variable cost of Major were to increase
by 5% and fixed costs remain unchanged, what will be the effect
on unit contribution margin and contribution to sales ratio respectively? Will it be

	Unit Contribution Margin	Contribution to Sales Ratio
(A)	Unchanged	Unchanged
(B)	Increased	Increased
(C)	Increased	Unchanged
(D)	Increased	Decreased

13. The following details relate to product X.

	£	£
Selling Price		240
Costs		
Materials	120	
Labour	30	
Variable Overhead	10	
Share of Fixed Overhead	20	180
Profit		£60

During the forthcoming year, it is expected that material costs will increase
by 10%, wages by $33\frac{1}{3}$% and other costs by 20%.

Calculate the percentage increase in the selling price of X which would
maintain the firm's contribution to sales ratio.

14. The budgeted profit and loss statement for 1983 for the Fairfield
Manufacturing PLC is as follows:

	Product X	Product Y	Product Z	Total
Sales	160	360	200	720
Cost of Sales				
Materials	60	60	40	160
Labour	40	80	40	160
Variable overheads	20	40	20	80
Fixed overhead	60	60	40	160
	— 180	— 240	— 140	— 560
Net Profit/(LOSS)	(20)	120	60	160

The fixed overheads derive from the use of resources common to the
manufacture of all products and have been apportioned on an equitable
but arbitrary basis.

A proposal has been made at the company board meeting that product
X should be discontinued. You are approached for advice on the proposal
and decide to re-draft the profit and loss account to give a clearer indication of the contribution, if any, X makes.

(A) Show your re-drafted profit and loss account and state whether you agree with the company proposal or not. (You may assume that the total fixed costs would be unaffected by a decision to stop producing product X).
(B) State what you would recommend management to do.
(C) Calculate the break-even point of the company and calculate the break-even point of X individually.

15. Falson Speedway own a motor-cycle track with a seating capacity of 3,750. The price per ticket has been £1·75 with an average attendance of 3,600 at the weekly races which are run 50 times per year. Direct costs are 25p per person and fixed costs are £120,000 per year.

The company can increase seating capacity to 4,000 seats for an annual rental of £15,000. Direct costs per person and ticket price remain the same.

How much would average attendances have to increase in order to make such a move worthwhile?

16. The Beacon company produces two products X and Y in the mixing department. X is sold for £8 per unit and Y for £14 per unit. X and Y are produced to the following recipe:

	sand kilos	cement kilos
Ingredients:		
Product X	0·5	1
Product Y	2	3
Cost per kilo of ingredient	£0·5	£0.75

The amount of cement that is available per week is limited to 4,800 kilos. The fixed costs of the mixing department are £3,500 per week.

(A) What is the best production plan and how much profit would it make assuming there is adequate demand; but not more than 200 difference in units of output between the two products is allowed.
(B) If the selling price of X is raised to £12, how if at all would your plan change?

CHAPTER 7

PLANNING, BUDGETING

CHAPTER OBJECTIVES

Having studied this chapter you should be able to:

* EXPLAIN THE BUSINESS MEANING OF THE TERM "BUDGET", AND THE MEANING OF A BUDGET VARIANCE

* EXPLAIN IN PRINCIPLE HOW A BUSINESS WILL MAKE UP ITS INTEGRATED BUDGET

* EXPLAIN THE ADVANTAGES OF BUDGETING

* LIST THE GENERAL CHARACTERISTICS OF A USEFUL BUDGET

* UNDERSTAND THE DIFFICULTIES AND DISADVANTAGES OF BUDGETING, AND SUGGEST SOME SOLUTIONS TO THEM

WHAT IS A BUDGET IN BUSINESS?

Most people associate the term "budget" with an amount they are allowed to spend. "I've got to budget my money this week and only spend £2 on my night out," is a typical use of the word in everyday language. For a business though, the term has a more positive side to it as well.

All businesses make plans for the future (though not all of them write them down) which might consist of: planning to sell so many items, to launch a new product, to produce so many items per day, employ so many people, buy some new machinery, start selling in new markets (e.g. export to a new country) give wage rises of so much, and so on. The firm's *budget* is the name given to the detailed forecast financial and cost accounting consequences of putting this plan into effect.

Generally firms will budget *one year ahead*. They will have rather less detailed plans for further ahead than that (medium term strategic plans) of course; but that aspect of planning is a separate subject on its own. Suffice it to say that for at least one year ahead firms generally know their objectives sufficiently clearly to be able to make very detailed plans, and therefore reflect these in very detailed budgets.

Again, as with all cost accounting techniques, budgeting is an optional activity. I have stated that not all firms write their plans down, they often remain in the owner's head for example. Similarly many firms do not produce a written budget; though in most cases a forecast is rapidly produced when it is needed even by the apparently most disorganised outfits! Anyone who has tried to borrow money from a bank rapidly finds the time to forecast (i.e. budget) his next year's profits!

HOW DETAILED ARE THE BUDGET FORECASTS?

Taking the Sales Budget as an example. A firm will plan to make sales revenue of (say) £1,100,000 in the year starting 1 January. This will probably be split down between its various products in terms of both *units* and *price per unit*. This may be further split into *areas of the country* and then finally *by salesman*. In this way a very detailed picture of the revenue planned for, and *where it should come from*, is built up. For example (diagrammatically) the build-up is like this:

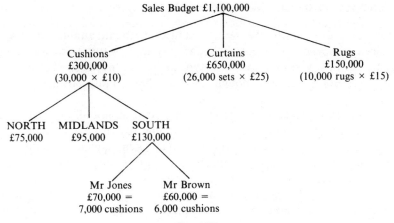

Fig. 125.

Once this has been done the individual salesmen or women can be given their expected targets for the forthcoming year. More than this, the budget will be broken down month by month to reflect the general trading pattern. For example the firm might expect to do more business in the spring and autumn. In which case the monthly split of the sales targets would be adjusted to take it into account. And if actual revenue is lower than budgeted one month; *a comparison will show up in precisely which area of the business things are going less well than planned.*

COMPARISON is the key word here. Much of the real usefulness of budgeting comes from comparing the budgeted (i.e. planned) position with what has actually happened. In this way managers learn what *is* happening compared with their expressed intentions (the budget) which in turn helps them to understand how the business is performing. The technical term for which is CONTROL. The great thing to realise is that regularly comparing plans with reality will enable managers to gain essential information about their businesses. This will help them make the most of the good news (e.g. 18,000 cushions are sold in the first 2 months – we raise cushion production sharply to take advantage of booming sales) and avoid disasters (e.g. our salesmen explain consumer resistance to the green patterned curtains in the range accounts for lower curtain sales – we change the pattern).

If the budget is regularly (at least once a month) compared with actual performance, it will help managers make the right decisions, i.e. it will help them *control the business.*

NOTE: The Budgeting discussions in this chapter take place mostly in the context of large organisations, and for this reason the large limited company is the main illustration used. This is because (A) large organisations need detailed written budgets much more than small ones (because in a small business there is much less difficulty in knowing how the business is performing in relation to one's intentions) and (B) the disadvantages of budgeting are more likely to appear in large organisations (because so many people in them perceive no link between what they do, and the success of the business as a whole).

A quick illustration of these points: A small business (say a garage) is most unlikely to order parts it will not use. This removes the need to have written co-ordination between sales and purchasing for example. Probably the same person does both. Similarly if petrol sales are low and the mechanics are not busy, everyone in the business will realise it has sales revenue problems, without needing a document to prove it. By contrast, large organisations often buy things they don't need, because the buyer has no contact with the stores.

INTEGRATED BUDGETS

It is essential that the different parts of the business do not make their plans separately. "Separately" in the sense of "regardless of the plans of the other parts". For example if the Sales department are intending to sell 30,000 cushions, 26,000 curtain sets and 10,000 rugs; the production team must plan to make at least this number! Similarly the buyers must plan to order the necessary materials. This may seem rather obvious to anyone who has not had experience of working (particularly in a larger organisation). However, believe me, the task of getting the sales and production people together and getting reasonable co-operation and co-ordination between them can be formidable in the extreme. In many organisations they are practically at daggers drawn!

The production budget, following the sales budget and allowing 10% extra for stock might be (again diagrammatically):

Production Budget
Total Cost of Output

	£500,000	
Cushions £150,000 33,000 units	Curtains £300,000 28,600 units	Rugs £50,000 11,000 units
Direct Materials £70,000	£210,000	£30,000
Direct Labour £60,000	£40,000	£10,000
Overheads £20,000	£50,000	£10,000

Costs based on the following forecasts:

Material Costs			
per yard	£1·50	£2·25	£2
Direct Labour Cost			
per hour	£3	£3	£3
Total Factory Overheads:			£80,000

Broken down as follows:	Rates and Rent	£20,000
	Machinery costs	£17,000
	Indirect Labour	£10,000
	Engineering Dept	£18,000
	Stores	£15,000

Fig. 126.

Again, the important thing is that the budget is done in enough detail to reveal *where and why* things are different when the comparison with the actual figures is made.

There are further things to integrate than just sales and production output of course. The expenditure of any surplus cash generated is another particularly important area. Salesmen need new cars, production wants new machinery, the firm maybe wants to expand into new premises. Any capital expenditure plans such as these must be carefully co-ordinated with sales and cost targets, and all three must be regularly compared with actual performance. It is disaster for a firm to run out of money and this can all too easily happen. If large sums are spent on new machinery and buildings, which sums should be available according to the budget; but have not been generated in reality, the firm will run out of money and collapse.

The purpose of integrating budgets therefore, is to ensure that the individual departments plans are properly co-ordinated and that the firm is not making plans which are internally inconsistent (e.g. planning to spend money it does not plan to be available).

The culmination of all this will be in a forecast month by month profit and loss account and balance sheet. You really need Stage 1 Financial Accounting to fully understand what these are. Briefly I can state that this means the firm will have a budgeted monthly statement – built up from each department's individual budgets, which for the entire organisation will show:

1. Sales Revenue gained
2. Expenses incurred (e.g. wages, materials, overheads broken down by item of expense)
3. Cash available

4. Stock levels

5. Amounts due to be paid to suppliers, and amounts owed by customers

6. Amounts spent on new fixed assets (machinery, buildings, vehicles)

7. To what extent the business has generated cash through trading profitably, and what has been done with the cash so generated.

And the important point to understand is that as a result of *comparing the intended position* (the budget) with *the actual figures* (recorded by the accounts department) the managers will be able to make sensible decisions. That is, will be better able to CONTROL the business.

CONSTRUCTING AN INTEGRATED BUDGET

Quite clearly for any business the *sales budget* is the foundation of the whole forecast. Once the plan for the *number of items, price,* and therefore *revenue* has been settled the *Production Budget* can be constructed.

This may involve a considerable amount of to-ing and fro-ing between the sales and production people involved. For instance, say the salesmen want 10,000 rugs, the production department might only be able to make 9,000 with the machinery they presently have. Between them they may have to decide if it is worth buying an extra machine for only 1,000 extra rugs. This may result in the sales department saying, "Buy the machine and we'll try to sell the 15,000 rugs we could then make" and so on. Wage levels will need to be predicted, as well as output levels, material costs and overhead expenses.

Once the sales and production departments have got themselves sorted out, then the various machinery and vehicle replacements will be agreed to make up the *fixed asset purchase budget.* Finally the expense budgets of the various service departments (including the expenses of *running* the sales department) will be agreed. These will include wages, motor expenses, pensions, staffing levels, telephones, electricity, insurances and so forth.

Finally the whole must be reviewed in terms of the cash available and whether from a profit point of view it seems a good plan.

The whole process is summarised in the table below, Fig. 127. The stages are logical steps – they may not necessarily occur in that order, and frequently the results of a later step will cause changes to be made in earlier ones. For instance, if unit costs are budgeted rather lower than expected, it may mean revising sales prices downwards and volume upwards. Similarly the budgeted cash available may necessitate that fixed asset purchases are reduced to prevent any cash shortage. The person most likely to be responsible for setting each budget is also shown. Though again in real life this will be a consultative process between most people involved in any particular area. The production manager won't set budgeted output levels without discussing the matter with the foreman and staff representatives, for instance.

STEP NO.	BUDGET DECISION / PEOPLE RESPONSIBLE	FORECAST DETAIL AND ACTION NECESSARY
1	Decide Sales Budget Sales Manager, Sales Director	No. of products. No. of items of each product. Price per item. Targets for each area and salesman. Unit sales per month.
2	Decide Factory Production Budget Works Manager, Production Director	No. of products. No. of items of each product. Output per week required. Output per week possible. Labour required. Machinery required, material costs, overhead costs (rent, rates, electricity). Unit Costs resulting.
3	Decide Fixed Assets purchases budget Departmental Heads, and Works Manager, all Directors	No. of salesmen's cars to be replaced. New machinery required. New buildings required. Cost of all these.
4	Decide departmental budgets Departmental Heads, e.g. Chief Accountant, Production Control Manager, Transport Manager	No. of Salesmen, production controllers, storemen, accounts staff, managers. Wages levels for these. Car expenses, office overhead expenses.
5	Construct Forecast Profit and Loss Account and Balance Sheet Chief Accountant, Finance Director	Uses the detail available from 1–4 to construct the overall picture of the next year's trading.
6	Construct Cash-Flow Budget Chief Accountant, Finance Director	Uses detail from 1–5 and dealt with separately in CHAPTER 9.
7	REVIEW THE BUDGET IN THE LIGHT OF 5 and 6. CHANGE ANY OF 1–4 if not satisfactory Managing Director, Executive Directors	If the Budgeted profit is not sufficient (for example) costs and revenue forecasts will have to be changed, and tougher targets set.

Fig. 127.

I repeat, this is a logical sequence. In reality there may be all kinds of negotiations and changes before the budget is finally agreed, all of which go on at once. The budget-setting time of year is pretty hectic in most firms, you can be sure.

Note: Apart from the areas specifically the responsibility of the accountant, there is a considerable involvement in providing data for all the other decisions. For example, take Step 2. Much of the data needed will be supplied by the accounts department – for instance factory overhead expense details. As well as this the accounts department may do the "number-crunching" on behalf of the works director (based on data the works director has approved) to calculate unit costs. However the costs so calculated are the *responsibility* of the works people, and it is their decision even if they are assisted by the accounts department.

I hope you realise that budgeting is an essential pre-requisite to calculating an Overhead Recovery Rate, and indeed to estimating a job, process and marginal cost. In fact as shown in Step 2, estimating unit costs will be an essential part of deciding if the plan is satisfactory. If the costs come out too high, the budget, i.e. the plan, must be changed.

A firm is free to choose whatever layout it likes to record its budget. Apart from the fact that the layout should be clear, there are no rules. A typical layout for the production department cushion budget for January, based on the year's budget (diagrammatically shown above in Fig. 126) would be as shown in Fig. 128:

Production Department Budget – year Beginning 1 January

MONTH: JANUARY

	Cushions			Comments
	Budget	Actual	Variance	
Output in Units	2,750			
Total Costs	£12,500			
Cost Breakdown				
Materials	£5,834			
Direct Labour	£5,000			
Overheads	£1,666			

Fig. 128.

The actual figures would be filled in and any worryingly large *Variances* (differences between budget and actual) would be investigated. Imagine that the actual January direct material costs were £6,500. The variance would be 6,500 *minus* 5,834 = £666 UNFAVOURABLE(U). "Unfavourable" means "the wrong way" (*tending to reduce budgeted profit*). In this instance actual cost is higher than budgeted cost so profits will be lower. In Revenue budgets unfavourable (the wrong way) is when actual revenue is lower than budgeted revenue and profits are lower as a result.

By contrast a "FAVOURABLE" variance (F) means "the right way" (*tending to increase budgeted profit* that is). So if actual costs were lower than budgeted, it produces a favourable variance because profits tend to be larger. If actual revenue were higher than budgeted, it too means higher profits, so the variance is favourable.

This £666 (U) variance would now be investigated to find out why it occurred. In principle the reasons could be one of the following three or a combination of them all:

(i) Actual price per yard of material is higher
(ii) More material per cushion was used than budgeted
(iii) More cushions were made than budgeted.

Obviously (i) or (ii) are more worrying reasons than (iii). A good deal more work will be done on variances in Chapter 8. At this stage just remember that the *reasons* for the difference are essential information for managers if a budget/actual comparison is to be useful.

Just as importantly much can be learned from favourable variances. For example investigation of their causes might lead managers to discover how to make similar savings in other areas of the business.

A similar layout could be used for the Sales Budget:

CUSHION SALES BUDGET JANUARY	Budget	Actual	Variance
Units	2,500		
Price Per Unit	£10		
Revenue	£25,000		
Revenue Breakdown NORTH MIDLANDS SOUTH	£6,250 £7,916 £10,834		

Fig. 129.

.... and for all of the others something quite similar.

All of this work culminates in the budget document itself, often quite a bulky folder. This consists of the budgeted profit and loss account, balance sheet, and cash flow (see Chapter 9). The information in these is cross-referenced to other parts of the document which give the breakdown of the main figures. For example the sales budget as shown in the profit and loss account is referenced to a sales breakdown schedule which shows sales per product, per area, per month (as illustrated in Fig. 129). In this way a considerable amount of useful information can be presented in one document – which although large, as it contains the whole plan of the business in complete detail for the next year, is quite small in relation to its contents.

WHAT ARE THE ADVANTAGES OF BUDGETING?

As outlined earlier in the chapter, the process of constructing a budget is quite laborious. So what are the principal advantages to be gained from the exercise?

(i) *Performance targets are clearly set.* If the job has been done properly, people in the organisation should be clear what is expected of them in the forthcoming months. The assumption is that the relevant part of the budget is communicated to those people responsible for achieving it. The salesmen know what they are expected to sell. The materials buyer knows what he or she is expected to buy and how much to pay for it. The works know what they should produce. Similarly the factory management will know how much has been allocated for them to spend on new equipment. The sales manager will know how many salesmen he can employ and what they should be paid. The other service departments, such as accounting, general administration and production control, will also know their allowed expenditure and manning levels. If (for example) a computer needs to be bought to help cope with the accounting workload, this will have been agreed and the expenditure allowed for.

(ii) *Budget/Actual comparisons reveal useful information.* The information gleaned from comparing the plan with reality helps managers control their business. For instance, if production costs are rising: (A) the management will know (B) they can investigate and do something to lower them (C) in the meantime they can ensure the firm does not run into cash difficulties as a result (by cutting back if necessary on planned expenditure in other areas).

(iii) *The activity of planning ahead is in itself beneficial.* Human beings do not naturally think ahead in any detail. Most of us have no firm plans for our weekend activity in 6 weeks time, for example. Similarly in business it is all too easy to jog along from day to day, week to week, with no clear idea of the MISSION, or DIRECTION it is being attempted to go in.

The fact that a budget for the forthcoming year has to be compiled, in great detail at that, FORCES MANAGERS TO THINK AHEAD. Imagine you are responsible for the factory. You have to (see Fig. 127, Step 2) say what the planned output will cost. You have to estimate (i.e. *think about*) all the points listed in the right-hand box: Output speeds, labour required, machinery needed, materials required, labour rates, material costs, factory overhead costs, and finally use this to give estimated absorption costs per unit.

All of which will be written into the budget and you, the factory manager, will have to make sure you *do* make reality coincide with your targets. This means that as far as possible you will take steps to ensure your estimated data is correct. For instance the Electricity Boards publish estimated price increases well in advance. The expected prices of all sorts of raw materials (e.g. oil, copper, paper, plastics, steel) can be found by referring to such bodies as the Economist Intelligence Unit, commodity brokers, suppliers and so forth. Once the serious business of *having* to plan ahead is embarked upon, it is surprising just how much information can be found to reduce the guesswork.

The fact that the budget *must* be compiled, therefore forces managers to undertake this type of investigation, which in turn makes them better informed and more aware of the future they face. Consequently they are able to make sensible decisions about their business.

THE GENERAL CHARACTERISTICS OF A USEFUL BUDGET

Even if a budget has been compiled, it won't necessarily be useful for the people in the firm, unless certain conditions exist within the business. It is all too easy for the budgeting exercise, and later comparison with actual figures, to be perceived by the vast majority of managers in a firm as an over-complicated time-wasting menace. The question is, what character-istics should *any* budget have if it is to be useful?

(i) The people using it (i.e. whose work and performance is being guided and measured by it) should *agree* with it, consider it is a *fair* target. Otherwise they won't bother to try to achieve the targets set.

(ii) The top management in the firm should be convinced the budget is a useful tool for the firm. If they don't the whole budgeting exercise will be done half-heartedly, and it will become a chore rather than a source of useful information.

You may wonder how any business would have a budget if the top management didn't think it was a good idea. Well, perhaps the Finance Director has said it must be done, the other directors don't disagree but don't *really* agree either. So they tend to "damn it with faint praise". This attitude quickly seeps down to the lowest ranks of managers, with disas-trous results. Disastrous because the exercise is seen to be time-wasting bureaucracy by most people in the firm.

(iii) People using the budget must *understand* what it is for. Following on from point (ii) above it is vital, if the benefits of the budgeting exercise are to be gained, that everyone realises what they are. If people realise that this information is important, why it is important, that it can prevent appalling errors by the firm (e.g. making too many of unsaleable Product 1 and not enough of enormous-selling Product 2) they are likely to do their best to make the system work. Believe me if the people don't want the system to work, it won't. For example if the actual output figures are inaccurate, late, or just not collected by a reluctant foreman, the vital comparisons will not happen. The result is that nobody knows what is happening to production costs.

(iv) Therefore the budget must be expressed *clearly*. This will seem obvious to a beginner. However I have seen more appallingly complicated budget-statements (which looked like a page of the telephone directory) than I have seen clear ones. Clarity essentially means ONLY THE VITAL FIGURES ON THE PAGE. Accountants are largely to blame for poor, over-complicated budget statements. This is because they never want to be accused of "not having told management". Therefore they include every conceivable figure which results in a statement few people understand. And we all know what human beings do with horrible complicated sheets of figures they don't understand, – they put them down on their desks and don't use them or look at them. Result – the information managers need, they don't get.

The golden rule is therefore: include only the essential figures *BUT* have the detail ready *if it is needed*. What the essential figures are is a matter of judgment of course; but in any individual case it is usually quite obvious. Imagine you are a partner in a firm of solicitors. The important thing would be that (i) Fixed Costs were on target (because 99% of costs would be fixed) and (ii) the number of hours charged to clients was as hoped for, so that (iii) the actual overhead rate per hour was close to the budgeted one being charged to customers.

A simple statement such as this would tell the senior partners all they needed to know about the profitability of their business each week:

	Budget	Actual	Variance	
Weekly Fixed Cost (A)	£700	£690	£10	FAVOURABLE
Hours Charged to Clients (B)	40	39	1	UNFAVOURABLE
Cost per Hour (A ÷ B)	£17·50	£17·69	£0·19	UNFAVOURABLE
CHARGE RATE TO CLIENTS	21·00	21·00		
PROFIT PER HOUR	£3·50	£3·31	£0·19	UNFAVOURABLE

Fig. 130.

If one or other figure is seriously out of line, *then more detail must be available for any investigation.* More mistakes have occurred because over-complicated statements have not been used, than because clear simple statements have not had enough detail on them.

I am not saying that the statement in Fig. 130 above is the only information necessary to run a firm. Each month for instance, a full Profit and Loss Account and Balance sheet needs to be produced and compared with budget. However it does illustrate how weekly control can easily be gained in a simple clear way.

(v) The budget must be expressed in *units the user can understand.* A salesman needs to be told how many cases per week his target is. A foreman on the line making electric motors needs to know how many per shift to produce. While this seems obvious, quite frequently in businesses it doesn't happen.

(vi) Actual/Budget comparisons must be available *quickly.* The sooner it is known that something is going unexpectedly well (e.g. a product is selling 20% more than budget) or badly (costs are 10% up per unit) the sooner the management can take the appropriate action. The weekly control illustrated in Fig. 130 above is very useful *because it is weekly.* If fixed costs jumped suddenly, not knowing about it for 6 weeks would be a great disadvantage.

(vii) Ideally the budget needs to be reasonably close to reality. If it is quite hopelessly wrong then the differences between actual and budget become so large they become meaningless. If we budgeted to sell 15,000 dresses a month and can only sell 2,000, then apart from telling us we have a disaster, the comparison will reveal no useful information. If the budget becomes irrelevant to reality no one will bother to use it, and the information it reveals will be swamped by the fact it is completely unrealistic.

(viii) The budget must be ready in good time before the start of the period being planned for. Then all concerned will be clear on their objectives. In many businesses the rush of events means the 1984 budget is not ready until April 1984!

(ix) If for some reason it seems necessary to deviate from the budget (e.g. to overspend a machinery replacement budget in order to gain a substantial drop in unit costs, or to overspend a travelling budget in order to gain an important new customer) a *decision to do so or not must be immediately available.* The system must not be so rigid that exceptional circumstances cannot be taken advantage of. Therefore good communication is essential between top middle and lower levels in the firm.

(x) The final point is that the budget should *concentrate on the business's essentials.* Spending time and effort on the paper clip budget is foolish and will divert energy from where it should be directed. The essentials for any given business will be different of course. For a mass-producer it might be direct materials and output speeds. Certainly car manufacturers spend a great deal of time concentrating on those aspects. Sales will of course be vital for every organisation. For a shop, the buying price of goods and the speed of stock-turnover would be vital areas, for example.

The important thing to ensure, in the effort of making up a budget, is that the essentials get the attention.

In years to come I invite you to compare the budgeting system in your organisation with these ten points – most of you will find it won't measure up to several of them. And you will then know and feel, rather than just be mentally convinced by my examples, that the system is the poorer for it.

THE DISADVANTAGES AND DIFFICULTIES OF BUDGETING

In many ways the disadvantages of budgeting are built into the system of creating a budget to begin with. There is the unspoken assumption that proper targets will be set by the budget. Whether sales, output, or departmental expense budgets, the assumption is that they will be satisfactory. In practice this is not necessarily true, and is very hard to be sure of. From this difficulty flow most of the disadvantages of budgeting.

(i) *The problem of setting budgetary targets.* Refer back to Steps 1, 2 and 3 in Fig. 127. The responsibility for *setting* the targets is borne by the same people responsible for *achieving* them. This is the centre of the problem. If you were the sales manager, you would be very tempted to set a sales target you were *sure* of achieving – which might not be as high as the sales that *could* be achieved. Similarly the production manager will be tempted to set output per hour targets that he or she is *certain* can be met – which might understandably be lower than those that could be.

Human beings are not usually going to set themselves targets which they feel will mean too much effort to meet. As a result it is all too easy for the budget to be set at a level which is not designed to produce the most out of the resources being used by the business.

This is where the review by the Managing Director and the other directors comes in. They have ultimate responsibility for ensuring the targets are sensible . . . but even they may be reluctant to make too large a change.

(ii) The comparison between actual performance and budget target too easily becomes a substitute for a proper assessment of a person's achievements. Once people realise that their efforts will be judged *on the budget variances alone,* they will put enormous effort into ensuring the actual figures come out close to the budget, regardless of whether this is good for the business. For example Salesmen will "soft-pedal" once they have met their monthly target. Production people will "soft pedal" once they have produced their weekly quota. A keen salesman who has the chance of extra business may be deterred from chasing it, if he will be blamed for over-spending his entertainment allowance as a result. If the senior management remain content with budget targets being met, and don't find enough out about the real situation to know that much more could be achieved, the resources of the business will be partly wasted.

All too easily therefore, the budget becomes a mechanism which makes the business rigid, discourages initiative, and discourages the management from properly assessing the performance of people within it.

This difficulty is linked to the first, of course. A sales manager is not going to set a challenging target that might just be missed, if it results in his being disciplined for "not meeting the budget". Which is best for the business, A or B below in Fig. 131?

	A	B
Sales Target	£1,000	£800
Actual Sales	£950	£830
Variance	(50) unfavourable	30 favourable

Fig. 131.

If you as sales manager could choose A or B, why would you choose A if you knew you would be damned for not meeting the target, when you could choose B and be praised?

(iii) Unnecessary expenditure can be encouraged. This, in bureaucratic organisations, such as government departments in particular, is the biggest single disadvantage of budgeting. It stems from the belief (usually true) that if less than the budgeted amount is spent, next year's allocation will be reduced. For instance if the works has an allocation of £150,000 for new machinery purchases, it will spend that money *regardless of whether it really needs to,* for fear of not having as large an allocation given to it next year when it might need it. If the accounts department has an allocation of £10,000 for new equipment, it will spend that money *regardless of whether it really needs to,* for the same reason.

This results, particularly from government departments, in an unholy rush during the last months of their financial year to spend their allocations. The fear of having them reduced in the following year, if they are not all spent this year, encourages the unnecessary expenditure.

(iv) Because last year's budget inevitably tends to be a guide to this year's ("plus 10% all round" is a pretty common solution to the problem of setting this year's budget!) totally unnecessary activities can be undertaken by the organisation because no one has questioned their necessity. This is particularly likely to occur in government-type organisations. For instance a large road planning department might be kept intact by a county council, when no major road schemes are, in fact, going to be built for many years.

SOLUTIONS TO THE DISADVANTAGES

Sensible management is the key to solving the difficulties. If people in a firm have confidence that the management is reasonable, then most of the disadvantages disappear. In more detail this means:

(A) "Zero budgeting" can be adopted. This is designed to remove disadvantage (iv) above. Each year a certain number of departments have to *justify their existence at all* in the organisation, and to further justify their size and expenditure if they are necessary. In this way it is hoped to remove the unnecessary expenditure and prevent waste being built into the budget.

(B) Management must instil confidence into people within the business that resources will be available for justified expenditure. In other words if money is saved one year it *won't* result in less being available when it is needed in the future. This requires good communications and trust to be present, which in turn means the management must be trained to help create these conditions.

(C) If budgetary targets are not seen as the sole measure of effort and performance, people will be more likely to set higher targets for achievement. This again relies on managers being reasonable, and understanding that a challenging target has been set, rather than an easy one. It further means that people's efforts must be judged on all the circumstances, not just on the basis of the budget. Which in turn means the effort must be made to communicate well by managers.

(D) Some clearly perceivable personal advantage must accrue to individuals who perform well. People are much more likely to work hard and make efforts if they will become richer as a result. If poor lazy efforts result in as much money as really hard work, what is the point of working hard? Fair bonus systems are notoriously difficult to devise of course, nevertheless managers must ensure that extra effort is rewarded if they want the most out of their staff. I hope you realise that the *attitude of the*

Taylorism - not always true.

individuals is the key to budgeting being a really useful activity, rather than a mechanism for ensuring mediocre minimum standards. Therefore reward for effort is the vital ingredient.

These solutions require years of effort by managers, directors and staff in learning to communicate properly, and developing their budgetary system sensibly. They also require constant effort and time to be expended, year in and year out, if the problems are to be solved. Too often budgeting is done in a rushed and hasty way which results in targets being imposed on reluctant individuals, with predictable results.

SUMMARY

The job of actually constructing a budget is easy, *once the targets and predictions have been made.* The accountant can easily multiply 5,000 units per month by £3·50 per unit to give a sales revenue budget of £17,500 per month, for example.

The problem with budgeting is one of *setting* the targets, i.e. of predicting the future. It involves predicting Demand for the product, Material costs, Wage rates, Expense levels, Energy prices, Output speeds, and the amount of Effort the individuals in the organisation are going to make.

This activity is difficult but ESSENTIAL. A large organisation with no budget is practically impossible to control. How do the factories know what to make, or the salesmen know what to sell?

If the budget is to be more than a mediocre plan only partly utilising the firm's resources, wasting them with unnecessary expenditure, and therefore resulting in poor profits (or more expenditure than the services provided *should* cost in the case of non-profit making bodies); the management must realise the dangers of budgeting and work towards eliminating them. And any accountant who understands the difficulties will be that much more useful to the business he or she works for.

SELF-ASSESSMENT QUESTIONS

* 1. If the sales budget is 20,000 units per month, at all times 7 weeks' sales must be ready in stock, and maximum output is 5,000 units per week (Assuming 4 week months):

(A) How many units will have to be produced before selling starts?
(B) How long will this take at maximum output?
(C) If the Factory absorption cost per unit is £6 at maximum output, what is the value of the stock?
(D) If the marginal cost of one unit is £2; what will the absorption cost per unit be if only 4,500 units are produced each week?

2. In the context of a business making and selling carpets:

(A) Name three possible causes of an unfavourable variance on Building and Establishment expenses.

(B) Name three possible causes of a favourable variance on Sales Revenue.

(C) Name three possible causes of a favourable direct labour variance.

3. If you were the person responsible for producing the carpets at the right unit costs, what steps would you take to remedy the causes outlined in (A) above?

4. The marginal cost per burger in our newly opened "fast food" restaurant is £0·20. Our fixed costs are £1,700 per month and we stay open 7 days a week. Selling prices per burger are £0·80; or £1·10 for the super-burger whose marginal cost is £0·25. We reckon to sell burgers in the ratio of 3 burgers to 1 super-burger.

(A) A profit of £1,500 per month is required:
   (i) How many of each type of burger has to be sold each month?
   (ii) What is the sales revenue budget for each type of burger for one month?

(B) Assume your budgeted sales were made: if actual fixed costs were £1,750 and actual marginal costs £0·22 and £0·29 for the two types of burger (i) what is the Fixed Cost Variance, the burger marginal cost variance, and the super-burger marginal cost variance for the month?

(C) If you were in charge of a chain of these fast food shops, do you think it would be best to give the staff a sales target expressed in Revenue per month or number of Burgers per week? Justify your answer.

Note: There are a number of other budgeting questions at the end of Chapter 9 – which needs to be read before attempting them of course.

CHAPTER 8

STANDARD COSTING AND VARIANCE ANALYSIS

CHAPTER OBJECTIVES

Having studied this chapter you should be able to:

* EXPLAIN WHAT STANDARD COSTS ARE, AND DESCRIBE IN PRINCIPLE HOW THEY ARE FOUND

* RELATE THE STANDARD-SETTING PROCESS TO THE BUDGETING PROCESS

* EXPLAIN THE GENERAL CHARACTERISTICS OF PRODUCTS WHICH ARE COSTED USING A STANDARD COSTING SYSTEM

* DESCRIBE WHY STANDARD COSTING AND VARIANCE ANALYSIS ARE PARTICULARLY SUITABLE FOR CONTROLLING COSTS OF COMPLEX MANUFACTURING BUSINESSES

* CONSTRUCT MASTER AND FLEXIBLE BUDGETS FOR BOTH REVENUES AND COSTS FROM GIVEN DATA

* CONSTRUCT A TABLE OF MAJOR VARIANCES FOR BOTH REVENUES AND COSTS

* CALCULATE SIMPLE SUB-VARIANCES

* UNDERSTAND THE USES AND LIMITATIONS OF THE VARIANCES CALCULATED

COSTING SYSTEMS FOR HIGH-VALUE IDENTICAL PRODUCTS

Cast your mind back to Chapter 4. There we dealt with two common absorption costing systems: job costing and process costing. Job costing for high-value "one-off" products, process costing for low-value identical ones. This left out an enormous section of manufactured products: relatively high-value identical ones, such as washing machines, dishwashers, cars, T.V.s, videos, mini-computers, Hi-Fi's, to name only a few.

This type of product tends to be (A) complex and (B) assembled in large numbers in large factories. As a result of these two factors it becomes almost impossible to know how efficiently they are being produced JUST BY BEING THERE AND WATCHING, even if you are really familiar with the set-up as a manager would be.

Take a car factory. There are literally thousands of people working in a great number of different departments; some are standing waiting for other things to happen, some are having breaks from work, others are busy mending production machinery that has broken, fork lift trucks are cruising around with loads of parts, and so on and so on.

You could spend five years wandering around and still not be able to say for certain whether in a particular week the cars were being turned out at the right price. For one thing (remember Make or Buy in Chapter 6?) car makers buy in over half of the cars' components – tracking prices alone is a major task. Contrast this with a small shop, or a small garage business. After two weeks of *just being there* you would know if they were busy, and profitable, or not. You would have assimilated the essentials because they would stand out so clearly. A few simple checks on cost prices of food, or fuel and spare parts, and you would soon know how much of the takings was contribution – and the fixed costs wouldn't be hard to estimate.

Because of the sheer size and complexity of the set-up, large manufacturing outfits making complicated products need *direction-finding apparatus* to help the managers find out if things are going to plan or not; and if they are not, *where the problem is showing itself.* Of course in an overall sense this is what the budget does, and why it is so essential to have one in a large business (see Chapter 7). However something like it is needed *on a product by product basis* and this is where standard costing comes in.

Standard costing is a costing system uniquely suitable for controlling the costs of high-value, identical mass-produced items made in complex manufacturing plants. We will take T.V.s as our example:

FINDING THE COMPONENTS OF THE SYSTEM

In factories making the type of product described, the costing problem is a blend of the problems solved by Job and Process costing. The items are identical (process costing characteristics); but they are of high value (job costing characteristics). It would clearly be wasteful to measure the cost of each one *individually* – an army of clerks would be following the T.V.s about for example. Equally, having made 10,000 T.V.s in a month, to then measure the actual costs and do a division sum to get a cost per T.V., doesn't help the management too much. What if the unit cost is higher than hoped? It doesn't tell you why, it might indicate higher Direct Labour than planned, but again would not indicate why, or in which of the many stages of production the extra cost was incurred.

Standard costing combines aspects of the two systems as follows:

STEP ONE: DECIDE THE STANDARD COST AND STANDARD OUTPUT

To begin with the cost of making *one* T.V. is estimated in great detail (rather as an estimated job cost would be, only because of the complexity of manufacture it is a much more complicated business). This becomes the standard cost. A **standard cost is the planned (budgeted) absorption cost of making one item.**

> *Note*: Remember that this must therefore be based on a given number; because strictly speaking an absorption cost can only be true for a given number of items. Make more items and the fixed costs are diluted (so the absorption cost drops) make fewer and the fixed costs are concentrated (so the absorption cost rises).

There is much written on the problems of setting standard costs. These are of course identical in principle to the problems of setting *any* budgetary target (see Chapter 7). Briefly it involves measurement of the work rates of production staff, estimates of machinery efficiency and speed (based on measurement taken) material cost estimates and waste percentages, overhead estimations, quality control rejection percentages, wage rates, and any other relevant information that affects the costs and output of a particular product. Standard-setters go about with stop watches, frequently, timing exactly how long it takes to insert a circuit board into a T.V. for instance.

Once these are all estimated there remains the problem of whether they are satisfactory and if a harder target should be set. These problems, answers to which are often forced on a management by the efficiency of the competition, all need to be taken into account in deciding what the standard cost should be.

Assume all has been done and the standard cost agreed. It might, for a T.V., look like this for Direct Labour:

		Total		Time		Rate/Hour
Direct Labour:	Operation 1	50p	=	15 mins	×	£2·00
	Operation 2	25p	=	7½ mins	×	£2·00
	Operation 3	10p	=	2 mins	×	£3·00
	Operation 4	70p	=	6 mins	×	£7·00
	Operation 5	30p	=	4 mins	×	£4·50
	Operation 6	£7·50p	=	1½ hours	×	£5·00

DIRECT LABOUR TOTAL £9·35

Fig. 132.

Direct Materials would be an equally complex breakdown of chassis costs, transistor costs, tube and circuit board and cabinet costs. Assume these totalled £50.

Overheads would be on the basis of productive capacity used, in the normal way; but again could be a complicated business. For instance if they were per Direct Labour Hour, there would be 6 overhead calculations within the standard cost, one for each operation. Assume the overheads totalled £64. Direct Labour plus Direct Materials plus Overheads equal the Standard Cost. So the T.V. Standard Cost is:

	£
Direct Labour	9·35
Direct Materials	50·00
Fixed Overheads	64·00
Standard Cost of T.V.	£123·35

Fig. 133.

Now this is an absorption cost – so the fixed costs must have been "spread" over a *particular number* of sets. So we will assume this standard cost has been calculated on the basis of making 1,400 sets per month, i.e. the STANDARD OUTPUT is 1,400 sets per month. Therefore total monthly fixed overheads are £64 × 1,400 sets = £89,600.

STEP TWO: CALCULATE THE MASTER BUDGET

From Chapter 7 you should be clear that firms with integrated budgets have monthly sales and output Budgets. The total Standard Cost for a T.V. was (Fig. 133) £123·35. This was on the basis of spreading the fixed costs over 1,400 T.V. sets. Therefore the total budgeted T.V. production costs per month will be £172,690, which is £123·35 × 1,400 sets.

This £172,690 budgeted output is called the MASTER BUDGET. So called because it represents precisely what it is planned, in the integrated budget, to spend in total on making T.V. sets each month. The master budget might be presented like this:

<u>Master Budget for Production of T.V.s</u>

Quantity Made		1,400
Direct Labour Costs		£
£9·35 Standard × 1,400	=	13,090
Direct Material Costs		
£50 Standard × 1,400	=	70,000
Fixed Overheads		
£64 Standard × 1,400	=	89,600
MASTER BUDGET TOTAL		£172,690

Fig. 134.

STEP THREE: CALCULATE THE FLEXIBLE BUDGET *if necessary*

What happens if we have a good month's output and manage to make 1,540 T.V. sets? *The master budget will not be a good guide to the costs which we would plan, or expect, to incur at the higher output level.* For instance if there were a bonus element in Direct Labour, we would expect that cost to be higher; obviously more would be spent on Direct Materials. (This is straightforward marginal costing of course, and should come as no surprise after Chapters 5 and 6). However the fixed overheads we would not expect to change *as a result* of making more T.V.s than master-budgeted. Therefore a straight multiplication of the Standard Cost (an absorption cost which is "True" for 1,400 sets per month only) by the 1,540 sets actually made, will not be a good guide either, to the *expected costs for the actual quantity*. The costs we would expect (i.e. plan or budget) to incur if 1,540 sets were made must be separately calculated, from the Master Budget, *using marginal costing principles*. The result of these calculations is called the FLEXIBLE BUDGET. **A flexible budget is therefore the expected costs for the actual quantity.**

Let's assume that labour is 100% variable (to make it easy!) and you should know that Direct Materials are, without being told. The Flexible Budget for 1,540 T.V. sets would therefore be:

Flexible Budget for Production of T.V.s

Quantity	1,540

Direct Labour		£
$\dfrac{13,090}{1,400} \times 1,540$	=	14,399
Direct Materials		
$\dfrac{70,000}{1,400} \times 1,540$	=	77,000
Fixed Overheads NO CHANGE		89,600
FLEXIBLE BUDGET TOTAL		£180,999

Fig. 135.

In other words if we made 1,540 T.V. sets one month, in spite of the Master Budget being £172,690, *we would expect to incur costs totalling £180,999.* The *flexible budget* would be the guide against which we measured the actual costs to see if output costs had gone according to plan.

STEP FOUR: MEASURE THE ACTUAL COST TOTALS *using the same breakdown as used in the standard cost*

This would mean measuring the costs actually incurred in each of the six Direct Labour operations for example. Remember this for use later. However to keep things straightforward at this stage, we will merely use the totals of each of the major components. So assume that the actual costs incurred for one month's output of T.V.s were as follows:

T.V. Production Actual Costs

Quantity Produced	1,540 T.V. Sets

	£
Direct Labour	15,900
Direct Materials	75,600
Fixed Overheads	91,700
ACTUAL TOTAL COST	£183,200

Fig. 136.

Now the necessary system components are known, the next part deals with using them.

USING THE COMPONENTS

PART ONE: MAJOR VARIANCES

First of all, what do the management want explained? They will have an integrated budget showing the intended costs of the standard output quantity, i.e. £172,690. They will have a report showing *actual* total costs of £183,200. The Standard Costing system is intended to explain to the management what has caused this difference, so they can take the appropriate action.

Therefore the starting point is this difference:

	Master Budget Cost Total
compared with	Actual Cost Total
equals	TOTAL VARIANCE

In our example then:

		£
Master Budget Cost Total	=	172,690
Actual Cost Total	=	183,200
TOTAL VARIANCE	=	£10,510 (U)

Fig. 137.

The system must therefore explain what has contributed to this total variance of £10,510 (U). In other words it must explain *why* costs are £10,510 higher than intended.

In principle the explanations will be covered by the following categories (each of which can be further subdivided; but that comes later). Note that Chapter 7 explains the use and meaning of the variance symbols (U) and (F) on pages 149 and 150.

EXPLANATION (A)

Either more or fewer items than the standard quantity could have been produced. That is why the flexible budget is calculated. The Flexible Budget will show how much the *actual* quantity *should* cost. Therefore the difference between the Master Budget cost-total and the Flexible Budget cost-total will show the *expected differences in cost from the Master Budget*

as a result of actually making a different quantity. This is called the
QUANTITY VARIANCE.

compared with	Master Budget Total Cost
	Flexible Budget Total Cost
equals	QUANTITY VARIANCE

In our T.V. set example:

		£	Based on
Master Budget Total Cost	=	172,690	1,400 sets
Flexible Budget Total Cost	=	180,999	1,540 sets
QUANTITY VARIANCE	=	£8,309 (U)	

Fig. 138.

"Unfavourable" because it is more than Master Budget – an overspending;
but probably not a cause for alarm, as it is an *expected overspending
resulting from making more T.V. sets.*

EXPLANATION (B)

*Either more or less has been spent than should have been on DIRECT
LABOUR.* "Should have been" is given by the Flexible Budget of course.
It's no good comparing the actual Direct Labour for making 1,540 T.V.
sets with anything other than the *expected* costs for 1,540 sets: that is,
with anything other than Flexible Budget Direct Labour.

compared with	Flexible Budget Direct Labour
	Actual Direct Labour
equals	DIRECT LABOUR MAJOR VARIANCE

For 1,540 T.V. sets made:

		£
Flexible Budget DL	=	14,399
Actual Direct Labour	=	15,900
Direct Labour Major Variances	=	£1,501 (U)

Fig. 139.

Unfavourable because we have actually spent more than expected on
Direct Labour.

EXPLANATION (C)

Similarly either more or less may have been spent on DIRECT MATERIALS than should have been. The same applies to "should have have been" for Direct Materials as for Direct Labour; the "should have been" is the Flexible Budget:

	Flexible Budget Direct Materials
compared with	Actual Direct Materials
equals	DIRECT MATERIAL MAJOR VARIANCE

In our example again:

Flexible Budget DM	=	77,000
Actual Direct Materials	=	75,600
Direct Material Major Variance	=	£1,400 (F)

Fig. 140.

Favourable because we have spent less than expected in Direct Materials.

EXPLANATION (D)

Either more or less may have been spent on overheads than intended. If (as in the T.V. example) all the overheads are fixed there will only be a Fixed Overheads Major Variance. If there were some variable overheads, there would be a separate Variable Overhead Major Variance. In which case the standard cost, Master Budget and Flexible Budget would contain a separate Variable Overhead category as well. *But remember* the variable overhead *will* be altered from Master to Flexible budget and the Fixed Overhead won't!

Either way the same applies as with explanation B and C for the major variance calculation:

	Flexible Budget Overheads
compared with	Actual Overheads
equals	OVERHEAD MAJOR VARIANCE

For our example then:

	£
	£
Flexible Budget Fixed Overhead	89,600
Actual Fixed Overheads	91,700
OVERHEAD MAJOR VARIANCE	£2,100 (U)

Fig. 141.

Unfavourable because more has been spent on Overheads than planned.

These explanations between them provide the first stage of the "direction finding" apparatus that managements of complex manufacturing plants need. They can be conveniently presented as a reconciled TABLE OF MAJOR VARIANCES:

Total Variance:		10,510 (U)
Explained by:	Quantity Variance	8,309 (U)
	Direct Labour Variance	1,501 (U)
	Direct Material Variance	1,400 (F)
	Fixed Overhead Variance	2,100 (U)
		10,510

Fig. 142.

We now know why the actual costs were higher than those budgeted. Partly because more were made (Quantity variance (U)) partly because Direct Labour costs were higher than they should be (D.L. Variance (U)), and partly because Overhead costs were higher than they should be (Overhead variance (U)); however these were mitigated by a saving on Direct Materials (D.M. Variance (F)). Management has some useful "direction finding" information already.

Diagrammatically this part of the system is broken down as shown below in Fig. 143.

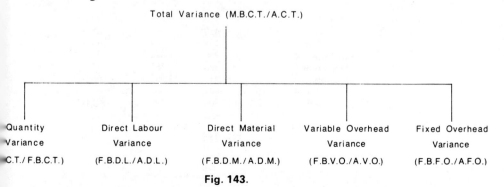

Fig. 143.

NOTE ABOUT FIG. 143:
M.B.C.T = M̲aster B̲udget C̲ost T̲otal, F.B.D.L. = F̲lexible B̲udget
D̲irect L̲abour, A.C.T. = A̲ctual C̲ost T̲otal and so on.
This is a handy guide to refer to in calculating major variances.

You should now be in a position to work through the questions in Part
A at the end of the chapter. Ensure you do these before going on to the
next section.

USING THE COMPONENTS

PART TWO: SUB VARIANCES

Just as the total variance is caused by the major variances, so the major
variances have causes – some of which can be calculated. These are called
the Sub-Variances.

DIRECT LABOUR AND DIRECT MATERIAL SUB VARIANCES

If you consult Fig. 132 you will see that the standard cost for Direct
Labour was in fact divided into six separate operations. This means that
in reality there would be 6 D.L. Major Variances, because the actual
direct labour costs would be recorded separately for each operation. (As
pointed out, they were treated together in the first explanation of major
variances for the sake of clarity).
Assume therefore that the *actual* Direct Labour cost total was broken
down as follows: (alongside it is the breakdown of the flexible budget
Direct Labour for each operation, which is the standard cost per operation
multiplied by the actual quantity).

	ACTUAL	FLEXIBLE BUDGET	MAJOR VARIANCE PER OPERATION
	£	£	
Operation 1	750	770	20 (F)
Operation 2	410	385	25 (U)
Operation 3	194	154	40 (U)
Operation 4	900	1,078	178 (F)
Operation 5	428	462	34 (F)
Operation 6	13,218	11,550	1,668 (U)
	£15,900	£14,399	1,501 (U)

Fig. 144.

This is a more real example of D.L. major variances, showing as it does to management *exactly which* operations are costing more than they should. Quite clearly the cause of the large variance on Operation 6 is the first target for investigation. The question therefore arises, what are the causes of this large unfavourable variance?

Because the standard cost is broken down into a Rate per Hour *multiplied by* a number of hours, we can calculate exactly what the breakdown of the flexible budget is, in terms of Hours × Rate per hour:

Standard Cost for Operation 6 (see Fig. 132):
1½ HOURS × £5 per Hour = £7·50

Flexible Budget for Operation 6:
£7·50 × 1.540 units = £11,550 (see table above)

At £5 per hour the flexible budget hours must be:
$$\frac{£11,550}{£5 \text{ per hour}} = 2,310 \text{ hours worked}$$

So the breakdown of the flexible budget is:
2,310 hours × £5 per hour = £11,550

Assume the measurement of the actual costs was as follows:
2,203 hours × £6 per hour = £13,218

We are now in a position to see the causes of the Operation 6 major variance of £1668 (U). Quite clearly (i) fewer hours are being worked than standard (2203 actual instead of 2310 budgeted), but (ii) more per hour is being paid (£6 actual instead of £5 budgeted). Unfortunately the net cost has come out rather higher than it should. These causes can be exactly quantified by calculating the Operation 6 Direct Labour Sub-Variances.

Taking the effect of the HOURS difference first:

Actual Hours	2,203
Flexible Budget Hours	2,310
HOURS SAVED	107

Therefore the HOURS (sometimes called "efficiency") sub-variance is the cost saved, *as a result of these hours saved.* That is 107 hours at the standard rate per hour:

D. L. HOURS SUB-VARIANCE = 107 hours × STANDARD RATE PER HOUR £5
= £535 (F)

The effect of the higher rate is next:

	£
Actual Rate	6
Budgeted Rate	5
Extra Hourly Rate	£1

Therefore the RATE sub-variance is the extra cost incurred, *as a result of the extra amount per hour being paid:*

D.L. RATE SUB VARIANCE = £1 × ACTUAL HOURS WORKED 2,203
= £2,203 (U)

These two will reconcile to the Operation 6 major variance and provide a further piece of "direction finding" information for management:

Operation 6 Major D.L. Variance	=		1,668 (U)
Explained by: Hours sub-variance		535 (F)	
Rate sub-variance		2,203 (U)	
			1,668 (U)

Management now know that it is a problem relating principally to wage rate on Operation 6. The increase in hourly rate has not been offset sufficiently by an hourly saving. Either wage rates must come down, or speed of work must increase, if the standard cost is to be maintained. This *could* be an example of an incentive scheme that has mis-fired of course. The extra speed of production hasn't offset the increase in wages per hour. Either way the management knows, in some detail, what has happened.

Sub-variances for Direct Materials are calculated in exactly the same way; but *Price* is the material equivalent of hourly rate; and *amount used* the equivalent of hours.

So general rules for calculating Direct Labour and Material sub-variances can be formulated; and really you need to learn them by heart.

SUB-VARIANCE CALCULATION RULES:

DIRECT
LABOUR   (1) D.L. HOURS sub-variance: Actual/Flexible Budget Hours
Difference
× Standard Rate per Hour

             (2) D.L. RATE sub-variance: Actual/Flexible Budget Rate Difference
× Actual Hours Worked

DIRECT
MATERIALS (1) D.M. USAGE sub-variance: Actual/Flexible Budget amount
used difference
× Standard price per unit of Direct
Material

             (2) D.M. PRICE sub-variance: Actual/Flexible Budget price per unit
difference
× Actual Amount Used.

To illustrate a direct material sub-variance, let's return to our T.V. example again. The flexible budget Direct Materials totalled £77,000, while Actual D.M. were £75,600.

To do the Sub-Variances we need to assume some information not so far given. This is greatly simplified for the purposes of learning, because in reality there might be hundreds of different components in a T.V. and so hundreds of different D.M. Major Variances. We will assume that there is only ONE type of material and that it costs £10 per kilogram at standard, and £7 per kilogram actually.

Now we are in a position to break down the actual and Flexible Budget D.M. cost into its sub-variance components. We know the cost per kilogram, actual and standard; we need to calculate the number of kilograms actually used and the number budgeted to be used:

Flexible Budget total D.M. Cost = £77,000 ÷ Budgeted Cost per kilogram £10 = 7,700 kilograms budgeted to be used.

Actual total D.M. Cost = £75,600 ÷ Actual Cost per kilogram £7 = 10,800 kilograms actually used.

Now we can follow the sub-variance calculation rules given above:

(i) D.M. Usage Sub-Variance:

Actual amount used:	10,800 kilos
Flexible budget amount:	7,700 kilos
Extra kilos used	3,100

Usage Sub-Variance = Extra kilos used × Standard Cost per kilo:
= 3,100 × £10
= £31,000 (U)

(ii) D.M. Price Sub-Variance:

	£
Actual Price per kilo:	7
Flexible Budget Price per kilo	10
Amount Saved	£3

D.M. Price Sub-Variance = Saving per kilo × Actual kilos used
= £3 × 10,800
= £32,400 (F)

Reconciliation: D.M. Major Variance (see Fig. 142) = 1400 (F)

D.M. Usage Sub-Variances 31,000 (U)
D.M. Price Sub-Variances 32,400 (F)

1400 (F)

This tells management that although a great deal more material is being used, it is more than offset by a lower price. This example is not too realistic in the case of T.V.s, of course. But for something made out of steel it could be different. Perhaps a lower quality steel is being tried out, and higher wastage is offset by a lower price.

OVERHEAD SUB-VARIANCES

These need a certain amount of discussion. In theory at least, fixed overheads are incurred regardless of output volume. If there is a fixed overhead major variance (in our T.V. example there was one: £2,100 (U); see Fig. 142) it must be caused by *spending* more on one or other of the many fixed overheads. It could be more petrol for salesmen than budgeted, higher rates, more machinery costs, insurance premiums going up, accounts staff wages being higher, and so on. All that can be done is to *compare the schedule of budgeted fixed costs* (which were £89,600 per month) with the *actual schedule of expenditure* and see where the differences are. No expenditure-based sub-variances, other than this, are possible. So, you will be relieved to hear, for fixed overheads no sub-variance calculations are within the scope of this book. To control fixed overhead expenditure it has to be a comparison of scheduled spending, or nothing. It is possible to calculate fixed overhead variances which are, in effect, over or under-recovery variances. These are beyond the scope of a beginner's book, as are many other types of variance. At the end of the chapter there is a general discussion of the further developments possible.

VARIABLE OVERHEADS are slightly more tricky. There are some

variable overheads which are almost like direct materials. For instance in aluminium smelting it takes over a hundred pounds worth of electricity to make 1 tonne of aluminium. In this case the electricity overhead is variable with output and the standard cost of 1 tonne of aluminium might have included in it a variable overhead as follows:

Variable Electricity Overhead: 3,000 kilowatts × 5p per kilowatt = £150

In this case the actual figures would be measured and a Price and Usage sub-variance would be calculated *exactly like the Direct Materials sub-variances.*

Apart from this type of variable overhead other convincing examples are quite hard to come by. It might be that there was a royalty fee to pay to an inventor per item manufactured. However once the flexible budget was calculated the major variance could only consist of a royalty price per unit difference, so no sub-variance would be possible.

In examinations you are far more likely to be given a problem which mixes together fixed and variable overheads and tempts you to treat them wrongly. For instance (say) you were given the following information:

(i) Standard Cost per unit for Overheads: £24 (75% fixed).
(ii) Standard Cost is based on making 1,000 items per month.
(iii) Actually 1,200 items were made.

Question: What is the flexible budget for overheads?
Answer:

(i) Find the Fixed Costs
Fixed Costs = 24 × 75% = £18 × Standard Quantity 1,000
                         = £18,000 WHICH DOES NOT CHANGE IN THE
                           FLEXIBLE BUDGET
(ii) Variable Overheads   24 × 25% = £6 × actual quantity 1,200
                         = £7,200
Flexible Budget for overheads = Fixed Overheads
                                £18,000
                                Variable Overheads
                                £7,200

OVERHEAD TOTAL   £25,200

Fig. 145.

So be on your guard against the temptation to take 24 and multiply it by 1,200! This of course is just basic marginal costing being applied. Don't fall into the trap of using an absorption cost as a marginal one.

At this stage we can fully work through an entire example which might be typical of a simple examination question. Here it is:

Question
The standard cost of a zoom gear box is as follows:

Direct Labour	£20 = 5 hours at £4 per hour.
Direct Materials	£18 = 6 kilos at £3 per kilo.
Overheads	£12 = £10 are fixed overheads.
Standard Cost =	£50

This is based upon making 800 gearboxes per month.

Actual costs for July were as follows:
Direct Labour £16,200 (actually 2,700 hours were worked). Direct Materials £11,800 (actual price per kilo was £4). Overheads totally £8,250 (£7,800 were fixed). Only 720 gearboxes were produced.

Required
   (i) What is the master budget?
  (ii) What is the flexible budget?
 (iii) Produce a reconciled table of major variances *and*
 (iv) The Direct Labour and Direct Material sub-variances.

Answer
  (i) The master budget will be the standard quantity at the standard cost:

Master Budget (Quantity 800 Units)

	£
Direct Labour £20 × 800 =	16,000
Direct Materials £18 × 800 =	14,400
Variable Overheads £2 × 800 =	1,600
Fixed Overheads £10 × 800 =	8,000
TOTAL	£40,000

Fig. 146.

(ii) The flexible budget will be the master budget adjusted for the actual output along marginal costing lines (as you have not been told to the contrary, assume Direct Labour is variable):

Flexible Budget (Quantity 720 Units)

	£
Direct Labour £20 × 720 =	14,400
Direct Materials £18 × 720 =	12,960
Variable Overheads £2 × 720 =	1,440
Fixed Overheads NO CHANGE =	8,000
TOTAL	£36,800

Fig. 147.

(iii) The Table of Major Variances is now straightforward following the chart in Fig. 143; but you need to ensure the actual figures given to you are in the correct form. It is sensible therefore to schedule them neatly:

Actual Costs (Quantity 720)

	£
Direct Labour:	16,200
Direct Materials:	11,800
Variable Overhead:	450
Fixed Overhead:	7,800
Total	£36,250

Fig. 148.

Reconciled Table of Major Variances

	£	
TOTAL VARIANCE (Master Budget total £40,000/Actual Total £36,250)	= 3,750	(F)
QUANTITY VARIANCE (Master Budget total £40,000/Flexible Budget total £36,800)	= 3,200	(F)
DIRECT LABOUR VARIANCE (Actual £16,200/Flexible Budget £14,400)	= 1,800	(U)
DIRECT MATERIAL VARIANCE (Actual £11,800/Flexible Budget £12,960)	= 1,160	(F)
VARIABLE OVERHEAD VARIANCE (Actual £450/Flexible Budget £1,440)	= 990	(F)
FIXED OVERHEAD VARIANCE (Actual £7,800/Flexible Budget £8,000)	= 200	(F)
	£3,750	

Fig. 149.

(iv) The Direct Labour and Material sub-variances come last. Taking the Direct Labour ones first, it is necessary to break down the flexible budget and actual figures into their rate and hours components:

Flexible Budget Direct Labour:	£14,400
Standard Rate per hour:	£4
Therefore No. of hours budgeted:	14,400 ÷ 4
	= 3,600 HOURS

Actual Direct Labour:	£16,200
Actual hours worked:	2,700
Therefore Actual Rate per hour:	16,200 ÷ 2,700
	= £6 per hour

Now that the information is clear, follow the sub-variances rules:

Direct Labour Hours (efficiency) sub-variance:

Actual Hours:	2,700
Flexible Budget Hours:	3,600
HOURS SAVED	900

Hours Sub-variance = 900 × Standard Rate £4
= £3,600 (F)

Direct Labour Rate Sub-Variance:

Actual Rate	£6
Standard Rate	£4
EXTRA RATE	£2

Rate Sub-variance = £2 × Actual Hours 2,700
= £5,400 (U)
(Reconciliation: 3,600 (F) − 5,400 (U) = £1,800 (U) major variance.)

Next the components for the Direct Material sub-variances:

Flexible Budget Direct Materials:	£12,960
Standard Cost per kilo:	£3
Therefore kilos budgeted:	12,960 ÷ 3
	= 4,320 kilos

Actual Direct Materials:	£11,800
Actual Price per kilo:	£4
Therefore kilos actually used:	11,800 ÷ 4
	= 2,950 kilos

Again, now the information is clear the sub-variance rules are easy to follow:

Direct Material Usage Sub-Variance

Actual Amount Used	2,950 kilos
Flexible Budgeted Amount Used	4,320 kilos
KILOS SAVED	1,370 kilos

Usage Sub-variance = 1,370 × Standard Price £3
$$= £4,110 \ (F)$$

Direct Material Price Sub-Variance

Actual Price per kilo =	£4
Standard Price per kilo =	£3
EXTRA PRICE	£1

Price Sub-variance = £1 × Actual Amount used 2,950 kilos
$$= £2,950 \ (U)$$

(Reconciliation: £4,110 (F) − 2,950 (U) = 1,160 (F) Major Variance.)

That completes the answers to the question. It seems long because of the explanations included. In fact the whole system is very straightforward providing you have clearly grasped what each part of it shows. What would the management *learn* from the information produced in your answer though? Briefly, the following:

There has been a saving on output costs of £3,750 this month (i.e. a total variance of 3,750 (F)). However we would *expect* to save £3,200 anyway, because we made fewer items than planned (i.e. a quantity variance of 3,200 (F)). There were significant savings on Direct Materials and both variable and fixed overheads (as shown by their favourable major variances of D.M. 1,160 (F) V.O. 990 (F) and F.O. 200 (F)). There was a large overspending on Direct Labour of £1,800 (as shown by its 1,800 (U) variance).

Further light is shed on both the Direct Labour and Material major variances by their sub-variances. For Direct Labour this showed that the increase in rate (shown by a rate sub-variance of 5,400 (U)) had not been sufficiently offset by a decrease in hours worked (shown by an hours sub-variance of 3,600 (F)). By contrast in Direct Materials it showed that the more expensive materials bought (shown by a price sub-variance of 2,950 (U)) did result in a much lower amount having to be used (shown by a usage sub-variance of 4,110 (F)) an overall saving being made as a result.

I hope you agree that there is lots here for management to go on, which, remember, is the purpose of the exercise.

You should now be in a position to answer the questions in Part B at the end of the chapter.

REVENUE VARIANCES

This is the final part of the chapter, and you may be relieved to hear it is quite easy. Revenue (or sales) variances show the causes for the difference between actual and budgeted revenue (sales income). For instance the (master) budgeted revenue from shirt sales may be £12,000 per month, broken down as 1,000 shirts selling for £12 each. In principle there can only be two reasons for the actual revenue differing:

(i) More or fewer shirts actually sold: a *Quantity Variance* in other words.

(ii) A higher or lower actual price per shirt: a *Price Variance.*

If we had in fact sold 1,150 shirts for £11 each giving actual revenue of £12,650, the revenue variances are quite easy to construct.

The method is first to construct a Revenue Flexible Budget; that is the *expected* revenue from the actual quantity:

Actual Quantity × *Budgeted Price* = *Expected Revenue.*
1,150 shirts × £12 each   = £13,800 = Revenue Flexible Budget.

So put clearly we now have:

	£
Master Revenue Budget:	12,000
Flexible Revenue Budget:	13,800
Actual Revenue:	12,650

Fig. 150.

The *Total Revenue Variance* is the difference to be explained, i.e. the difference between Master Budget and Actual Revenue:

	£
Master Budget:	12,000
Actual:	12,650
Total Revenue Variance	£650 (F)

Fig. 151.

(Remember: with Revenues: F means *more* than budget, tending to increase profits;
U means *less* than budget, tending to reduce profits.)

The *Revenue Quantity Variance* is the difference between the master and flexible budgets and shows the *expected* difference in revenue as a result of having sold a different-from-master-budget number of shirts.

	£
Master Budget	12,000
Flexible Budget	13,800
Quantity Variance	£1,800 (F)

Fig. 152.

Finally the *Price Variance* is the difference between the Flexible Budget and the Actual revenue. Remember: both deal with the same number of shirts (i.e. 1,150) but one prices them at the standard and the other at actual selling price. So the difference between them is the Price Variance:

	£
Flexible Budget	13,800
Actual	12,650
Revenue Price Variance	£1,150 (U)

The table of Revenue Major Variances now is:

	£
Total Revenue Variance:	650 (F)
Quanity Variance:	1,800 (F)
Price Variance:	1,150 (U)
	£650 (F)

Fig. 153.

Management now know that the extra revenue has been gained by selling more shirts than planned (Quantity Variance of 1,800 (F)) but that to do this prices had to be reduced (Price Variance 1,150 (U)). Diagrammatically the Revenue Variances are worked out as follows:

Fig. 154.

REVENUE AND COST VARIANCES AND PROFIT VARIANCES

If you think about it, changes in costs and revenues must account for changes in profits. The cost total-variance and revenue total-variance show the differences between actual and master budgeted costs and revenues. Therefore they will reconcile with the difference between actual and master budgeted profits.

In our gearbox example, assume the master budget revenue was to sell 800 boxes for £60 each; and that we actually sold 720 for £65 each.

What are the revenue total variances? First tabulate the information:

		£
Master Budget:	800 × £60 =	48,000
Flexible Budget:	720 × £60 =	43,200
Actual:	720 × £65 =	46,800

Then the revenue variance reconciliation is straightforward:

		£
Total Revenue Variance	(48,000 − 46,800) =	1,200 (U)
Quantity Variance	(48,000 − 43,200) =	4,800 (U)
Price Variance	(43,200 − 46,800) =	3,600 (F)
		£1,200

Fig. 155.

If you refer to Figs. 146 and 148 you will find that the master budget costs were £40,000 and the actual costs 36,250 giving a total cost variance of £3,750 (F).

If you work across the table below you will see how the master budgeted profits, and actual profits give a profit variance which is the net of the two Total Variances:

	Master Budget	Actual	TOTAL VARIANCES
	£	£	£
Revenue	48,000	46,800	1,200 (U)
Costs	40,000	36,250	3,750 (F)
Profits	£8,000	£10,550	£2,550 (F)

Fig. 156.

Similarly if we assume the T.V. sets were budgeted to be sold for £160 and were actually sold for £150, we find:

	£
Master Budget Revenue of 1,400 sets × £160 =	224,000
Flexible Budget Revenue of 1,540 sets × £160 =	246,400
and Actual Revenue of 1,540 sets × £150 =	231,000

The Revenue variances for T.V. sales are therefore:

		£
Total T.V. Revenue Variance	(224,000 − 231,000) =	7,000 (F)
Quantity Variance	(224,000 − 246,400) =	22,400 (F)
Price Variance	(246,400 − 231,000) =	15,400 (U)
		£7,000 (F)

Fig. 157.

If you refer to the T.V. set example, in Figs. 134 and 136, they show Master Budget total costs of £172,690 and Actual total costs of £183,200. And a table of reconciled total and profits variances can be done once more:

	Master Budget	Actual	TOTAL VARIANCES
	£	£	£
Revenue	224,000	231,000	7,000 (F)
Costs	172,690	183,200	10,510 (U)
Profit	£51,310	£47,800	£3,510 (U)

Fig. 158.

You should now be in a position to complete all the remaining questions in Section C at the end of the chapter. However, before doing so read the last section which comments upon the system of standard costing from a number of standpoints.

PRACTICAL POINTS ABOUT STANDARD COSTING SYSTEMS

There are a number of problems in practice with standard costing. It is a very complicated system to operate, and requires large numbers of people to set the standards, record the data, and produce the variances. A product such as a car, with hundreds of components, sub-assemblies, and production operations (all of which need to have standard costs set) requires a small army of people to operate the standard costing system. Data collection of the actual costs is also often difficult and certainly time-consuming.

There is the further considerable problem of keeping standards up to date. Wage rates change frequently, methods of working change. A production manager is not going to refrain from buying a new machine which will increase output (but alter the standard cost) just because it would upset the accountants. New materials are often introduced which further outdate the standard. And a standard which is *not* an expression of what is being attempted, is of very little value.

These two factors, complication and the need for continuous up-dating of standards, mean the system is inevitably extremely expensive to operate. Finally, particularly with some of the more complicated forms of variance (not dealt with here) there is the danger that management are swamped with data they do not fully understand. Quite often information on speed of output is far better presented as (say): "Budget Output per hour 25,000 items; Actual Output per hour 23,000 items", than by terms that are hard to *really* understand such as: "overhead efficiency variance of 2,700 (U)".

Certainly the application of computers to store and adjust standard costs has greatly simplified the task of keeping them up to date. For instance when wage rates change, all standards can be updated quite easily. No one who has one would say computers that do this type of task were cheap though!

Remember, accounting is a practical subject and clarity is all-important. Cost accounting information is for managers to understand, not a beautiful system to appeal to the accountant's sense of numerical symmetry and elegance. In practice, particularly with standard costing and variance analysis; this must be remembered!

Finally, there is the inevitable problem which is part of any target setting process. Is the target correct? As already mentioned all the problems of setting budgetary targets apply to setting standard costs. A standard which is too low may guarantee inefficiency – not the intention, at all, of the system.

INTERPRETING VARIANCES

Variances must be interpreted with care. Whilst standard costing and variance analysis is excellent "direction finding apparatus" for management, it is not "reason-identifying apparatus" necessarily. For instance an unfavourable material major variance may be principally accounted for by a large unfavourable Usage sub-variance. However the *cause* of the over-usage may be nothing to do with faulty material. Perhaps a machine is consistently going wrong and ruining the material.

Management having identified a problem usually must find out the cause for themselves. It is important to be aware that problems which show themselves up as particular variances may be *caused* by quite different factors. An unfavourable labour hours variance *may* be caused by a lazy workforce; but equally could be caused by continuous machinery breakdowns or poor quality materials slowing down the job.

This doesn't lessen the value of standard costing; the system ensures managers know there is a problem, showing up as (say) a labour hours variance. It is the management's job *to identify the reason*, by going and looking at how the work is progressing. Both "alarm bell" and action are essential if a large complicated factory is to be controlled properly.

Further Learning

This chapter is only an introduction to the basis of standard costing and variance analysis. In particular there are many more complicated variances possible, depending on the type of work and product in view. For instance Mix and Yield variances show the effects of Direct Material "recipe" changes and waste percentage changes. Overhead efficiency and volume variances show the effects of over and under recovery of overheads resulting from non-standard hours and output speeds.

If you have understood this chapter and can work through the examples, you have made a sound start, and will be in a good position to go further into the subject if you need to.

SELF-ASSESSMENT QUESTIONS

PART A

* 1. The standard cost of the super-wash combination washer and dryer is:

	£
Direct Labour	27
Direct Materials	40
Fixed Overheads	33
Standard Cost	£100

This is based upon making 500 machines each month. In July the actual costs for the 450 machines made were: Direct Labour £13,000, Direct Material £17,200 and Fixed Overheads £15,400.

Produce the Master Budget, Flexible Budget and a reconciled table of major variances for July.

2. The standard cost of one Sno-Drive rear axle, based upon making 1,000 per month is:

		£
	Direct Labour:	18
Type 1	Direct Material:	15
Type 2	Direct Material:	25
	Fixed Overhead:	17
	Standard Cost	£75

The actual cost per unit for December, when 1,200 axles were made was:

		£
	Direct Labour:	17
Type 1	Direct Material:	18
Type 2	Direct Material:	21
	Fixed Overhead:	17
		£73

Produce the Master Budget, Flexible Budget and total actual costs for December, and a reconciled table of major variances.

3. The Master Budget for March's output of electric drills is:

Quantity	5,000 Drills
	£
Direct Labour	2,500
Direct Materials (i)	3,000
Direct Materials (ii)	4,000
Variable Overhead	1,000
Fixed Overhead	9,500
	£20,000

In March 4,750 Drills were actually made. Direct Labour is 20% variable. What is the Flexible Budget for March?

PART B

* 4. The Standard Cost of one barrel of cutting fluid has been set as follows:

	£	
Direct Labour	15	(£3 per hour × 5 hours)
Direct Materials	25	(£5 per kilo × 5 kilos)
Fixed Overhead	10	
Standard Cost	£50	

Actual output in week 29 was 840 barrels which was 40 barrels more than the standard output. Actual costs were Direct Labour £12,000, Direct Materials £22,200, and Fixed Overheads £9,200. The actual Direct Labour rate per hour was £4, and 7,400 kilos of material were actually used.

Produce a Master and Flexible Budget, a reconciled table of major variances, and the Direct Labour and Direct Material sub-variances.

5. The master budget for May's output of kitchen tables was:

Quantity	2,000	
	£	
Direct Labour	10,000	(Rate per hour = £5)
Direct Materials	14,400	(Price per kilo £6)
Variable Overhead	3,000	(10,000 kilowatts of power at £0·30 per kilowatt)
Fixed Overhead	7,000	
	£34,400	

(A) What is the standard cost per table?

(B) Actual Costs for May's production of 1,800 tables were: Direct Labour £9,400, Direct Materials £13,800, Variable Overhead £2,800, and Fixed Overhead £6,000. Actual Direct Labour hours worked were 2,350, Direct Materials actually cost £5 per kilo, and the electricity board reduced the cost of electricity unexpectedly to £0·25 per kilowatt.

Produce the flexible budget for May, a reconciled table of major variances, and the Direct Labour, Direct Material, and Variable Overhead sub-variances.

6. The Standard Cost of a bowser of detergent ready to leave the factory gates, *for Direct Labour and Direct Materials only is*:

    Material Type 1: 200 kilos × 40p per kilo =   £80
    Material Type 2: 400 kilos × 30p per kilo = £120
    Labour: 20 hours at 2·80 per hour = £56

Last week 1,020 bowsers were made and the actual costs were as follows:

    Material Type 1: £74,970 (214,200 kilos used)
    Material Type 2: £124,032 (387,600 kilos used)
    Labour: £55,080 (Actual Rate £3 per hour)

Calculate the flexible budgets for Direct Labour, Direct Material 1, and Direct Material 2, and the Major sub-variances for each of them.

7. The Durham Company produces one product.
You are given the following Budget information for one year.

Variable overhead	£150,000
Fixed overhead	£300,000
Normal activity	100,000 direct labour hours.

The standard costs per unit are:

	£
Direct Labour (5 hrs at £3·00)	15·00
„ Material (20 lbs at £1·00)	20·00

The actual results of April's operations were as follows:

Variable overhead	£11,000
Fixed overhead	£26,000
Actual activity	8,000 direct labour hours
Actual production	1,450 units
Actual labour costs	£25,600
Actual material costs (30,000 lb)	£33,000

You are required to compute cost variances and present a statement reconciling Standard costs and Actual costs.

8. The York Plastics Company produces a product for which the following standards per unit are given:

Direct Material 6 kilogrammes at £1·50 per kilogram
Direct Labour 4 hours at £1·60 per hour

In the month of May 1992, the following actual details were recorded:

Direct Materials
used 231,000 kilograms – total cost £378,000
Direct Labour
156,000 hours worked at a cost of £273,000
Actual output 38,000 UNITS.

There was no work in progress at the beginning or end of the month.
Calculate the following variances:

(i) direct materials price,
(ii) direct materials usage;
(iii) total material cost;
(iv) direct labour rate;
(v) direct labour efficiency (hours used);
(vi) total labour cost.

9. The Air Speed Company actually produced 21,000 units of product during the month of May.

Three cubic metres of material at a standard cost of £5·00 per cubic metre are required for each unit of product. The actual material purchased and used had a total cost of £330,000 and each metre of material cost £5·50. Each unit of product is budgeted to use 6 hours of labour time. The standard labour hourly rate is £7·00 an hour. The actual labour hourly rate paid was £6·80 and 5% more labour hours were used than budgeted. You are required to calculate the budgeted and actual labour and material costs, and to calculate the labour and material sub-variances.

10. The Quorn Manufacturing Company had two main products and for control purposes uses a flexible budgetary control system. The original budget and actual results for April are as follows:

	Original budget	Actual
Output in units		
A	1,200	1,000
B	800	1,000
Costs: Materials	6,600	6,650
Labour	14,000	16,800
Machining	9,600	9,450
Overheads	6,000	6,000
	36,200	38,900

Production details are as follows:

1. Material per unit – A 4 kilos; B 5 kilos.
2. Direct labour hours required per unit – A 1 hour; B 2 hours.
3. Machining costs include a variable element of £4 per machine hour. Machining time – A 0·5 hours; B 0·25 hours. The remainder is fixed.
4. Overhead costs include a variable element of £1 per direct labour hour worked. The remainder is fixed.

Construct the flexible budget and a table of major variances for April.

SECTION C

* 11. The Sales Budget of your factory calls for standard output of 5,000 radios per month to be sold for £15 each. In fact in April the output was 5,500 radios which were sold for £14 each.

(i) What is the master and flexible sales budget?
(ii) What is the Sales Total Variance?
(iii) What are the Sales Quantity and Price variances (which must reconcile to the total variance)?

12. Using the data in Question 5, the standard selling price for a kitchen table is £25. The tables made in May were actually sold for £22 each.

(i) Calculate the total Sales Variance, and the Sales Quantity Variance and Sales Price variance.

(ii) Calculate the budgeted profit, actual profit and profit variance for October, and reconcile the total Cost Variance and total sales variance to the profit variance.

13. Using the Data in Question 4, the standard selling price of a barrel of cutting fluid is £70. The 840 barrels actually made sold for £65 each.

(i) Calculate the Total Sales variance, and the Sales Quantity variance and Sales Price variance for week 29.

(ii) Calculate the actual and budgeted profits for week 29, the profit variance, and reconcile the Total Cost Variance and Total Sales variance to the profit variance.

14. The Bow-Jolly Wine Co. actually made 320 demijohns of wine in November, which were sold for £46 each. Fixed Factory Overheads totalled £4,300, Fixed selling overheads £2,000, and the cost of materials was £1,200 – which represented 4,800 kilos of grapes used. Labour costs totalled £3,900 at a rate of £3 per hour.

The standard costing system showed that 260 demijohns was the normal output and that the standard selling price was £50. Based on the normal output the standard cost of a demijohn was:

	£	
Direct Labour	12	(paid at £4 per hour)
Direct Materials	3	(material cost of £0·2 per kilo)
Fixed Factory Overheads	16	
Fixed Selling Overheads	10	
Standard Cost per Demijohn	£41	

You are required to produce (i) Master Budget and Flexible Budget for both Costs and Revenues. (ii) A reconciled table of major variances for costs and revenues. (iii) The Direct Labour and Direct Material subvariances. (iv) The budgeted and actual profit for November and the profit variance. (v) A statement reconciling the Total Cost and Total Revenue variances with the profit variance.

CHAPTER 9

CASH FLOWS AND WORKING CAPITAL

CHAPTER OBJECTIVES

Having studied this chapter you should be able to:

* EXPLAIN WHY CASH FLOW BUDGETING IS SO IMPORTANT TO A BUSINESS

* CONSTRUCT SIMPLE CASH FLOW BUDGETS

* EXPLAIN THE MEANING OF WORKING CAPITAL

* CONSTRUCT SIMPLE WORKING CAPITAL PROJECTIONS

* EXPLAIN THE IMPORTANCE OF CONTROLLING WORKING CAPITAL LEVELS AND THE EFFECT OF CREDITOR, STOCK, AND DEBTOR LEVEL CHANGES, ON CASH BALANCES

THE IMPORTANCE OF CASH

The first duty of any manager is to ensure that the business survives. There is an old and true saying, that anyone can manage a business in boom times, it is those managers who survive a recession who can really manage. Understanding how to sensibly manage cash is of the first importance; because a business will always keep going unless it runs out of it.

It is even possible for a business to be profitable, yet to run out of cash. If by trading a firm makes £10,000, and then spends £25,000 on new machinery, it will *spend* £15,000 more than it earns, for example. Equally a firm that is losing £1,000 per month can go on trading for a long time if it has £1,000,000 in the bank to start with!

The vital point to understand is that firms must not run out of money if they want to remain in business. When they do run out of money, the workforce can't be paid, stocks can't be bought, expenses can't be paid, and the whole business is forced to stop, whether it wants to or not.

The planning (budgeting) of cash payments (outflows of cash from the business) and cash receipts (inflows of cash into the business) is therefore of very great importance. In a logical sequence (i) the management make their operational plans, as outlined in Chapter 7 on budgeting, then (ii) the cash flow budget is constructed which shows the *cash consequences* of these plans. If the cash consequences are such that the firm runs out of money at a crucial stage – the plans can be changed or borrowing facilities arranged.

The budgeting of cash involves two important factors:

    (i) HOW MUCH is flowing in and flowing out
and (ii) WHEN it is flowing in and out.

As a result cash flow budgets break down a year's cash movements into monthly slices. In this way the *timing* of cash movements is made absolutely clear, and the embarrassment of running out of money can be avoided. For instance, when first done the cash flow may show a large payment to be made in July which would necessitate an overdraft, and a large receipt due in August which would more than cover the previous month's payment. It is probably a simple matter (once the potential problem is clearly shown by the cash budget) to re-schedule the payment to August, so that no overdraft is necessary.

Without doubt the best form of layout for a cash flow budget is that shown in Fig. 159 opposite:

	Aug	Sept.	Oct.	Nov.	Dec.
Inflows					
Sales					
Total Inflows	W				
Outflows					
Wages					
Materials					
Power					
Rent					
Advertising					
Fuel					
Capital Expenditure					
Total Outflows	X				
Monthly Surplus (Deficit)	W−X				
Balance Brought Forward	Y				
Final Balance	Z				

Fig 159.

It works as follows. Each month the total inflows are added up to give sub-total W. The outflows are added up to give sub-total X. The monthly "surplus/deficit" sub-total (W minus X) shows how the cash balance will be affected *by that particular month's cash movements.* The balance brought forward Y, is the cash balance at the start of the month. So the month's opening cash Y, adjusted for the monthly surplus or deficit (W minus X) will give the projected final balance at the end of the month, Z. Next month's balance brought forward is last month's final balance.

CONSTRUCTING A CASH FLOW

To illustrate the layout further, imagine you have been given the following data and been asked to construct a cash flow for the four months July, August, September, October:

(A) Sales each month are as follows; *but all are on credit and we are paid one month after the sale month.*

Sales Month	June	July	August	September	October
Amount £	1,000	1,500	2,000	1,300	1,200
Cash Received £		1,000	1,500	2,000	1,300

Note it is the month in which the cash is *received* which is important from the cash flow point of view. We will actually *receive* June's sales money in July, because debtors pay a month after the sale. Therefore £1,000 is our July inflow.

(B) Wages each month are as follows, and are paid in the month:

Wages Month	July	August	September	October
Amount £	250	300	300	280
Cash Paid £	250	300	300	280

(C) Purchases of stocks were as follows; *but are paid for two months after purchase*:

Purchase Month	May	June	July	August	September	October
Amount £	400	500	470	510	420	440
Payment Made £			400	500	470	510

Note, because we don't pay for May's purchase of stock until July, May's purchases form July's cash outflow. Similarly September and October's purchases will not appear on the cash flow because they are not paid for until after October, which is as far as the budget is going.

(D) Six months rent of £700 is payable in July:

Rent Month	July
Amount £	700
Payment Month £	700

(E) We wish to purchase a new machine for £6,000 in August which will have to be paid for in September.

Machine Purchase Month	August	September
Amount £	6,000	
Payment Month £		6,000

(F) Other expenses run at £180 per month, paid in the month incurred:

Expense Month	July	August	September	October
Amount £	180	180	180	180
Payment Month £	180	180	180	180

Now we have clearly scheduled both the transactions and the payment months, it is very quick and easy to fill in the cash flow table, shown in Fig. 160. Assume the opening balance is £4,700. Make sure you follow through each entry and understand the way the balances are carried forward:

Narrative	July	August	September	October
Inflows	£	£	£	£
Sales	1,000	1,500	2,000	1,300
Other	—	—	—	—
Total Inflows	1,000	1,500	2,000	1,300
Outflows				
Wages	250	300	300	280
Purchases	400	500	470	510
Rent	700	—	—	—
Expenses	180	180	180	180
Machine			6,000	
Total Outflows	1,530	980	6,950	970
Monthly Surplus (Deficit)	(530)	520	(4,950)	330
Balance Brought Forward	4,700	4,170	4,690	(260)
Final Balance	4,170	4,690	(260)	70

Fig. 160.

What does management learn from this cash flow forecast? The firm is making money in August and October, and suffering a net outflow in July and September, because of the large payments in those months. However only in September will it need overdraft facilities because the *final balance* shows a negative position only in that month. The management now have a clear statement showing them the cash movements of the business, and have plenty of warning that they need to make arrangements for an overdraft in September. Alternatively they could negotiate with the machine manufacturer to spread the payments evenly: £3,000 in September and £3,000 in October. If you re-do those months for this change you will find that an overdraft is now unnecessary. This shows that WHEN payments are made is just as important as HOW MUCH is paid, in terms of ensuring a business does not run out of money.

More importantly, it shows how a clear cash flow statement allows managers to (A) understand the cash-consequences of their plans and (B) take sensible action as a result. This, remember, is the point of all cost accounting – to help managers make sensible decisions about the running of their businesses.

MONITORING ACTUAL PERFORMANCE

Once the cash flow forecast has been finalised, it is used like any other budget to keep track of actual expenditure. Usually an extra blank column is included by each month's forecast column and the actual figures are inserted there. So in our example we would have July Actual, August Actual, September Actual and October Actual columns alongside each month's forecast column. If the cash available is not as predicted, the comparisons will show up why. Perhaps a sale hasn't been made, or more stock has been purchased than intended – the comparison will show it up. Managers are sure to have their attention drawn (i) to the fact that cash levels are not as planned (and they can take action if necessary to alter their plans) and (ii) to the *reason* why they are not as planned (and they can take action about this too if necessary).

You should now be in a position to answer the questions in Part A at the end of the chapter.

WORKING CAPITAL

This is essentially a Balance Sheet concept, and you need to study Foundation Financial Accounting to understand it fully. What follows is an introduction to the principle of the subject only.

Working Capital is the name given to the value of Stocks, Debtors and Cash held by a business:

(i) STOCKS

This includes stocks of raw materials, work in progress (i.e. the value of partly-finished work or goods) and stocks of unsold finished goods.

NOTE: Every business has to tie up money in stocks otherwise it doesn't have anything to sell. Even a small corner shop may well have £10,000 worth of goods on its shelves and in its store-room. Service businesses such as doctors and solicitors partnerships tend to have quite low stocks; but even they have some, stationery, stamps, and files for instance.

(ii) DEBTORS

This means goods which have been sold; but for which the firm has not been paid.

NOTE: Most businesses have debtors. Apart from shops (which may have a few) practically all businesses grant a period of credit to their customers. A £500 sale may be made in July; but the money doesn't come in until September, for instance. Therefore from July until September there is a debt of £500 due to the business; which is another £500 which needs to be funded by the business on top of the stock on the shelf.

(iii) CASH

The problem from most points of view when dealing with working capital comes from cash. There are several points about cash levels. (i) There is a minimum amount of cash a firm needs to hold to pay wages, expenses, supply cash floats and so on, before cash from sales starts to roll in. (ii) As well as this minimum cash level, there can be extra cash generated as a result of trading profitably, or as a result of selling off some non-trading item such as a now-unused factory.

WORKING CAPITAL PROJECTIONS

Quite often people are asked to produce working capital projections. By this is meant an estimate of the amount of money that will be needed to buy stocks, finance debtors, and, *it must be assumed* provide the minimum amount of cash thought necessary. Why I say "it must be assumed" is because the projected cash levels will immediately start to increase when profitable trading starts. For instance imagine we want to start a market stall, and decide we need £2,000 of stocks and £100 cash float. Our working capital needs are therefore:

	£
Stocks	2,000
Debtors	—
Cash	100
Working Capital	£2,100

Fig. 161.

So when we start to trade we will need to have £2,100 ready. We buy the stock with £2,000, and keep £100 as a necessary cash float for odd expenses.

If after our first week we have sold half the stock for £1,500. The position now is:

	£	
Stocks	1,000	(half have been sold)
Debtors	—	
Cash	1,600	(our original £100 plus the money from the sales)
Working Capital	£2,600	

Fig. 162.

Immediately our working capital has changed. We now have £500 more than we did when we started. This £500 represents the profit we have made on the first week's sales, and strictly speaking is not *necessary* working capital. For instance it would be quite possible to pay ourselves the extra £500 without damaging our ability to pay for more stock.

Therefore any working capital projection must be stated AT A GIVEN TIME. This is essential because from one time to the next (in our example from the first week to the next) the working capital a business has (i.e. its stock, debtor, and cash levels) will change.

GROSS AND NET WORKING CAPITAL

So far we have been assuming that the owners of the business will have to provide all the working capital the business needs. In our previous market stall example the addition of stocks, debtors and cash came to £2,100, which is in fact the GROSS working capital required by the business at the start.

However it could be that the supplier of the stock allowed us more generous payment terms than "cash with goods". Imagine he said we could pay for half straightaway and half of them after one month. In this case we would have a creditor (i.e. someone to whom we owe money) of £1,000, and as a consequence could start trading with *less money than before*:

	£
The gross working capital remains the same:	2,100
less Amount due to Creditor:	1,000
Net Working Capital	£1,100

Now we can start trading with £1,100. At the start (i.e. at Day 1) this is our net working capital requirement.

When there are debtors, and wages to pay, the position is slightly more complicated. Consider the following illustration of a shop wishing to expand and open a freezer section. The plans are outlined below in the numbered paragraphs.

1. Extra initial stocks of frozen food will be needed at a cost of £4,000 – payable *half on delivery and half in month 2*. Thereafter any deliveries will be paid for one month later. Assume stocks are topped up on the last day of the month.

2. Monthly Sales of £2,000 of goods at cost, £3,000 at selling prices, are projected. That is a mark up of 50% on cost.

3. Of the sales, £2,100 will be for cash and £900 to a local hotel who will pay two months after they receive the goods.

4. Weekly wages for a new assistant will be £75.

5. A float of £200 is required in the till.

What will be the working capital position of the business at the end of month 2?

Solution

(A) *Stocks:* This is quite straightforward – the stocks will remain at the level of £4,000, because we will always replace them on the last day of the month.

(B) *Debtors:* A schedule makes it clear what the position will be:

	Month 1	Month 2	Month 3	Month 4
	£	£	£	£
Additions to Debtors	900	900	900	900
Add Balance B/F	—	900	1,800	1,800
less PAYMENTS RECEIVED	—	—	(900)	(900)
Closing Debtor Balance	£900	£1,800	£1,800	£1,800

Fig. 163.

In month 3 we are paid for month 1 sales, in month 4 for month 2 sales, and so on. At any one time we are owed two months sales = £1,800.

(C) *Cash:* The only certain way to be sure what the cash position will be is to construct a mini cash-flow which you should already know how to do:

	Month 1	Month 2	Month 3
	£	£	£
Inflows			
Cash Sales	2,100	2,100	2,100
Debtor receipts	—	—	900
INFLOW TOTAL	2,100	2,100	3,000
Outflows			
Stock Payments	2,000	4,000*	2,000
Wages	300	300	300
Float	200	—	—
TOTAL OUTFLOWS	2,500	4,300	2,300
Surplus (Deficit)	(400)	(2,200)	700
Balance B/F	—	(400)	(2,600)
FINAL BALANCE	£(400)	£(2,600)	£(1,900)

Fig. 164.

So a £2,600 overdraft will be needed at the end of month 2. Put another way the owner would need £2,600 to begin with to avoid an overdraft being necessary.

(D) *Creditors:* It is easiest to schedule the creditor movements to ensure that no mistakes are made:

	Month 1	Month 2	Month 3
	£	£	£
Balance B/F	—	4,000	2,000
Initial Stocks	4,000	—	—
Add month end top up	2,000	2,000	2,000
	6,000	6,000	4,000
less Payments	(2,000)	(4,000)*	(2,000)
Closing Creditor	£4,000	£2,000	£2,000

Fig. 165.

* Note this payment is for the second part of the initial delivery, and the end of month 1 top-up.

Now the working capital position at the end of month 2 is easily produced:

	£	£
Stocks		4,000
Debtors		1,800
Cash Float		200
Gross Working Capital		6,000
less Creditors	2,000	
Overdraft	2,600	
		4,600
Net Working Capital		£1,400

Fig. 166.

What does this really tell anyone? First, that either an overdraft of £2,600 is needed, or that £2,600 must be ready in advance to pay the bills. Obviously this is no more than a cash flow itself shows. Second, working capital projections are useful as budgets for stock and debtor figures. If the actual stock figure goes higher than that projected, then extra cash will be used up to finance those stocks which may result in a cash shortage. Therefore projected stock and debtor levels are an important yardstick for management to measure stocks and debtor levels against. This aspect is discussed more fully in the next section of the chapter.

The interesting thing is, who provided the net working capital of £1,400? It is clear who provided the rest – either the bank or the supplier of the stock.

The £1,400 has not had to be found by the owner. It has been financed by profits. Profits are the difference between Sales and Expenses and represent the resources the business has generated for itself:

	£
Two Months Sales =	6,000
Expenses	£
Stock Used	4,000
Wages	600
	4,600
Profit Made	£1,400

Fig. 167.

For those of you who are also studying financial accounts, the balance sheet for this enterprise at the end of month 2 is:

	£		£
Profit	1,400	Stocks	4,000
Creditors	2,000	Debtors	1,800
Overdraft	2,600	Cash Float	200
	£6,000		£6,000

Fig. 168.

Anyone who can do double entry book-keeping will find working capital projections are very easy to do. You just fill in the transactions in "T" account form and take out the balances at the appropriate date. Those of you not studying book-keeping will just have to rely on the scheduling method shown in this chapter.

The important point to remember is that the working capital position of a business will alter from one time to another as trading goes on and profits are made. Therefore be sure that when you are doing a projection you *know what the projected date is*.

CONTROLLING WORKING CAPITAL

Extremely large sums are tied up in working capital. In our last example either £2,600 needs to be borrowed (e.g an overdraft) or the owners must provide £2,600 of their own money to finance the expanded shop. In a small business quite large sums are involved. In a large business the sums involved run into millions very quickly. Take a shop like Marks & Spencer in the U.K.: the value of unsold stock in their stores is enormous, and it has to be financed by somebody. Similarly, large trading companies like Unilever, are owed millions by their customers.

Therefore the control of working capital is a crucial objective for all managements. If Stocks go above the targeted levels for instance, presuming the creditor and debtor figures do not change, the cash level must drop. In our shop example, if the supplier was *only* prepared to extend credit of £2,000 and we wanted stocks of £5,000 at the end of Month 2, how could we get them? Answer, only by paying him cash for them, in which case the working capital figure would be:

	£			£	
		Stocks		5,000	(+ £1,000)
Creditors	2,000	Debtors		1,800	
Overdraft	3,600	(+ £1,000)	Cash Float	200	
	£5,600			£7,000	

Fig. 169.

An extra £1,000 needs to be borrowed (or to be available if we are supplying it from our own resources). Clearly therefore, keeping stocks and debtors to their budgeted levels is important for the cash-management of the business.

Controlling working capital means three things in principle:

1. Ensuring stocks are not above the planned levels.
2. Ensuring debtors do in fact pay when they have agreed to.
3. Ensuring creditors are not paid before the business has agreed to pay them.

Figure 169 illustrated what happens to the overdraft if stocks go up by £1,000. Equally if debtors pay more slowly than they should, cash will not reach the planned levels either. Refer to the mini cash-flow in Fig. 164. The month 3 overdraft should drop to £1,900, because the first debtor payment of £900 comes into the inflow side of the cash flow. What if the debtor *didn't* pay us in month 3? The overdraft would in reality go up at the end of the month. So it is crucial to cash levels that debtors pay on time.

Creditors work similarly. Of the gross working capital of £6,000 at the end of month 2 (Fig. 166) £2,000 of it is supplied by the creditor who has given us stocks and not been paid for them. If we were suddenly not allowed any credit, and had to immediately pay the creditor, the only way to do so would be to increase the overdraft by £2,000. So again, if creditors are paid more quickly than they should be, cash levels will drop as a result.

Therefore control of working capital centres on the three principles outlined above. And this control is vital because running out of cash spells disaster for all businesses.

In principle, and very much in outline, how are the elements of working capital controlled?

Obviously there are the monthly budgeted levels of stocks, debtors and creditors which are the broad control. However, in detail, managements usually install the following types of control mechanisms:

STOCK CONTROL

In Chapter 3 simple stock-cards were illustrated. Most businesses will set maximum stock levels item by item, to ensure that over-ordering cannot occur by mistake. Often stock-movement charts are produced to show which items of stock are selling or being used and which are not. Those stock items which are not being used can be sold off, and "stops" can be put on them to ensure no more are ordered.

Call off arrangements with suppliers can be negotiated whereby stocks will be delivered, guaranteed, within (say) 72 hours of order. In this way it may only be necessary to carry (say) one week's material requirements in stock. If deliveries are only made once a month, then stock levels must be much higher, because 4 or 5 weeks requirements must be held.

There is of course a tension here between the need to tie up the smallest amount of money possible in stock, and the need to provide a service for your customers. No one shops in a shop with empty shelves remember! Stock control is a whole subject on its own, which needs thoroughly studying if your work involves you in working capital control.

DEBTORS

Detailed debtor control starts by ensuring you only deal with customers who will be *able* to pay. A bad debt means you have given the goods away. Therefore these days most firms require references, and an up to date set of accounts, to prove a business' ability (and inclination) to pay for the goods they have received from suppliers.

Thereafter the control consists of ensuring that (A) you notice when a debtor doesn't pay you on time, and, (B) you quickly inform the customer that you have noticed and ask for payment. (A) requires a good debtor's ledger system which automatically "throws up" overdue accounts. Computerised systems have greatly helped this to be achieved: in goes the intended credit period for a customer, e.g. 45 days, and automatically (say) 60 days later if the amount is unpaid, it is printed out as overdue. Overdue payment tabulations are a great feature of all computer salesmen's pitches to prospective customers! (B) Consists usually of a series of letters (each more threatening than the last). Often overlooked (in textbooks at least!) is the telephone, which is by far the best way of 'getting money out of customers" – the official name for which is "Credit Control". A telephone call works wonders usually, and often gives less offence than a letter.

If a business has a good credit controller with a good telephone manner – quite often a long-distance friendship is struck up with an opposite number in the customer's accounts department. This can do wonders for credit control!

Again there is a tension between the need to be paid (to preserve cash levels) and the need not to annoy your customers. People pretty quickly become annoyed with suppliers who are always moaning for cash. Therefore credit control needs to be tactfully done. In reality a 30 day credit period usually gets to nearly 60 before anyone gets really difficult about non-payment.

CREDITORS

In the main computerised systems have made it easier to ensure creditor payments are not made too quickly. A list of "amounts due for payment" works in a similar way to an "overdue debtors" list. The machine throws up a list of accounts that have fallen due. In our example of the shop, it would show (see Fig. 165) £4,000 as due for payment in month 2 and £2,000 in month 3, for example.

In many firms the policy is "Pay nobody until they scream". In other words payments are made as slowly as possible in order to preserve cash. In either case a proper system which records amounts due and shows clearly *when* they are due is essential. Managements need to be informed – the decisions they make are up to them. It must be stated though, that a business which pays slowly may have difficulties in finding suppliers. Much depends on the competitive position, and on whether the supplier is confident of receiving the money due eventually, even if late. The art of it is to pay as slowly as possible without upsetting your suppliers unduly! Again the personal touch is imporatnt. If people like you, they'll let you pay more slowly – it's just human nature!

You should now be in a position to answer the questions in Part B at the end of the chapter.

SELF-ASSESSMENT QUESTIONS

SECTION A

* 1. Simon Brown has decided to start a business selling his "Simon the Pieman" pies. He gives you the following information.

(i) He will start the business with £30,000 of capital to be paid into the bank on 1 January 1984.

(ii) Also on 1 January he will buy for cash the following fixed assets: Kitchen Premises £15,000, Machinery £5,000 and a delivery van £4,000.

(iii) He will employ two people for a salary of £250 per month each from 1 February.

(iv) Usage of materials are as follows and materials are paid for in the month following use.

Jan.	Feb.	March	April	May	June
£1,000	£2,500	£2,200	£2,900	£3,500	£4,000

(v) Sales, all paid for in cash at time of purchase, are forecast to be:

Feb.	March	April	May	June
£3,500	£3,300	£4,000	£4,500	£5,300

(vi) Fixed expenses of £230 per month are anticipated and payable two months in arrears.

(vii) Brown will sub-let part of the Kitchen space to Muffit for £1,800 per year, payable monthly.

(viii) Brown will pay himself a salary of £200 per month.

(ix) The rates are £2,000 per annum, paid half yearly in March and September.

Produce a suitable cash flow budget for the six months to 30 June 1984 to clearly show S. Brown his cash position each month.

2. Your company, the Sharp Shirt Company, has made the following plans for the immediate future:

(a) Production in Shirts:

April	May	June	July	Aug.	Sept.	Oct.	Nov.
400	460	540	700	640	560	500	420

(b) Direct materials cost £3 per shirt, paid the month after manufacture.

(c) Labour costs are £4 per shirt paid in the same month as the shirts are made.

(d) Variable Overhead is £2 per shirt paid *half* in the month of production and *half* in the following month.

(e) Fixed overhead costs are £1,000 per month.

(f) Sales revenue is £15 per shirt. All production is sold; but revenue is not received until the second month after manufacture.

(g) New machinery costing £5,000 will be paid for in July.

At 1 June the cash balance was £12,000. You are required to produce a cash flow for the business for the months June, July, August, September and October.

3. Your firm has been sub-contracted to produce a special shield to protect users of hospital X-ray equipment from harmful effects. The details of the scheme are:

(1) Machinery costing £125,000 will be purchased specially for this work. Delivery is in January, payment in March.

(2) Two eight hour shifts per day are planned, 5 days per week. Each shift would consist of 5 people being paid £4 per hour each. Wages are paid in the week they are earned.

(3) One months training (in January) will be necessary before production starts in February.

(4) Power consumption will be £600 per month normally; but only £300 per month in the training month, payable quarterly.

(5) Raw materials for one month's output of 400 shields will cost £2,000 payable one month after use in production. £3,000 of materials will be used in training.

Assume four week months in all your calculations:

REQUIRED: The firm wishes to recover the cost of the machine within 2 years in selling prices, and to make a profit of 25% on total costs incurred. (A) How much will the selling price have to be per shield? (B) Produce a cash flow for the first six months of the project (assume 4 week months). It is estimated that the customer will pay one month after delivery. The first delivery of 400 shields will be made in March, and thereafter monthly.

4. On 1st January 1992 a company has a favourable bank balance of £20,000. The budgeted operating statement for the next six months are as follows.

	JAN £	FEB £	MAR £	APRIL £	MAY £	JUNE £
SALES	168,000	192,000	200,000	216,000	216,000	240,000
Production Expenses						
Purchases	68,000	76,000	80,000	84,000	84,000	92,000
Labour	36,000	42,000	42,000	44,000	44,000	46,000
Overheads	24,000	30,000	30,000	32,000	32,000	34,000
COST OF PRODUCTION	128,000	148,000	152,000	160,000	160,000	172,000
− Increase + Decrease in stock of Finished Goods	−4,000	−4,000	−4,000	—	—	+8,000
Cost of Goods Sold	124,000	144,000	148,000	160,000	160,000	180,000
Administration	16,000	16,000	16,000	18,000	18,000	18,000
Selling and Distribution	12,000	12,000	12,000	14,000	14,000	14,000
Total Expenses	152,000	172,000	176,000	192,000	192,000	212,000
PROFIT	16,000	20,000	24,000	24,000	24,000	28,000

Materials purchased are paid for in the month following usage. Purchases used in December 1991 amounted to £64,000.

On average, half the debtors pay their accounts the month after being invoiced and half the subsequent month. Sales for November 1991 and December 1991 were £176,000 and £160,000 respectively. Manufacturing overheads include depreciation at £4,000 per month. Payment for labour and overheads is to be made in the month in which they are incurred.

Payment of Corporation Tax £40,000 is due in January and the capital budget provides for a payment of £40,000 in March and £20,000 in June. Prepare a cash budget for the first six months of 1992.

5. Fieldhead Plastics Ltd. manufactures moulded containers. In April the company approached its bank with the object of raising a loan of £200,000. The bank agreed that subject to a satisfactory cash budget they would grant the loan from 1st May at an interest rate of 12% per annum, payable monthly. To prepare the cash budget the company has available the following information:

(A) Stock of finished goods on 1st April was 48,000 containers. The finished goods stock at the end of each month is to be maintained at 20% of sales of the following month. There is no work-in-progress.

(B) Sales were budgeted at 240,000 containers per month. Selling price is £4 per container. Sales are invoiced on the fifteenth and the last day of each month and the payment terms are 2% discount if paid within 10 days. It is expected that sales will be even throughout the month and 50% of customers pay within the discount period. The remainder pay at the end of 30 days, except for bad debts which usually average ½% of each months' gross sales.

(C) The stock of raw materials on 1st April was 45,600 kilos. At the end of each month, the raw material stock is to be maintained at not less than 40% of production requirements for the following month. Purchases of each month are paid in the next month without discount.

(D) Manufacturing overheads and selling and administrative overheads are paid on the tenth of the month following the month in which incurred. Selling expenses average 10% of gross sales and administrative expenses total £66,000 per month.

(E) Wages are paid on the fifteenth and the last day of each month for the period ending on the date of payment.

(F) The standard manufacturing cost of a plastic container, based on an average production of 200,000 containers per month, is

Direct Materials ½ Kilo	£1·00
Direct Labour	£1·20
Variable Overhead	£0·60
Fixed Overhead	£0·30
	£3·10

(G) The bank balance on 1st May is expected to be an overdraft of £72,600.

Using the information above produce a cash budget for the month of May.

SECTION B

* 6. The Ace manufacturing company is considering making a new type of automatically-temperature stabilised bath tap, which would ensure baths of the exact pre-set temperature always being run.

The output per month would be 700 taps, and the materials would cost £12 per tap. It would be necessary to have a minimum of one month's materials always in stock, and material deliveries would be made only on the first day of the month. Payment is due in the month after the delivery month. The wages for the tap-making section are £2,100 per month. A permanent cash float of £150 is needed also. Variable overheads are £180 per month for the tap making section and are payable 2 months after they are incurred. Fixed overheads are £170 per month also payable 2 months in arrears.

Ace Manufacturing have agreed to sell all of their output to Heels, a well known chain store for £20 per tap; however Heels will only pay two months after delivery.

Manufacture will start on 1 April and the deliveries to Heels start in May when the first month's output will be delivered.

What will be the working capital position of Ace Manufacturing at the end of August? Note: delivery of the August output will not have been made at the end of August, and finished goods are valued at Factory Cost of Production.

7. Output of the "sheer-beauty" jersey will begin on 1 September. At that date three months raw materials will be delivered. Monthly output of jerseys will be 5,000. Material cost is £1·80 per jersey, and the supplier is to be paid one month after delivery. Thereafter further deliveries will be monthly, of one month's material requirements, starting 1 November.

Sales will start on 1 November when 10,000 will be delivered to customers, thereafter monthly deliveries of 5,000 jerseys will be made. Labour costs per jersey are £1·90 payable in the month of production. The overheads are £4,500 per month, and the selling price is £6 per jersey. All customers will pay 1 month after delivery. Overheads will be paid for 2 months after they are incurred.

What is the predicted working capital position of the sheer-beauty jersey at the end of January, four months after production began? Finished goods are valued at cost of production.

8. Consider the following statement of the Norticat Co.'s working capital at 1 August 1984:

		£
Stocks		17,000
Debtors		14,000
Cash		2,000
		33,000
less Creditors	£15,000	
Net Working Capital		£18,000

Alter up the statement of working capital for each of these *separate, unconnected,* possibilities. (Assume overdraft facilities are available):

(i) Stocks need to be £8,000 higher; but the creditors will not allow any increase in the amount owed to them.

(ii) You collect £3,000 from various debtors.

(iii) You pay your supplier £5,000 of the amount due; but also have delivered stock worth £4,000.

(iv) You sell goods in stock at £3,000 for £4,000, payment to be in 1 months time.

(v) You sell goods in stock at £1,000 for £1,400, cash sale.

(vi) You collect £5,000 from your debtors; pay your supplier £6,000, and pay wages £800.

CHAPTER 10

CAPITAL INVESTMENT APPRAISAL

CHAPTER OBJECTIVES

Having studied this chapter you should be able to:

* EXPLAIN THE BUSINESS MEANING OF THE TERM "CAPITAL INVESTMENT"

* BRIEFLY OUTLINE THE DATA-COLLECTION NECESSARY BEFORE ALTER-
NATIVE CAPITAL PROJECTS CAN BE EVALUATED – AND COMMENT ON THE
IMPORTANCE OF DATA RELIABILITY

* LIST AND SIMPLY ILLUSTRATE THE METHODS MOST COMMONLY USED TO
CHOOSE BETWEEN COMPETING ALTERNATIVE CAPITAL PROJECTS

* APPLY EACH METHOD TO SIMPLE EXAMPLES

* COMMENT ON THE USEFULNESS OF EACH METHOD

* EXPLAIN AND SIMPLY ILLUSTRATE THE IMPORTANCE OF SENSITIVITY AN-
ALYSIS TO PROJECT APPRAISAL

THE MEANING OF CAPITAL INVESTMENT

In the last chapter we used the example of a shop opening a new freezer section to illustrate how working capital needs increase when a business expands. Possibly you realised there was no reference to buying the actual freezer chests themselves – which clearly would be necessary. This brings us to the important distinction (particularly important in financial accounts) between **Revenue Expenditure** and **Capital Expenditure**.

Revenue Expenditure has already been dealt with in our working capital examples. It means money spent on such things as Rent, Insurance, Wages, Stocks, Electricity, Telephones – all the day to day expenses of running a business.

Capital Expenditure refers to the money needed to buy the lasting things a business will use for a number of years. Money spent on Buildings, Cars, Trucks, Machinery (freezer chests) Office Furniture and Shop Fittings – all of which last for several years – is called *Capital Expenditure*. The technical term for this type of "lasting thing" a business uses is a FIXED ASSET. A proper cash flow includes *both* capital and revenue expenditure of course; the "mini-cash flow" done for the purposes of predicting working capital needs, only includes revenue expenditure.

Although working capital involves substantial sums, often Capital Expenditure involves much larger ones. More importantly once a business has bought a particular type of freezer chest (for example) it is stuck with it. Usually selling fixed assets early on in their useful lives, rather than getting the value out of them by using them over a long period, results in substantial losses. (Think how much a new car drops in price after only a few months use.) Therefore businesses must be very careful to ensure they do not make mistakes with capital expenditure, that is they try to ensure the money is spent in the best possible way.

CAPITAL INVESTMENT APPRAISAL refers to the techniques used to help decide "the best possible way". Usually there are alternatives, certainly in our shop expansion there would be various possibilities:

: Do we rent or buy the new premises?
: Do we buy 6 Rolls Royce type freezer chests for £400 each which last 10 years; or do we buy 6 medium quality ones which last 6 years at £300 each?

In large manufacturing businesses the alternatives are incredibly numerous. Does British Petroleum buy coal mines or cosmetic companies when it wants to expand into areas other than oil? There is only so much money available – on which capital project is it to be spent?

Well, we are only dealing with simple examples, thank goodness; but it is important for you to understand in principle the stages that have to be gone through, before the choice between alternative capital investments can be made.

COLLECTING THE DATA

Take the shop expansion example – the owner does not have to expand by opening a freezer centre. It could be children's clothes, a newsagency, a butchers shop, a hardware store and so on. The owner has only enough money for *one* expansion though. What type of data will be needed before choosing? Let's say the owner fancies only one of these three: Freezer centre, butchers shop or newsagency: what will he try to find out (i.e. predict) about each before choosing?

(1) DEMAND: The level of trade, likely selling prices and therefore likely weekly sales revenue will be first on the list – no sales, no business remember.

(2) TRADING COSTS: Assistants' wages will be higher for a skilled butcher than for a check-out assistant at a freezer centre. The price of the stock, level of stock and therefore the working capital required will be important. Stock deterioration must be allowed for. It will be higher in a butcher's shop than in a freezer centre. The *rate* at which stock will be sold is an important factor. A hardware shop may have a much slower turnover than a freezer centre, for instance.

The amount of credit available from the suppliers of each type of stock is another important consideration. There will, in this example, be certain common revenue expenses – rates, rent, insurances, heating for instance. But there may be certain overheads which vary between alternatives. Electricity costs are going to be much higher for the butcher/freezer alternatives than for the hardware shop, for instance.

All this will have to be predicted before a working capital projection could be done, and trading costs estimated.

(3) CAPITAL COSTS. A butcher's shop requires an enormous walk-in cold store to be installed. A hardware shop needs masses of racking and shelving, a freezer centre large refrigerated chests and a cold store for reserve stocks. The costs and payment terms of this equipment will need to be predicted.

When all of this is done the owner will be in a position to produce a cash flow forecast for each alternative. While this will be in considerable detail in practice, particularly for the first year of operation, it will have to be extended in total form for some years ahead. It would be no use choosing between alternatives on the basis of one years trading. Let's assume the owner has in mind at least a six-year period. The predictions need to be made for the whole life of the project – six years in fact. There may not be very much data to go on for later years, of course; but there will be certain points for the owner to consider:

Is there an expanding market for hardware/freezer foods/fresh meat?
Is there likely to be much competition opening up in the area?
Is there any more housing being built in the immediate area?
Are there plenty of suppliers willing to deliver goods to this particular area?

This is just a selection of the sort of thing an owner might consider when thinking further into the future.

Assume all this has been done, and a summary of the six year's cash flows turns out to be as shown in Fig. 170

Note on layout: The basic idea is to present a project in terms of (i) the amount of capital expenditure it will require and (ii) How much cash it will generate each year as a result of trading. In this way the firm is considering (rather as you would when investing money in a building society or national savings scheme) what *return* it is making on the money it permanently ties up in the project. The key therefore to capital investment appraisal is to identify;

    (i) The capital expenditure required
and (ii) The yearly trading *net cash inflows* (i.e. the difference between each years trading outflows for stocks and expenses) and inflows (sales revenue).

	Freezer	Butcher	Hardware
	£	£	£
Capital Costs	15,000	10,000	6,000
Yearly Cash 1	4,000	5,000	2,000
net Inflows: 2	7,000	5,000	3,000
3	8,000	6,000	4,000
4	7,000	6,000	6,000
5	7,000	6,000	6,000
6	9,000	7,000	6,000
Total Inflows	42,000	35,000	27,000
less Capital Costs	15,000	10,000	6,000
Project Lifetime Surplus	£27,000	£25,000	£21,000

Fig. 170.

Figure 170 is the raw material for the next section which explains the common methods of evaluating these alternatives. What needs emphasising here is that all this data is ASSUMED TO BE EQUALLY RELIABLE. If it is not, then IN FACT the project which seems worst, after evaluation, might really be the best. In other words the real problem with capital investment appraisal is the reliability of the basic data. The evaluation of it, as the next section shows, is quite straightforward. It's a bit like a pools coupon – very easy to fill in the details – the problem is accurately predicting the future!

THE CAPITAL INVESTMENT APPRAISAL TECHNIQUES

There are three commonly used methods:

(i) Return on Capital Employed
(ii) Payback Period
(iii) Discounted Cash Flow.

(A possible fourth is a predicted Profit and Loss account and Balance Sheet. This is a financial accounting technique which is not within the scope of this Stage One book.)

METHOD 1. RETURN ON CAPITAL EMPLOYED

This method considers how much money each proposed scheme earns as a percentage of the capital investment to begin with. (We assume the capital costs were incurred at the start of the project in all these techniques). This is rather like finding out the best interest rate on investing money in a bank:

	Freezer	Butcher	Hardware
(A) Lifetime Surplus	£27,000	£25,000	£21,000
(B) Initial Investment	£15,000	£10,000	£6,000
(C) As a percentage of B, i.e. the percentage return on the capital employed:	180%	250%	350%
(D) Life of Project in Years:	6	6	6
(E) Yearly Return C ÷ D:	30%	42%	58%

Fig. 171.

Quite clearly the hardware store shows the best earnings, in percentage terms, from the amount of capital invested. From a return on capital point of view the hardware store is the best option.

A problem with this method is that it deals in percentage terms rather than in absolute numbers. From an *absolute* point of view things could be different. The project which *earns the most money* in 6 years is the Freezer with a surplus of £27,000. The Hardware option requires less initial capital and that is why its *percentage* return is better. When considering projects using this method, care must be taken not to recommend a project with a wonderful return on capital; but which earns peanuts in absolute terms. For instance, which is *really* the better option 1 or 2 below?

	1	2
Initial Capital Investment	£100	£15,000
Lifetime Surplus	£60	£6,000
Return on Capital Employed	60%	40%

Fig. 172.

Obviously the *scale* of project is so different that a return on capital comparison is meaningless. No one who wants to invest £15,000 is going to be interested in a £100 alternative.

In our example, if we assume the shop owner has got £15,000 ready to invest, he would only use £6,000 of it on the Hardware store. The problem would then be what else to do with the remaining £9,000. If there were only low-interest rate investments available, it might be that the £21,000 hardware surplus *plus* the interest earned on the £9,000 came to less than the £27,000 Freezer surplus. In this case the *combined Hardware plus Bank interest surplus* might be less than £27,000. In which case an *overall* poorer return on capital would have been made. It is essential therefore to compare like with like. If £15,000 is to be invested, *all* the investment must be taken into consideration.

Summary. The return on capital employed method of choosing the best project is a good method *assuming* (i) projects are of the same scale and (ii) other suitable investment opportunities exist for any unused otherwise-idle funds.

METHOD 2. THE PAYBACK PERIOD

This method seeks to quantify risk by seeing how long it takes a project to pay back to the owner the money he initially invests. The idea being the one that pays back its initial capital fastest, is best. Refer to Fig. 170 to check the table below:

	Freezer	Butcher	Hardware
	£	£	£
Initial Capital	15,000	10,000	6,000
less Year 1 surplus	4,000	5,000	2,000
Capital Outstanding	11,000	5,000	4,000
less Year 2 surplus	7,000	5,000	3,000
Capital Outstanding	4,000	NIL	1,000
less ½ year 3 surplus:	4,000	less ¼ year 3 surplus:	1,000
Capital Outstanding	NIL		NIL

Fig. 173.

The Payback Periods therefore are:

Freezer:	2½
Butcher:	2 years
Hardware:	2¼

The Butcher project pays back its initial capital soonest, so from a payback point of view this is the best project.

The only problem with the payback method is it takes no account of ultimate profitability. What about this project which only lasts one year:

	£
Initial Investment	10,000
Total Year 1 Inflows	10,000
Lifetime surplus	NIL

Fig. 174.

It has a 1 year payback; but no profits! Obviously not a good project even though it has a fast payback.

Summary. The payback method is a sensible way to evaluate the *risk* of projects. A 6-year project, however apparently profitable, that didn't pay back its initial capital for 5½ years, would be extremely suspect. Nobody can be *absolutely certain* what will happen next year, and consequently must be much less certain about events in 5½ years' time. However, care must be taken than any project recommended is profitable enough to be worthwhile.

In our example the differences in payback periods are probably not significant enough to influence the final decision (unlike the return on capital percentages which vary widely). All have reasonable payback periods.

METHOD 3. DISCOUNTED CASH FLOW (D.C.F.)

This is a rather more complicated way of evaluating projects, which will only be covered in simple form in this book. In essence it measures how well each project performs, in relation to the alternative of investing the initial capital of that project at *compounded current interest rates*. There is one more thing to grasp as well – namely that by convention the sums are discounted rather than compounded. To explain using a simple illustration:

Question: How much is £100 invested at a *compound* interest rate of 10% worth in 3 years' time?

Answer:

	£
	100
Plus 1 year's interest	10
End year 1 sum	110
Plus 1 year's interest	11
End year 2 sum	121
Plus 1 year's interest	12·10
End year 3 sum	£133·10

Fig. 175.

£100 invested at *compound* interest of 10% for 3 years gives a *Compounded* Cash Flow of £133·10.

Discounting is the mathematical opposite of compounding. The question could be put like this: "Assuming we were to invest the money, and interest rates for the next three years will be 10%, how much is £133·10 receivable in 3 years' time equivalent to today?"

The answer of course is £100. There are a series of *factors* in a table at the end of the chapter which (together with a calculator!) enable you to work out the answers quickly for any prevailing interest rate and any number of years. For example look up the 3-year 10% factor. It is 0·751. Multiplying the sum receivable in 3 years' time by this factor, gives its equivalent in today's money:

$$£133·10 \times 0·751 = £100$$

If interest rates are only 7% then £133·10 in 3 years is equivalent to, in today's money:

$$£133·10 \times 0·816 = £108·61$$

"Equivalent to" means "if we were to invest £108·61 now, for 3 years at a compound interest rate of 7% we would end up with £133·10". *In that sense* we can say (at interest rates of 7%) that £133·10 in 3 years' time is equivalent to £108·61 *now*.

USING DISCOUNTING FACTORS TO EVALUATE CAPITAL PROJECTS

Take the Freezer project. It requires initial capital of £15,000 and its yearly surpluses come in for 6 years. Because the earlier years' cash flows *can* be re-invested at compound rates they are worth more than the later ones. For instance the first year's cash flow of £4,000 could be invested for 5 years before the end of the project, while the last year's cash flow couldn't be invested at all before the end.

The idea is to use discounting factors to put all of these years cash flows into "today's money" and see which project comes out best. The technical term for "today's money" is the PRESENT VALUE of the future cash flows. Just as £100 is the *present value* of one inflow of £133·10 in 3 years' time (if interest rates are 10%) so we can work out the present value of each year's inflows to give the whole project's Present Value. Assume interest rates are 10%:

Freezer

Capital Cost		£15,000	DISCOUNT FACTORS	DISCOUNTED CASH FLOWS
		£		£
Yearly Inflows:	1	4,000	0·909	3,636
	2	7,000	0·826	5,782
	3	8,000	0·751	6,008
	4	7,000	0·683	4,781
	5	7,000	0·621	4,347
	6	9,000	0·564	5,076
TOTAL INFLOWS		£42,000	PRESENT VALUE OF PROJECT	£29,630

Fig. 176.

This indicates that the cash flows from the Freezer project, when discounted to today's values, are worth £29,630 in today's money.

The final stage is to work out the NET PRESENT VALUE (N.P.V.) of the project:

		£
	Discounted Flows	29,630
minus	Initial Capital	15,000
	PROJECT N.P.V.	£14,630

Fig. 177.

The project with the highest N.P.V. is the best, because *if compounded*, the *highest N.P.V.* is bound to give the *highest end-of-project cash total.* Everyone understands that (say) £1,000 is better than £900 in 6 years time. Equally therefore if both are discounted by the 6-year factor:

$$1,000 \times \cdot 564 = £564 \qquad \text{Present Value}$$
$$900 \times \cdot 564 = £507 \cdot 6 \qquad \text{Present Value}$$

the *highest Present Value* is best too.

Now to calculate the N.P.V.s of the other two projects:

	Butcher			Hardware	
Initial Capital	£10,000			£6,000	
	INFLOWS	DISCOUNTED INFLOWS	YEARLY DISCOUNT FACTORS	INFLOWS	DISCOUNTED INFLOWS
	£	£		£	£
Year 1	5,000	4,545	0·909	2,000	1,818
2	5,000	4,130	0·826	3,000	2,478
3	6,000	4,506	0·751	4,000	3,004
4	6,000	4,098	0·683	6,000	4,098
5	6,000	3,726	0·621	6,000	3,726
6	7,000	3,948	0·564	6,000	3,384
Total Inflows	£35,000			£27,000	
Present Values		24,953			18,508
less Initial Capital		10,000			6,000
Project Net Present Value		£14,953			£12,508

Fig. 178.

We therefore have three projects with Net Present Values as follows:

	Freezer	Butcher	Hardware
N.P.V.	£14,630	£14,953	£12,508

Summary. This method of appraisal says the Butcher project is best, closely followed by the Freezer! Why the Hardware example has fared badly is because in cash inflow terms the last three years of that project are its best ones by far. However that leaves those later, larger sums relatively little time to be invested before the end of the project's life. Discounting (i.e. compounding in reverse) takes into account what can be earned by re-investing the yearly cash flows, *as well as* how much each years cash flow actually is. What the calculations really tell us is that *if we do re-invest at compound* the yearly cash flows of each project until the end of their lives in 6 years' time, we come out best (having paid off the initial capital) doing the Butcher project.

If the N.P.V. comes out as a negative number (i.e. the discounted inflows are not even equal to the original investment) the project is not worth doing at all. It indicates the original capital would be better invested at compound interest rates in a bank, for example, than invested in the project.

PROBLEMS WITH D.C.F.

Problem one is D.C.F. is hard to understand. Compound Cash Flows (C.C.F.) is much easier to understand, gives the same result (you take the largest compound figure at the end of the project life instead of the largest discounted figure at the beginning) but no one uses it, unfortunately.

The second problem is that it mixes up (i) the re-investment potential of what a project earns with (ii) what it actually earns by itself. In my view these are separate considerations. A rather mediocre project that earns high inflows *early on* can often appear to be good because of the re-investment potential of these early flows. It might be better from a number of other points of view to do the project which is a steady earner for a longer period.

Problem three is that discounting is an exponentially severe test of a project. In other words increasing the discount rate from say 10% to 12% makes the test more than 2 tenths harder. And increasing a rate from 15% to 20% may more than double the severity of the "hurdle" the project has to overcome. This makes it difficult to interpret the real meaning of D.C.F. results.

It should not concern you that our three methods do not all indicate that the same project should be done. This is often the way in business. There are conflicting indications, priorities, interests, and it is the management's job to make a decision based upon rational information. The three methods seek to highlight different aspects of each project's performance. It is a matter for management to weigh up the evidence before making a choice. Undoubtedly all three techniques should be used and

their results considered before a choice is made.
You should now be in a position to tackle the self assessment questions.

SENSITIVITY ANALYSIS

Earlier in the chapter I mentioned how the reliability of the base data is crucial to the accuracy of *any* of the conclusions the various appraisal methods lead a manager towards. Another very important data evaluation test is "Sensitivity Analysis". This gives managers an idea of how sensitive each project is to changes in price, or output efficiency for example.

Sensitivity analysis consists of saying (for instance) "If labour costs are 10% higher than predicted what happens to the project's profitability?" In our freezer shop example we might ask "What if electricity is 20% more dear in 2 years' time?" The figures are re-done for each "What if". It quite often happens that a particular project's profitability is *very* sensitive to the price of a certain resource. It could be labour, power, materials, and so on.

Once the sensitivity is identified it puts managers on the alert. It makes them double-check their predictions, and, if the project is undertaken, makes them pay special attention to ensure the sensitive area goes as planned.

As a quick example take the following:

	£	£
One Year's Sales Inflow		40,000
One Year's Costs Outflow:		
Labour	20,000	
Materials	10,000	
Overheads	4,000	
		34,000
Net Year's Inflow:		£6,000

What if labour costs are 15% higher than predicted?

	Sales	£ 40,000
	£	
Labour	23,000	
Materials	10,000	
Overheads	4,000	
	37,000	
Profit	£3,000	

Fig. 179.

Future years	Percentage rate of discount								
	1	2	3	4	5	6	7	8	9
1	0·990	0·980	0·971	0·962	0·952	0·943	0·935	0·926	0·917
2	0·980	0·961	0·943	0·925	0·907	0·890	0·873	0·857	0·842
3	0·971	0·942	0·915	0·889	0·864	0·840	0·816	0·794	0·772
4	0·961	0·924	0·888	0·855	0·823	0·792	0·763	0·735	0·708
5	0·951	0·906	0·863	0·822	0·784	0·747	0·713	0·681	0·650
6	0·942	0·888	0·837	0·790	0·746	0·705	0·666	0·630	0·596
7	0·933	0·871	0·813	0·760	0·711	0·665	0·623	0·583	0·547
8	0·923	0·853	0·789	0·731	0·677	0·627	0·582	0·540	0·502
9	0·914	0·837	0·766	0·703	0·645	0·592	0·544	0·500	0·460
10	0·905	0·820	0·744	0·676	0·614	0·558	0·508	0·463	0·422
11	0·896	0·804	0·722	0·650	0·585	0·527	0·475	0·429	0·388
12	0·887	0·788	0·701	0·625	0·557	0·497	0·444	0·397	0·356
13	0·879	0·773	0·681	0·601	0·530	0·469	0·415	0·368	0·326
14	0·870	0·758	0·661	0·577	0·505	0·442	0·388	0·340	0·299
15	0·861	0·743	0·642	0·555	0·481	0·417	0·362	0·315	0.275
16	0·853	0·728	0·623	0·534	0·458	0·394	0·339	0·292	0·252
17	0·844	0·714	0·605	0·513	0·436	0·371	0·317	0·270	0·231
18	0·836	0·700	0·587	0·494	0·416	0·350	0·296	0·250	0·212
19	0·828	0·686	0·570	0·475	0·396	0·331	0·277	0·232	0·194
20	0·820	0·673	0·554	0·456	0·377	0·312	0·258	0·215	0·178
21	0·811	0·660	0·538	0·439	0·359	0·294	0·242	0·199	0·164
22	0·803	0·647	0·522	0·422	0·342	0·278	0·266	0·184	0·150
23	0·795	0·634	0·507	0·406	0·326	0·262	0·211	0·170	0·138
24	0·788	0·622	0·492	0·390	0·310	0·247	0·197	0·158	0·126
25	0·780	0·610	0·478	0·375	0·295	0·233	0·184	0·146	0·116
30	0·742	0·552	0·412	0·308	0·231	0·174	0·131	0·098	0·075
35	0·706	0·500	0·355	0·253	0·181	0·130	0·094	0·068	0·049
40	0·672	0·453	0·307	0·208	0·142	0·097	0·067	0·046	0·032
50	0·608	0·372	0·228	0·141	0·087	0·054	0·034	0·021	0·013

This project is very sensitive to labour costs. A 15% rise means *halved* profits.

The watchword, in reality, is check everything when considering different alternatives, and be sure you work out the effects of key costs being predicted slightly inaccurately.

Percentage rate of discount									Future
10	11	12	13	14	15	16	17	18	years
0·909	0·901	0·893	0·885	0·877	0·870	0·862	0·855	0·847	1
0·826	0·812	0·797	0·783	0·769	0·756	0·743	0·731	0·718	2
0·751	0·731	0·712	0·693	0·675	0·658	0·641	0·624	0·609	3
0·683	0·659	0·636	0·613	0·592	0·572	0·552	0·534	0·516	4
0·621	0·593	0·567	0·543	0·519	0·497	0·476	0·456	0·437	5
0·564	0·535	0·507	0·480	0·456	0·432	0·410	0·390	0·370	6
0·513	0·482	0·452	0·425	0·400	0·376	0·354	0·333	0·314	7
0·467	0·434	0·404	0·376	0·351	0·327	0·305	0·285	0·266	8
0·424	0·391	0·361	0·333	0·308	0·284	0·263	0·243	0·225	9
0·386	0·352	0·322	0·295	0·270	0·247	0·227	0·208	0·191	10
0·350	0·317	0·287	0·261	0·237	0·215	0·195	0·178	0·162	11
0·319	0·286	0·257	0·231	0·208	0·187	0·168	0·152	0·137	12
0·290	0·258	0·229	0·204	0·182	0·163	0·145	0·130	0·116	13
0·263	0·232	0·205	0·181	0·160	0·141	0·125	0·111	0·099	14
0·239	0·209	0·183	0·160	0·140	0·123	0·108	0·095	0·084	15
0·218	0·188	0·163	0·141	0·123	0·107	0·093	0·081	0·071	16
0·198	0·170	0·146	0·125	0·108	0·093	0·080	0·069	0·060	17
0·180	0·153	0·130	0·111	0·095	0·081	0·069	0·059	0·051	18
0·164	0·138	0·116	0·098	0·083	0·070	0·060	0·051	0·043	19
0·149	0·124	0·104	0·087	0·073	0·061	0·051	0·043	0·037	20
0·135	0·112	0·093	0·077	0·064	0·053	0·044	0·037	0·031	21
0·123	0·101	0·083	0·068	0·056	0·046	0·038	0·032	0·026	22
0·112	0·091	0·074	0·060	0·049	0·040	0·033	0·027	0·022	23
0·102	0·082	0·066	0·053	0·043	0·035	0·028	0·023	0·019	24
0·092	0·074	0·059	0·047	0·038	0·030	0·024	0·020	0·016	25
0·057	0·044	0·033	0·026	0·020	0·015	0·012	0·009	0·007	30
0·036	0·026	0·019	0·014	0·010	0·008	0·006	0·004	0·003	35
0·022	0·015	0·011	0·008	0·005	0·004	0·003	0·002	0·001	40
0·009	0·005	0·003	0·002	0·001	0·001	0·001	0·001		50

SELF-ASSESSMENT QUESTIONS

* 1. What are the present values of the following:

£4,000	receivable in	5 years'	time when interest rates are	12%?
£7,000	„	„ 8 years'	„ „ „ „ „	8%?
£1,200	„	„ 3 years'	„ „ „ „ „	16%?
£26,000	„	„ 4 years'	„ „ „ „ „	6%?
£3,500	„	„ 6 years'	„ „ „ „ „	13%?
£6,900	„	„ 10 years'	„ „ „ „ „	15%?

* 2. Zoom Lens Co. Ltd have developed two new products; but only have the resources to launch one of them. The estimated costs and revenues are as follows for the two products:

	Long Range	Hi Definition
	£	£
Initial Capital Cost:	10,000	12,000

Net Inflows:		
Year 1	4,000	4,000
2	6,000	6,000
3	6,000	8,000
4	4,000	6,000

Calculate the (i) Yearly Return on Capital Employed,

(ii) The payback period,

(iii) The Net Present Value, of these alternatives.

Current interest rates are 9%.

3. The following two projects are under consideration by your firm (Mammoth Motors) and they present you with the following data:

	Sun-Roof Project	Auto-Window Wind Project
	£	£
Initial Capital Expenditure	400,000	600,000

Cash Flow Details:		
Year 1 Inflow	140,000	200,000
Outflow	20,000	40,000
Year 2 Inflow	260,000	200,000
Outflow	60,000	80,000
Year 3 Inflow	240,000	320,000
Outflow	80,000	120,000
Year 4 Inflow	180,000	480,000
Outflow	100,000	200,000
Year 5 Inflow	200,000	400,000
Outflow	120,000	220,000

(i) Calculate the net yearly inflows for each year of each project.

(ii) Calculate the yearly return on capital employed, the payback period, and the Net Present Value of each project.

Interest rates are 16%

4. You have the option to buy the lease of a piece of land for £5,000. The lease will last 5 years. You are considering two alternative uses:

(i) Installing a car-wash which will cost an extra initial £8,000 capital; but produce yearly net inflow of £3,500.

(ii) Sub-let the land to a caravan park owner; who will pay you £1,500 per year for it.

Interest rates are 10%. What is the Net Present Value of each alternative?

5. You have been asked to consider which of the following projects to recommend.

	Project 1 £	Project 2 £
Initial Capital	100,000	150,000
Net Yearly Inflows: 1	20,000	40,000
2	30,000	30,000
3	40,000	30,000
4	40,000	40,000
5	20,000	70,000
6	20,000	70,000
7	20,000	60,000

Calculate the yearly return on capital employed, the payback period, and the Net Present Value of each project. Interest rates are 14%.

6. Global Ltd. occupies factory premises in Brixton. It has the option to lease for 6 years the ground floor of an adjacent factory at a cost of £15,000 payable when the lease is signed. It intended to install machinery which would cost £24,000 to produce a new line; the machinery would last until the end of the lease when it would be valueless. It estimates that the project would generate cash flow of about £10,500 per annum.

However, Global has now been approached by another company in another trade which wishes to sub-let the property and is willing to pay £4,500 per annum for the life of the lease.

Assume that cost of capital is 10%, that outlays on lease and machinery would occur immediately and that all annual amounts would occur end-year.

Which option gives Global the better return.

7. Evaluate the investment below using

(A) Pay-back
(B) Return on Capital Employed
(C) Net Present Value.

(A) INVESTMENT	£10,000	
Year	Cash Flow	Profit
1	£2,200	£200
2	3,500	1,500
3	3,500	1,500
4	4,000	2,000
5	4,300	2,300

(B) Cost of Capital = 13%

8. Second City Investments has to make a choice between two possible projects. The first (Wheel Pressing) requires an investment of £400,000

and will give a return of £250,000 in year 1 and £280,000 in year 2. The second (Axle grinding) requires an investment of £200,000 and will give a return of £125,000 in year 1 and a return of £180,000 in year 2.

For each of these projects calculate the pay-back period, the return on capital employed and the net present value using a discount rate of 15%. Which project do you think is more attractive?

9. Supplies Ltd. is considering the installation of a micro computer which will yield savings of £400 per annum. It has two alternatives: it can buy Model A which has an estimated life of 4 years and costs £1,000 or it can buy Model B which has an estimated life of 7 years and costs £1,200. (The company cost of capital is 15% per annum.)

Advise the company on the purchase, using the facts given. Would you view change if it was likely that Model B might only last 5 years?

10. Timber is an attractive investment for many reasons. If you expect an acre of pine trees to realise £5,000 in 20 years time after paying the felling costs, and you want a return on your investment of 12% per annum, how much are you prepared to pay now for the acre of saplings?

CHAPTER 11

INTEGRATING AND RECONCILING COST AND FINANCIAL ACCOUNTS

CHAPTER OBJECTIVES

Having studied this chapter you should be able to:

* DESCRIBE IN PRINCIPLE HOW COST AND FINANCIAL ACCOUNTING SYSTEMS CAN BE *EITHER* RECONCILED *OR* INTEGRATED; AND WHY THEY NEED TO BE

* DESCRIBE HOW MANUFACTURING ACCOUNTS GIVE CERTAIN COST-ACCOUNTING DATA WITHIN THE FORMAT OF THE FINANCIAL ACCOUNTING SYSTEM

* CONSTRUCT SIMPLE MANUFACTURING ACCOUNTS

AGREEING COST AND FINANCIAL ACCOUNTING DATA

It is absolutely essential that the *actual* cost-accounting data (for example analysis "type one", the basic cost classification as shown in Chapter 2, or "type two", the split between fixed and variable costs as shown in Chapter 5) for a given period is correct. Equally it is important that the *estimated* cost accounting data used to help set selling prices, plan budgets and so forth, is as accurate as possible.

Ultimately, it is the financial accounting system which records a business's real transactions with the "outside world". Cash, debtors, creditors, sales revenue, expenses, purchases of fixed assets, all these are recorded by the financial accounting system. Cost accounting re-analyses these "real" transactions to give useful *internal information*, as described in this book's first ten chapters.

If this "internal information" is to be useful, it must be accurate. For instance our predicted total overheads can only be proved to be true if all the financial transactions which should total up to overhead expenses (rent payments, wages, electricity, machinery expenses and so on) really *do* total up to the figure being used in our cost accounting system.

Therefore it is essential to ensure, on a regular basis, that the two systems are in tune, i.e. RECONCILED. The only other alternative is to use a system which never separates them at all. In this case it is said the firm runs an INTEGRATED cost and financial accounting system.

RECONCILING THE TWO SYSTEMS

In theory (using as our example throughout this part of the chapter a firm using a job costing system) the profit shown in the (financial accounting) profit and loss account should equal the addition of the individual actual profits shown on the job-cards for the same period.

Similarly the sales figure in the P + L should agree with the sales revenue shown by adding up all the sales revenues on the job cards for the period. Likewise actual direct labour and material costs should be able to be reconciled, and overhead costs too (with some adjustment for over or under recovery).

The point of doing all this is so managers can be sure the actual information on their cost accounting records (the job cards) is true. And this is proved by agreeing it with the financial accounting records, which derive directly from the real transactions the business has with the outside world.

The problem with regular reconciliation is that it can be a lengthy business, essential as it is. A simple 3-job illustration of how this reconciliation might occur is as follows:

	Job 1 ACTUAL	Job 2 ACTUAL	Job 3 ACTUAL	Job Card Actual Totals
				£
D.L.	500	450	200	1,150
D.M.	120	700	65	885
O/H	300	180	85	565
TOTAL COSTS	920	1,330	350	£2,600

Fig. 180.

The P + L might show costs for the period as follows (after analysis into comparable headings).

	£
Direct Labour	1,170
Direct Materials	850
Overheads	620
Total Costs	£2,640

Fig. 181.

The differences would be investigated and explained. The reasons shown below are imaginary ones of course; but give an idea of the likely causes:

Direct Labour: P + L £1,170; Costs £1,150; Difference £20.
Reasons: A bonus of £20 paid for a safety suggestion not included in the costing data.
Direct Materials: P + L £850; Costs £885; Difference £35.
Reasons: Special bulk buying discount not included in cost accounting prices used to calculate job D.M. costs.
Overheads: P + L £620; Costs £565; Difference £55.
Reasons: Four hours machine breakdown resulted in an under-recovery of £40 and £15 caused by the estimated overhead recovery rate being too low.

This then, is the way in principle that the costing records are kept accurate if a non-integrated system is used. The two systems' results are regularly reconciled.

INTEGRATING THE TWO SYSTEMS

By contrast, integrating the cost and financial accounting systems prevents the necessity for periodic reconciliation by, in effect, continuously doing so. Integrated accounts work in principle like this:

Step 1. The normal financial accounting system records the expenses incurred. For instance, assume the financial accounting records showed the following expenses:

	£
Wages	1,300
Materials	900
Rent	200
Rates	50
Insurance	90
Power	40
Telephone	60
	£2,640

Fig. 182.

Step 2. These would be transferred to the normal cost accounting headings to give (for example) the following analysis of actual expenditure:

	Direct Labour	Direct Material	Overheads	Total
Transfers In	£1,170	£850	£620	£2,640

Fig. 183.

Step 3. Then, as the jobs were done, the TRANSFERS OUT of these accounts would begin, and the job cards would be filled in at the same time using the same data. The transfers out would be made at the PRE-DETERMINED COSTING RATES (i.e. predicted D.L., D.M. and O/H costs would be used, multiplied by the ACTUAL time taken and quantities used). The transfers out would be made into "Cost Recovered" or "Cost of Sales" accounts. Assume the transfers out were as shown below in Fig. 184.

	Direct Labour	Direct Materials	Overheads	Total
	£	£	£	£
Transfers In	1,170	850	620	2,640
less TRANSFERS OUT	1,150	885	565	2,600
BALANCES LEFT	£20	£(35)	£55	£40

Fig. 184.

Step 4. The *balances left* on the accounts would show the extent to which the costs had been over- or under-recovered by charging them to the jobs done in the period. In our example we have not charged enough direct labour or enough Overheads, and have over-charged direct materials. (The reasons would still have to be found of course, and the job-cards which are still filled in normally, would still be needed to give a breakdown of how estimated and actual performance differed on any particular job).

However the great advantage is that the *balances left* on the accounts in Fig. 184 above, *automatically* provide the necessary reconciliation between the costing and financial records. The addition of costs on the job cards will always equal the amounts *transferred out* because they are both derived from the identical data (actual times and quantities × predicted rates and prices).

Step 5. The integrated accounts now make a complete statement possible without further work being needed:

	Cost Recovered Account Balances	(Over) Under Recoveries	Total Costs per Financial Accounts
	£	£	£
D.L.	1,150	20	1,170
D.M.	885	(35)	850
O/H	565	55	620
TOTAL	£2,600	£40	£2,640

Fig. 185.

SECTION SUMMARY

Integration of, or regular reconciliation between, cost and financial accounts, ensures the costing data being used is regularly proved against the expenditure the firm really incurs. Only the financial accounts (which record the transactions the firm has with the "outside world") can supply this "proving" data. As emphasised in previous chapters, for costing data to be useful, accurate predicted costs are essential, and any variations must be known about as soon as possible. Integration, or regular reconciliation, of costing and financial accounts, allied to the more detailed information in the individual costing records (be it job, process, marginal or standard) will ensure that management is aware when predicted and actual performances differ, and why they do.

MANUFACTURING ACCOUNTS

A manufacturing account is really a specialised form of profit and loss account, which aims to highlight the performance of particular sections of the business. It is produced under the normal historical financial accounting principles and conventions, and is used to give information about factory, sales and office overhead performance in a layout suitable for inclusion in a set of Financial Accounts.

If you have done simple trading accounts in your financial accounting studies, you will be familiar with the way the goods *actually used* to produce sales revenue are separated from those purchased, by adjusting purchases for opening and closing stocks. For instance:

		£	
	Opening Stocks:	2,000	
Add	Goods Purchased:	15,000	
= Cost of goods available to sell		17,000	
less	Closing Stocks	5,000	(i.e. goods not sold still held)
= Cost of Goods Sold		£12,000	

Fig. 186.

With manufacturing accounts there are in fact three types of stock that need adjusting: (i) Raw materials stocks; (ii) Work in Progress, i.e. the "stock" of partly completed goods (see Chapter 4 for an illustration of this in a process costing example); and (iii) Finished goods stocks.

A manufacturing account, in order to identify the costs of producing the completed goods has to adjust all three in a similar manner to that used to adjust purchases, illustrated in Fig. 186 above.

For instance raw materials are purchased; but only some of them are issued to production. Of those materials issued to production, not all of them may be converted to finished goods at the accounting date. It is only the cost of those raw materials included in the goods *actually complete* that must be charged to them. The same goes for labour and overhead costs incurred in the factory. If 27 machine hours and 38 direct labour hours have been spent on a batch of uncompleted items, the overhead and wages cost of those hours must not be charged to the completed ones. Rather it must be held over as part of the closing work-in-progress, to be included in the cost of the batch of items *when they are complete*. The closing work in progress figures thus represent the material, labour and overhead costs so far incurred in making not-yet-complete goods.

Opening work-in-progress represents the costs of partly completed goods at the end of *last* month. These will be turned into complete ones this month and are added into the costs incurred this month. So work in progress (W.I.P.) stock levels are adjusted in a similar way to purchases (shown in Fig. 186 above) in order to find the costs of the goods actually finished this month. For instance:

		£
	Costs incurred in the month	15,000
Add	Opening W.I.P.	2,000
		17,000
less	Closing W.I.P. (i.e. costs incurred on goods not yet complete)	5,000
	Cost of completed goods	£12,000

Fig. 187.

Using imaginary figures a typical Manufacturing, trading and profit and loss account layout would be:

ZOOM PRINT CO. MANUFACTURING ACCOUNT: JULY 1985

	£	£
Direct Materials Purchased:	15,000	
Add Opening D.M. Stocks:	2,000	
Direct Materials Available:	17,000	
less Closing D.M. Stocks:	5,000	
Direct Materials issued to production:		12,000
Add Direct Labour Costs:		9,000
Prime Costs Incurred:		21,000
Add Indirect Labour:	2,000	
Indirect Materials:	1,000	
Depreciation:	6,000	
Establishment Costs:	4,000	
		13,000
Total Factory Costs Incurred:		34,000
Add Opening Work in Progress:		17,000
		51,000
less Closing Work in Progress:		12,000
Factory Cost of Finished Goods Produced:		£39,000

TRADING ACCOUNT

	£	£
Sales:		108,000
Factory Cost of Finished Goods Produced:	39,000	
Add opening stock of finished goods:	10,000	
Finished goods available:	49,000	
less closing stock of finished goods:	8,000	
Cost of goods sold:	41,000	
Trading Profit:		£67,000

PROFIT AND LOSS ACCOUNT

		£
	Trading Profit:	67,000
less: Office Costs:	£	
Sales	30,000	
Administration	15,000	
Interest	4,000	
Sundry	2,000	
	£51,000	
Net Profit:		£16,000

Fig. 188.

The management can now measure the performance of the factory separately from the trading performance. The factory cost of goods sold £39,000, may be in line with budget, or not. Either way the manufacturing account clearly shows the cost of manufactured goods, which can be compared with that planned.

The trading account then concentrated on the profitability of selling those goods, and once again will highlight whether the trading margin and sales revenue are as budgeted or not.

Finally the profit and loss part of the whole shows the actual office costs (which can also be compared with budget) and identifies the net profit.

The important point to grasp is that without the adjustment for the value of opening and closing direct materials, work in progress and finished goods stocks, the costs and profit will be meaningless.

A manufacturing account is another example of integrating cost accounting and financial accounting information. This illustrates, of course, that financial accounts (which a manufacturing account forms part of) and cost accounts are not necessarily clearly distinguishable. There is much cost-accounting information in the basically financial-accounting-orientated manufacturing, trading and profit and loss account. Particularly if comparisons with budgeted figures are included.

In Chapter 1 it was mentioned that cost accounting represented a collection of techniques to help managers run their businesses. In as far as financial accounts also do so, they are arguably cost accounts too! The labels are not important. Understanding the techniques available, how they work, and when to use them is the key to all accounting success in business: namely, supplying managers with clear, relevant, accurate information, to help them make well informed decisions which will benefit and strengthen their businesses.

SELF-ASSESSMENT QUESTIONS

* 1. Present the following information about March's trading performance in the form of a Manufacturing, Trading and Profit and Loss Account:

Machinery costs 12,000
Salesmen's car expenses £4,000
Opening stocks of raw materials £3,100
Opening work in progress £1,800
Factory wages £14,000 (20% indirect labour)
Direct materials purchased £19,000
Indirect materials costs £1,500
Opening finished goods stocks £6,600
Factory Rent £1,700   Sales office rent £400
Factory Rates £1,000   Admin. office rent £300
Factory Telephone £3,000   Sales office rates £200
                                        Admin. office rates £150

Office wages £4,000 (60% sales office 40% admin. office). Interest costs £500. Office telephone and electricity costs £3,000 (40% admin. and 60% sales office).

Closing raw material stocks are £2,900. Closing Work in Progress is £2,400. Closing finished goods stocks are £7,000.

Sales Revenue totalled £69,000.

2. The financial accounts (after re-analysis) show the following amounts as actual expenses in July:

| Direct Materials | £16,200 | Direct Labour | £17,500 |
| Overheads | £12,000 | | |

The firm uses a process costing system and has cost accounts which show the following amounts charged to the process:

| Direct Materials | £16,000 | Direct Labour | £17,100 |
| Overheads | £12,400 | | |

(A) What are the amounts under or over-charged to the process this month?

(B) Produce a table (as shown in Fig. 185) to show the reconciliation between the cost and financial accounting records.

(C) Suggest a reason to account for each of the differences between the two sets of records.

APPENDIX OF ANSWERS

CHAPTER 1

Q.3.

(A)

		£
Total Cost:	Wages	15,000
	Rent	5,000
	Machinery	3,000
	Electricity & Gas	4,000
	Rates	2,000
	Cleaning Fluid	7,000
	TOTAL COSTS	**£36,000**

$$\text{Absorption Cost per article cleaned} = \frac{£36,000}{18,000} \text{ items}$$

$$= £2$$

(B) Marginal cost of 18,000 items:

		£
½ × Gas and Electricity	=	2,000
plus cleaning fluid	=	7,000
		£9,000

$$\text{Therefore marginal cost of one more item} = \frac{£9,000}{18,000}$$

$$= £0·50$$

(D) Factory Overheads = £61,630 (Cost of Production *less* Prime Cost)

(E) Total Overheads = £140,250 (Total Cost *less* Prime Cost)

(F) Absorption cost per rocket $= \dfrac{£230,000}{20,000}$

$$= £11·50 \text{ each}$$

(G) Prime cost of one rocket $= \dfrac{£89,750}{20,000}$

$$= £4·49$$

(H) Factory Overhead cost per rocket $= \dfrac{£61,630}{20,000}$

$$= £3·08$$

(I) Total Overhead cost per rocket $= \dfrac{£140,250}{20,000}$

$$= £7·01$$

(J) Cost of Production of one rocket $= \dfrac{£151,380}{20,000}$

$$= £7·57$$

CHAPTER 2
Q.2. (A, B, C)

	Wages £	Rent £	Purch. £	Machin. £	Office Wages £	Tele. Post £	Cars £	Delivery £	Advert. £	COST CLASSIFICATION £
						WORKINGS				
D. Labour	26,000									26,000
D. Materials			63,750							63,750
Prime Cost										*89,750*
I. Labour	14,000									14,000
I. Materials			7,500							7,500
Machinery Costs				29,000						29,000
Building Est. Costs		8,880				2,250				11,130
Cost of Production										*151,380*
Sales & Distrib.		1,560	1,875		9,000	12,750	9,000	15,000	17,000	66,185
Admin.		1,560	1,875		9,000					12,435
Finance										—
Sundry										—
TOTAL COST	£40,000	£12,000	£75,000	£29,000	£18,000	£15,000	£9,000	£15,000	£17,000	£230,000

CHAPTER 3

SECTION A

Q.2.
Labour cost in total £8,000. If 30% is Indirect Labour, 70% is Direct Labour. So £8,000 × 70% = £5,600. 35,000 packets are made so Direct Labour cost per packet = $\frac{5,600}{35,000}$ = £0·16 per packet.

Q.3. (i) + (iii)

Collins total hours	= 28 × £3·50 =	£98·00
Heath total hours	= 42 × £3·50 =	£147·00
Gill total hours	= 31 × £3·50 =	£108·50
Bache total hours	= 40 × £3·50 =	£140·00
	Week 25 Total Wages	£493·50

(ii)

Monday Hours	= 29 × £3·50 =	£101·50
Tuesday Hours	= 29 × £3·50 =	£101·50
Wednesday Hours	= 24 × £3·50 =	£84·00
Thursday Hours	= 29 × £3·50 =	£101·50
Friday Hours	= 30 × £3·50 =	£105·00
		£493·50

(iv)

Direct labour cost per record where 2,000 are made = $\frac{493·50}{2,000}$ = 25p

SECTION B

Q.5.
(A)

	£
All Materials Issued	9,500
less Indirect Materials	500
	9,000
less Unused Direct Materials	2,000
Cost of D. Materials used	£7,000
Quantity Made	35

Direct Material Cost each = 7,000 ÷ 35 = £200

(B)

	£
All Wages paid =	4,500
less Indirect Labour =	1,000
Direct Labour Cost	£3,500

Direct Labour Cost per life raft = 3,500 ÷ 35 = £100

(C)

	£
Prime cost per life raft = DL	100
DM	200
Prime Cost	£300

Q.6 A + B

F.I.F.O. ISSUING METHOD

Narrative	Quantity of Chains	Price per Chain	Value of Chains	Analysis of Issues and Balances		
Jan. 15 Receipt	400	£3	£1,200	Balance (A) =		
Jan. 19 Receipt	150	£2	£300	200 × £3	=	600
				150 × £2	=	300
Balance	550		£1,500			
Jan. 23 Issues (N)	200	£3	£600	350		£900
Balance (A)	350		£900	Issues (P) =		
Feb. 7 Receipt	300	£2·50	£750	200 × £3	=	600
				140 × £2	=	280
Balance (B)	650		£1,650			
Feb. 14 Issues (P)	340		£880	340		£880
				Balance (C) =		
				10 × £2	=	20
Balance (C)	310		£770	300 × £2·50	=	750
Feb. 22 Issues (Q)	210		£520			
				310		£770
Balance (D)	100		£250			
March 10 Receipts	330	£3·20	£1,056			
				Balance (D) =		
Balance	430		£1,306	100 × £2·50	=	£250
March 14 Receipts	150	£4	£600	Balance (E) =		
				100 × £2·50	=	250
Balance (E)	580		£1,906	330 × £3·20	=	1,056
March 20 Issues (R)	370		£1,114	150 × £4	=	600
Balance (F)	210		£792	580		£1,906
April 9 Issues (S)	150		£552			
				Issues (R) =		
Balance (G)	60	£4	£240	100 × £2·50	=	250
				270 × £3·20	=	864
				370		£1,114

Balance (F) =
60 × £3·20 = 192
150 × £4 = 600

210 £792

Issues (S) =
60 × £3·20 = 192
90 × £4 = 360

150 £552

Q.6. A + B

L.I.F.O. ISSUING METHOD

Narrative	Quantity of Chains	Price Per Chain	Value of Chains
Jan. 15 Receipt	400	£3	£1,200
Jan. 19 Receipt	150	£2	300
Balance	550		£1,500
Jan. 23 Issues (N)	200		£450
Balance (A)	350		£1.050
Feb. 7 Receipt	300	£2·50	£750
Balance (B)	650		£1,800
Feb. 14 Issues (P)	340		£870
Balance (C)	310		£930
Feb. 22 Issues (Q)	210		£630
Balance (D)	100		£300
March 10 Receipts	330	£3·20	£1,056
Balance	430		£1.356
March 14 Receipts	150	£4	£600
Balance (E)	580		£1,956
March 20 Issues (R)	370		£1,304
Balance (F)	210		£652
April 9 Issues (S)	150		£472
Balance (G)	60	£3	£180

Analysis of Issues and Balances

Issue (N):
$$150 \times £2 = 300$$
$$50 \times £3 = 150$$
$$200 \qquad £450$$

Balance (A):
$$\underline{350} \times £3 = \underline{£1050}$$

Issues (P):
$$300 \times £2·50 = 750$$
$$40 \times £3 = 120$$
$$340 \qquad £870$$

Balance (C):
$$\underline{310} \times £3 = \underline{£930}$$

Balance (D):
$$\underline{100} \times £3 = \underline{£300}$$

Balance (E):
$$100 \times £3 = 300$$
$$330 \times £3·20 = 1,056$$
$$150 \times £4 = 600$$
$$580 \qquad £1,956$$

Issues (R):
$$150 \times £4 = 600$$
$$220 \times £3·20 = 704$$
$$370 \qquad £1,304$$

Balance (F):
$$100 \times £3 = 300$$
$$110 \times £3·20 = 352$$
$$210 \qquad £652$$

Issues (S):
$$110 \times £3·20 = 352$$
$$40 \times £3 = 120$$
$$150 \qquad £472$$

Q.6. A + B

A.V.C.O. ISSUING METHOD

Narrative	Quantity of Chains	Price Per Chain	Value of Chains	Analysis of Issues and Balances
Jan. 15 Receipt	400	£3	£1,200	
Jan. 19 Receipt	150	£2	£300	
Balance	550		£1,500........	... Average price =
Jan. 23 Issues	200	£2·73	£546	£1,500 ÷ 550 = £2·73 each
Balance (A)	350		£954	
Feb. 7 Receipt	300	£2·50	£750	
Balance (B)	650		£1,704........	... New Average price =
Feb. 14 Issues	340	£2·62	£891	£1,704 ÷ 650 = £2·62 each
Balance (C)	310		£813	
Feb. 22 Issues	210	£2·62	£550	
Balance (D)	100		£263	
March 10 Receipts	330	£3·20	£1,056	
Balance	430		£1,319	
March 14 Receipts	150	£4	£600	
Balance (E)	580		£1,919........	... New Average price =
March 20 Issues	370	£3·31	£1,224	£1,919 ÷ 580 = £3·31 each
Balance (F)	210		£695	
April 9 Issues	150	£3·31	£496	
Balance (G)	60	£3·31	£199	

Q.6. A + B Summary:

	F.I.F.O.	L.I.F.O.	A.V.C.O.
	£	£	£
Cost of Issues January	600	450	546
February	1,400	1,500	1,441
March	1,114	1,304	1,224
April	552	472	496
TOTAL COST OF ISSUES	3,666	3,726	3,707
CLOSING STOCK	240	180	199
TOTAL PURCHASED	£3,906	£3,906	£3,906

SECTION C

Q.8. (i) Direct Labour Hours.

(ii) Hours per week actually producing goods = 36 per person.
Therefore period's productive hours = 36 hours × 18 people × 4 weeks
= 2,592 Direct Labour Hours.

$$\text{ORR} = \frac{£22,000}{2,592} = £8\cdot49 \text{ per Direct Labour Hour.}$$

(iii) (A) If actual overheads were £24,000, the under recovery in total
= £24,000 *minus* £22,000 = £2,000.

(B) Per Hour the under recovery = $\dfrac{£2,000}{2,592 \text{ HOURS}} = £0\cdot77$

(iv) Cost of one Cassette Recorder:

	£
D.L. 4 hours × £3 per hour =	12
D.M.	8
Overheads 4 hours × £8·49 =	33·96
Estimated Absorption Cost	£53·96

(v) Actual Cost is the Estimated Cost £53·96 *plus* 4 hours of the under recovered overheads:
4 × £0·77 = £3·08.
Actual Cost = £57·04.

Q.9. (i) The years overheads total £13,100.
Productive hours are 37 hours per week × 48 weeks per year × 3 Partners
= 5,328 Direct Labour hours per year (Partner hours).
ORR per partner hour = £13,100 ÷ 5,328 = £2·46

(ii) A rate to include salaries of £15,000 each would be:

	£
Overheads	13,100
Plus 3 × £15,000	45,000
=	£58,100 ÷ 5,328 Hours = £10·90 per hour

(iii) (A) If all partners worked 40 hours for clients per week instead of the 37 hours planned, Over
Recovery would be:
3 hours × 3 partners × 48 weeks × £2·46 per hour = £1,062·72

(B) Extra Salary earned: Salary rate per hour = Combined Rate £10·90
less Overhead rate £2·46 = £8·44
Extra salary earned *per partner* = £8·44 × 3 hours × 48 weeks
= £1,215·36

CHAPTER 4

SECTION A

Q.1.

			£
Direct Labour: 31 hours × £3·50	=		108·50
Direct Materials: 35 yards × £20	=		700·00
15 yards × £18	=		270·00
Overheads: 31 hours × £15	=		465·00
Estimated Total Cost of Dresses			1,543·50
Add 15% profit Margin			231·52
Estimated Selling Price			£1,775·02

Q.2.

Estimated Costs:		£
Direct Labour: 18 hours × £7	=	126
20 hours × £5	=	100
Direct Materials: Steel	=	2,500
Overheads: 18 hours × £26	=	468
60 hours × £46	=	2,760
Total Estimated Cost	=	5,954
Profit 5%	=	298
Selling Price		£6,252

Actual Costs		£
Direct Labour: 16 hours × £7	=	112
24 hours × £5	=	120
Direct Materials: £28 × 95 kilos	=	2,660
Overheads: 16 hours × £26	=	416
58 hours × £46	=	2,668
Actual Total Cost		5,976
Selling Price		6,252
Actual Profit		£276

SECTION B

Q.10. (A) Total costs input by end of January:

Direct Labour: 1,200 + 5,520 = £6,720
Direct Materials: 10,800 + 38,000 + 21,000 = £69,800
Overheads: 1,000 + 4,880 = £5,880

(B, C, D) Equivalent units produced:

Direct Labour: 4,000 actually	=	4,000
400 × 50%	=	200
D.L. Equiv. Units		4,200

Direct Material: 4,000 actually	=	4,000
400 × 100%	=	400
D.M. Equiv. Units		4,400

Overheads: 4,000 actually	=	4,000
400 × 50%	=	200
O/H Equiv. Units		4,200

Cost of Finished kilos:

	£	Closing W.I.P.
D.L. $\dfrac{£6,720}{4,200} \times 4,000$ =	6,400 :	£320
D.M. $\dfrac{£69,800}{4,400} \times 4,000$ =	63,454 :	£6,346
O/H $\dfrac{£5,880}{4,200} \times 4,000$ =	5,600 :	£280
Total Cost of finished kilos	£75,454	

Unit Cost per kilo = £75,454 ÷ 4,000 = £18·86

CHAPTER 5

SECTION A

Q.1. (A) Revenue 27 *less* Variable Cost 9 = £18 unit contribution.

(B) Total Contribution = 3,800 × £18 = £68,400.
Contribution £68,400 *less* Fixed Costs 54,000 = Profit £14,400

(C) (i) Selling 3,600 tyres:
Lost contribution = 200 × £18 = £3,600. Therefore profit will be £14,400 *minus* 3,600 = £10,800
(ii) Selling 4,000 tyres: Extra contribution = 200 × £18 = 3,600.
Therefore profit = £14,400 *plus* 3,600 = £18,000
(iii) Selling 3,400 tyres: Lost contribution = 400 × £18 = £7,200.
Therefore profit = £14,400 *minus* £7,200 = £7,200.

SECTION B

Q.3. (A) Sales £6,200 *less* Variable Costs £2,790 = Contribution £3,410.

(B) C/S Ratio = 55% (3,410 as percentage of 6,200).

(C) £2,000 × 55% = £1,100.

SECTION C

Q.6. Basic Information: Divide costs into Fixed and Variable:

	FIXED	VARIABLE
	£	£
Direct and Indirect Labour	3,200	800
„ „ „ Materials	300	6,700
Rent	2,000	–
Machinery	4,000	–
Sales and Distribution	900	100
Finance	2,000	
	£12,400	£7,600

(A) Variable cost per gear box = £7,600 ÷ 50 = £152.

(B) Unit Contribution: Normal £500 minus £152 = £348
             (i) £450 „ „ = £298
             (ii) £600 „ „ = £448
Total Contribution: Normal £348 × 50 = £17,400
             (i) £298 × 65 = £19,370
             (ii) £448 × 40 ÷ £17,920
Plan (i) is the most profitable.

(C) C/S Ratios   Normal : 69% (348 as percentage of £500)
               (i) : 66% (298 as percentage of £450)
               (ii) : 75% (448 as percentage of £600)

(D) Break even in units for each alternative:

$$\text{Normal} : \frac{12,400}{348} = 36 \text{ units}$$

$$\text{(i)} \quad \frac{12,400}{298} = 42 \text{ units}$$

$$\text{(ii)} \quad \frac{12,400}{448} = 28 \text{ units}$$

Q.7. Divide basic informations into fixed and variable costs:

	FIXED	VARIABLE
	£	£
Direct Materials		250,000
Direct Labour	120,000	30,000
Overheads	480,000	70,000
	£600,000	£350,000

(A) Output = Revenue £1,000,000 ÷ £10 per dress = 100,000 dresses.
   Unit variable cost = £350,000 ÷ 100,000 units = £3·50.

(B) Unit Contribution = £10 minus £3·50 = £6·50.

(C)   Contribution from one extra dress sold for £4:
   £4 minus £3·50 = £0·50 per dress.
   20,000 dresses would give extra contribution of 20,000 × £0·50 = £10,000 which would be
   extra profit.

  (ii) Unit Contribution at £9 per dress = 9 minus £3·50 = £5·50

£5·50 × 150,000 dresses	=	£825,000
less Fixed Costs		600,000
Profit		£225,000

   Yes, this is worthwhile.

(D) C/S ratio under original budget = 65% (£6·50 as percentage of £10).
   C/S ratio under (ii) = 61% (£5·50 as percentage of £9).

(E) Break even revenue under original budget $= \dfrac{600,000}{£0·65}$
$$= £923,077$$

Break even revenue under (ii) $= \dfrac{600,000}{£0·61}$
$$= £983,606$$

CHAPTER 7

Q.1. (A) Four weeks Sales = 20,000 units. Therefore 7 weeks sales = $\dfrac{20,000}{4} \times 7$ = 35,000 units, which is the required stock figure to be produced before selling starts.

   (B) At output of 500 units per week it will take 7 weeks to build up the required stock.

   (C) At an absorption cost per unit of £6 the value of the stock will be £6 × 35,000 = £210,000.

   (D) At maximum output of 5,000 units the unit absorption cost is £6, and the marginal cost per unit £2, therefore £4 is the fixed cost per unit, *at 5,000 units* per week. Therefore one week's fixed costs are 5,000 × £4 = £20,000. At output of 4,500 units total costs are:

$$
\begin{array}{lcr}
4{,}500 \times £2 \text{ marginal cost} & = & 9{,}000 \\
\text{plus Fixed Costs} & = & 20{,}000 \\
\hline
 & & £29{,}000 \\
\hline
\end{array}
$$

$$\text{New absorption cost} = \frac{£29{,}000}{4{,}500} = £6{\cdot}44$$

CHAPTER 8

PART A

Q.1.

QUANTITY	Master Budget 500		Flexible Budget 450	Actual 450
	£		£	£
D.L. £27 × 500:	13,500	£27 × 450:	12,150	13,000
D.M. £40 × 500:	20,000	£40 × 450:	18,000	17,200
Fixed O/H £33 × 500:	16,500	No change:	16,500	15,400
TOTAL	£50,000		£46,650	£45,600

	£
Table of Variances: Total Variance:	4,400 (F)
Quantity Variance	3,350 (F)
D.L. Variance	850 (U)
D.M. Variance	800 (F)
O/H Variance	1,100 (F)
	£4,400 (F)

PART B

Q.4.

QUANTITY	Master Budget 800		Flexible Budget 840	Actual 840
	£		£	£
D.L. £15 × 800:	12,000	£15 × 840:	12,600	12,000
D.M. £25 × 800:	20,000	£25 × 840:	21,000	22,200
Fixed Overhead, £10 × 800:	8,000	No change:	8,000	9,200
TOTAL	£40,000		£41,600	£43,400

	£
Table of Variances: Total Variance:	3,400 (U)
Quantity Variance:	1,600 (U)
D.L. Variance:	600 (F)
D.M. Variance:	1,200 (U)
O/H Variance:	1,200 (U)
	£3,400 (U)

D. L. Sub Variances:

Flexible Budget information: £3 rate

$$\text{Therefore Hours} = \frac{12,600}{3} = 4,200 \text{ hours}$$

Actual Information: £4 rate.

$$\text{Therefore Hours} = \frac{12,000}{4} = 3,000 \text{ hours}$$

D.L. Hours Sub Variance (also called Efficiency Sub Variance)

Actual Hours	=	3,000
Flexible Budget Hours	=	4,200
Difference		1,200 × £3 standard rate

D.L. Hours Sub Variance = £3,600 (F)

D.L. Rate Sub Variance

Actual Rate	=	4
Flexible Budget Rate	=	3
Difference		1 × 3000 Actual Hours

D.L. Rate Sub Variance = £3,000 (U)

Note 3,000 (U) minus 3,600 (F) = D.L. Major Variance 600 (F).

<u>D.M. Sub Variances</u>

Flexible Budget Information: Price £5 per kilo

$$\text{Therefore Kilos} = \frac{21,000}{5} = 4,200 \text{ kilos}$$

Actual Information: 7,400 kilos were used

$$\text{Therefore Price per kilo} = \frac{22,200}{7,400} = £3$$

D.M. Usage Sub Variance:

Actual kilos:	7,400
Flexible Budget kilos:	4,200
Difference	3,200 × £5 standard price

D.M. Usage Sub Variance = £16,000 (U)

D.M. Price Sub Variance:

Actual Price:	3
Flexible Budget Price:	5
Difference	2 × 7,400 Actual kilos

D.M. Price Sub Variance = £14,800 (F)

Note 16,000 (U) minus 14,800 (F) = 1,200 (U) Major D.M. Variance.

SECTION C

Q.10.

					£
A	Master Sales Budget	=	5,000 × £15	=	75,000
B	Flexible Sales Budget	=	5,500 × £15	=	82,500
C	Actual Sales	=	5,500 × £14	=	77,000

				£
A–C	=	Total Sales Variance	=	2,000 (F)
A–B	=	Sales Quantity Variance	=	7,500 (F)
B–C	=	Sales Price Variance	=	5,500 (U)

£2,000 (F)

CHAPTER 9

Q.1

Narrative	Jan.	Feb.	Mar.	April	May	June
INFLOWS						
	£	£	£	£	£	£
Capital	30,000					
Sales		3,500	3,300	4,000	4,500	5,300
Rent Income	150	150	150	150	150	150
Total Inflows	30,150	3,650	3,450	4,150	4,650	5,450
OUTFLOWS						
Premises	15,000					
Machinery	5,000					
Van	4,000					
Materials						
(paid 1 month after use)	–	1,000	2,500	2,200	2,900	3,500
Wages of Assistants	–	500	500	500	500	500
Fixed Expenses						
(paid 2 months in arrears)	–	–	230	230	230	230
Browns Salary	200	200	200	200	200	200
Rates	–	–	1,000	–	–	–
Total Outflows	24,200	1,700	4,430	3,130	3,830	4,350
Surplus (deficit)		1,950	(980)	1,020	820	1,020
	5,950					
Balance B/F		5,950	7,900	6,920	7,940	8,760
	–					
Final Balance		£7,950	£6,920	£7,940	£8,760	£9,780
	£5,950					

7900

SECTION B

Q.6

Stocks (i) Raw materials 700 taps × £12 = £8,400

(ii) Finished Goods: August output 700 in stock completed not delivered:

	£
Value of Goods at Factory Cost of Production = D.M.	8,400
D.L.	2,100
Variable O/H	170
Fixed O/H	180
	£10,850

Total Stock Value £19,250

Debtors 2 months' deliveries (June output delivered in July, and July output delivered in August) will not have been paid for.

2 months' sales = 700 × £20 × 2 = £28,000 = Debtors at August.

CASH	April £	May £	June £	July £	August £
Inflows Sales	–	–	–	14,000	14,000
Outflows					
Wages	2,100	2,100	2,100	2,100	2,100
*Materials	–	16,800	8,400	8,400	8,400
Variable O/H	–	–	180	180	180
Fixed O/H	–	–	170	170	170
CASH FLOAT	150				
Total Outflows	2,250	18,900	10,850	10,850	10,850
Surplus (deficit)	(2,250)	(18,900)	(10,850)	3,150	3,150
Balance B/F	–	(2,250)	(21,150)	(32,000)	(28,850)
Final Balance	£(2,250)	£(21,150)	£(32,000)	£(28,850)	£(25,700)

* *Note* To ensure 1 month's raw materials are always in stock, enough for 1,400 taps is delivered in month 1. Thereafter enough for 700 taps is delivered each month.

Creditors:

		£
2 months × Fixed O/H	=	340
2 months × Variable O/H	=	360
1 months Raw Materials	=	8,400
		£9,100

Working Capital Summary at end of August:

	£	£
Stocks		19,250
Debtors		28,000
Cash Float		150
Gross Working Capital		47,400
Financed by:		
Creditors:	9,100	
Overdraft or Cash used from pool available	= 25,700	
		34,800
Net Working Capital		£12,600

Note We have invoiced deliveries in May, June, July and August. Each had sales of £14,000 less factory cost of £10,850 = Profit £3,150. £3,150 × 4 months = £12,600 = Net Working Capital financed by profits made to date.

CHAPTER 10

Q.1.

£4,000 × 0·567 (5 year 12% factor) = £2,268 Present Value.
£7,000 × 0·540 (8 year 8% factor) = £3,780 Present Value.
£1,200 × 0·641 (3 year 16% factor) = £769 Present Value.
£26,000 × 0·792 (4 year 6% factor) = £20,592 Present Value.
£3,500 × 0·480 (6 year 13% factor) = £1,680 Present Value.
£6,900 × 0·247 (10 year 15% factor) = £1,704 Present Value.

Q.2.
(i)

	Long Range	Hi Definition
	£	£
Total Yearly Inflows:	20,000	24,000
less Initial Capital:	10,000	12,000
Lifetime Surplus:	£10,000	£12,000
Lifetime Percentage return on Initial Capital:	100%	100%
Yearly Return (4 years):	25%	25%

(ii)

Payback Period	2 years	2¼ years

(iii)

	Long Range		9%	Hi Definition	
	NET INFLOWS	PRESENT VALUE	FACTOR	NET INFLOWS	PRESENT VALUE
	£	£	£	£	£
Year 1	4,000	3,668	0.917	4,000	3,668
Year 2	6,000	5,052	0.842	6,000	5,052
Year 3	6,000	4,632	0.772	8,000	6,176
Year 4	4,000	2,832	0.708	6,000	4,248
PRESENT VALUES		16,184			19,144
less Initial Investment		10,000			12,000
Net Present Value		£6,184			£7,144

CHAPTER 11

Q.1.

MANUFACTURING ACCOUNT

	£
Direct Materials: Opening Stocks	3,100
Add Purchases	19,000
	22,100
less Closing Stocks	2,900
Direct Materials Issued	19,200
Add 80% Direct Labour	11,200
Prime Cost	30,400
Indirect Labour 20%	2,800
Indirect Materials	1,500
Machinery Costs	12,000
Rent, Rates, Telephone	5,700
Factory Costs Incurred	52,400
Add Opening W.I.P.	1,800
	54,200
less Closing W.I.P.	2,400
Factory Cost of Finished Goods	£51,800

TRADING ACCOUNT

	£			£
Opening Stocks of Finished Goods	6,600		Sales	69,000
Add Cost of Goods Completed	51,800			
Goods Available	58,400			
less Closing Finished Goods Stock	7,000			
Cost of Goods Sold	£51,400			
			TRADING PROFIT	£17,600

PROFIT AND LOSS ACCOUNT

	£		£
Sales Dept Costs:		Trading Profit	17,600
Cars	4,000		
Rent	400		
Rates	200		
60% Wages	2,400		
60% Telephone	1,800		
	——	8,800	
Admin. Dept Costs:			
Rent	300		
Rates	150		
40% Wages	1,600		
40% Telephone	1,200		
	—	3,250	
Finance Costs:			
Interest		500	
Office Total Costs		£12,550	
		Net Profit	£5,050